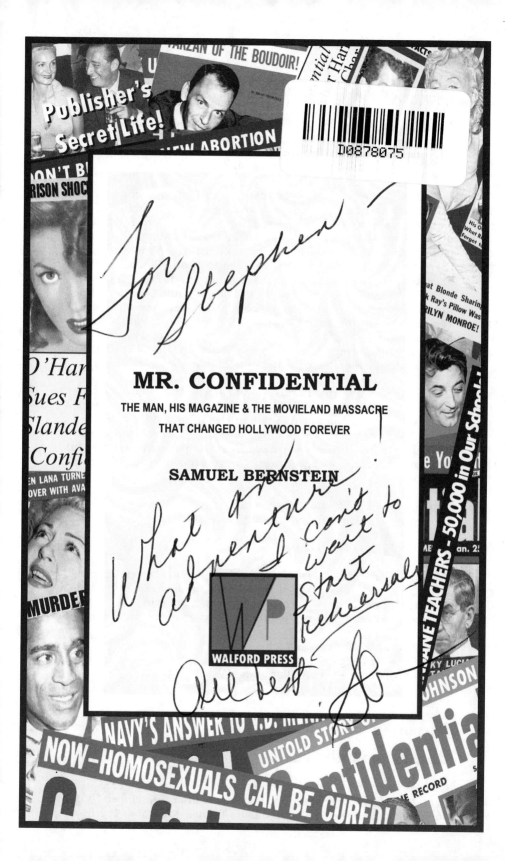

MR. CONFIDENTIAL

THE MAN, HIS MAGAZINE & THE MOVIELAND MASSACRE

THAT CHANGED HOLLYWOOD FOREVER

SAMUEL BERNSTEIN

WALFORD PRESS

Walford Press and the author gratefully acknowledge the contribution of Michael and Barbara Tobias for their recollections and generosity, and attorney Arthur Crowley, whose memory of the 1957 *Confidential Magazine* libel and obscenity trial, and of Robert Harrison personally, adds enormously to the book. We are also grateful to Mr. and Mrs. Tobias, and Mr. Crowley for allowing us access to their private collections of photographs.

The author wishes to thank the research and photography departments of the New York and Los Angeles Public Libraries, the research staffs of *The Los Angeles Times, The New York Times*, and the Academy of Motion Picture Arts and Sciences Margaret Herrick Library, as well as Harlan Böll, Gwenevere Bridge, Anneke Campbell, Diane Casey, Janet Charlton, Bryan Cooper, Anna Cottle and Mary Alice Kier, Linda De Blase, Alan Friel, Mickey Freiberg, Jim Green, David Groff, Julie Kenner, Josh Kesselman, Liz and Dave Kirschner, Robert Kosberg and David Permut, Stuart Lampert and Stephen Tomar, Jane Lawton Moore, Karen McCullough Lutz, Pat Quinn, Steve Rohde, Lenore Ross, Henry E. Scott, Beverly and Joseph Shore, Joshua Silver, Liz Smith, Stella Stambler, Eric Weinstein, and most especially Stephanie Snyder and Ronald Shore.

Copyright 2006 by Samuel Bernstein
Library of Congress Control Number 2006930554
ISBN 0-9787671-2-8
ISBN13 978-0-9787671-2-9

Published by Walford Press
LONDON – NEW YORK – LOS ANGELES
walfordpress.com – shop.walfordpresssales.com

Walford Press
1133 Broadway, Suite 708
New York, NY 10010-7903

Cover design by Jeff Holtzman

Cover photographs: Robert Harrison publicity shot circa 1955, *Confidential Magazine* cover art: Marilyn Monroe (September 1955), James Dean (January 1958) and Lana Turner (November 1954).

TO RONUEL
The worst kind of boy.

TELLS THE FACTS / NAMES THE NAMES

Robert Harrison practically invented modern celebrity journalism. Deeply tanned, handsome, and charming beyond belief, he was catnip to the ladies. Men wanted to be just like him—or at least have his day job—since Harrison initially found success publishing girlie magazines, often posing himself in risqué photo spreads with sirens like pin-up queen Bettie Page, in *Beauty Parade, Titter, Wink, Eyeful, Whisper,* and *Flirt.* Nice work if you can get it.

Harrison was tall, with dark, thick hair and a smile that never quit. He didn't say "yes" or "no," it was always "Damn right!" or "Hell, no!" in a rich baritone. For him, things were "the greatest" or "for the birds," people were "geniuses" or "clinkers," with friends and acquaintances sometimes going from one to the other and back again all in the same day. He was a guy who basked in attention and wanted to be famous.

Instead, he ended up making everyone else famous.

When censorship battles threatened his empire of girlie magazines, the driven, obsessively detail-oriented Harrison looked around for another idea, and found it in the dirt, creating *Confidential Magazine* in late 1952. No one could possibly have been more surprised than the publisher himself, when *Confidential* became a cultural obsession and media phenomenon. He suddenly found himself rewriting the rules of Hollywood mythmaking.

Humphrey Bogart famously quipped that no one ever admitted to buying *Confidential,* that people always said the cook or the maid brought it into the house. But whether or not readers were willing to come out of the closet about having a taste for the tawdry, they couldn't tear themselves away: White Glamour Gals with Big Black Bachelors, Homos in Hollywood, Society Swells in Hock. The magazine's popularity spread from sea to shining sea, and then over to Europe. Like Plague. At least that's how half of Hollywood felt. The other half was busy planting their own stories in the magazine, and then publicly denouncing Harrison for printing the information they themselves had secretly provided.

Confidential. The name alone promised so much. And this rag delivered; giving everyone in America a chance to get the real-life lowdown on the lowbrow habits of their icons. Maybe the magazine stopped short from saying outright that sultry Lizabeth Scott was a lesbian, for instance, but a sentence like, "The unmarried actress prefers the company of Hollywood's weird society of Baritone Babes," didn't leave much to the imagination. Scott's career was a little on the skids anyway. Did a terrible scandal from *Confidential's* 1955 article kill it off for good? Lizabeth Scott made headlines when she announced that she was filing a libel lawsuit. Threatening to sue could be fun. You got a bunch of publicity and could then drop the whole thing when no one was looking, *before* it got to trial and you had to testify under oath. No Scott v. *Confidential* suit ever materialized, with jurisdictional issues given as the reason. Did *Confidential* end her career? In 1957 Scott quit the business *for good.* Except that she came back again in the '60s and worked a lot before quitting the business another time *for good*, until the '70s, when she did it all over again. *For good.*

Readers were titillated and shocked by the magazine's tawdry tales, but perhaps too, it was a relief to find out that Desi was a boozer who stepped out on Lucy, or to read the magazine's "June is Busting Out All Over" allegations about goody-goody June Allyson's, "uncontrollable itch to push the sugar bowl aside and reach for the spice shelf." Scoping out the scoop on how far your idols could fall made not measuring up in your own life seem less of a crime. And how soothing and self-satisfying to get rock-solid proof that fame and money really don't guarantee happiness.

By 1955, *Confidential's* national newsstand sales roared past five million; more than *TV Guide, Life, Time, Look,* or *The Saturday Evening Post*; figures confirmed by *The Wall Street Journal.* Standards of obscenity were stricter and libel was easier to prove in the 50s, yet *Confidential* pushed the envelope farther and faster than anybody else.

Along with the Hollywood gossip, there were exposés on cigarettes causing cancer (this in 1954), abortion drugs that could kill, infant death hazards, auto safety, prescription drug addiction, and breast augmentation nightmares. Taboos like homosexuality, miscegenation or "race mixing," alcoholism, drug addiction, and child abuse surfaced in *Confidential* for the first time anywhere in the national press, opening a generation's eyes to a few facts about America.

World War II was fading from sight. Rock and roll and the Sexual Revolution were on the horizon. In between, *Confidential* helped turn once shocking taboos into ordinary conversation fodder at water coolers and over neighborhood fences all across the country, certainly helping to pave the way for the complete lack of embarrassment that today accompanies once unthinkable behavior. Look around. Whatever some may think privately, little is said about the rabidly *conservative* African American Supreme Court Justice with the white wife; few condemn the flocks of children born to famous mothers and fathers out of wedlock; nude pictures and videos of the stars appearing on the Internet provoke not shame, but court battles over profits; in one of the few "morality" battles left, even many on the Right propose same-sex civil union, in itself a groundbreaking social construct, as an alternative to legalized gay marriage.

The shocking subject of homosexuality was a *Confidential* mainstay. Maurice Zolotow, a journalist and later the writer of definitive biographies of Marilyn Monroe, Billy Wilder, and John Wayne, was unsuccessfully wooed by Harrison in the '50s for a writing gig, and coined the phrase "queer for queers" to describe the publisher's boundless enthusiasm for homosexual exposés. Most articles about Bob Harrison for the next 50 years use the description. There was always space in *Confidential* for anything and everything limp-wristed. Liberace and "Mad About the Boy," Lavender Lad Love Nest, Swishful Thinking.

The puns alone were worth the price of admission.

Harrison "outed" Van Johnson, still a huge A-list MGM star at the time, while announcing Johnson's conversion to heterosexuality. He printed details from rising teen heartthrob Tab Hunter's onetime arrest record for attending an alleged gay "pajama party" before he was famous. The magazine detailed two decades of the tangled, dual gender love affairs of part-time Baritone Babe, Marlene Dietrich.

Who came up with "Baritone Babe" is lost to history but imagine Robert Harrison alone at night, and as usual, obsessively dreaming about his magazine.

Yellow. Red. Blue. Always primary colors. Bold lines. Surprising angles. Midnight. Exhausted, Harrison's vision blurs as he studies the graphic design layouts for the next issue of 'Confidential.' It's a spread on film legend Marlene Dietrich. He keeps changing the placement for photos of her and two female sexual playmates.. He crosses out the word 'lesbian' in the headline, saying to himself, 'Who the hell is gonna even know what that means? Like we're trying to make out she's Arab?'

Suddenly, the lines, boxes, and photos start to rise from the page, swirling around him, dancing in front of his eyes. From the shadows, Dietrich and her pals appear, motioning for Harrison to join them in their amorous play. As the three women surround him, touching him, undressing him, Dietrich whispers into his ear, 'Bob, baby, just call me a Baritone Babe...'

Homosexuality's kissing cousin in the magazine was Race Mixing. Few issues were devoid of articles on the subject, and the language depicting Black and White couples was as colorful as that for gays and lesbians: Copper Cuties, Nubian Nymphs, Sepia Sirens, "Some Girls Go For the Gold, But Ava Gardner Prefers *Bronze!*" "Marlon Brando's Tawny Tootsie!" "Orson Welles and his Chocolate Bon-Bon!"

Wordplay and alliteration drew readers in, along with pulsating graphic design and photos that often depicted stars mouths agape, as if reacting to the *Confidential* headline personally. But after drawing in the customers, the magazine kept them buying by always managing to get and give up the goods.

Harrison loved all of it—from the frothy silliness of a piece attributing a star's sexual prowess to his breakfast cereal, to articles that made serious allegations of rape and murder among the elite, getting the inside story, entertaining readers, and keeping himself decked out in custom suits and Cadillacs made all the compulsively hard work well worth it. He was passionately in love with his creations, but little did he know the Pandora's Box he was opening: Without *Confidential* there would be no *TMZ, The Smoking Gun, Drudge Report, Data Lounge,* or *Gossip List;* no *National Enquirer, Star, Us, People* or *In Touch*; no "Entertainment Tonight," "E! True Hollywood Story," or "Access Hollywood;" no modern incarnation of *Vanity Fair.*

"Half-fictionalized as they are, the tabloids, with their twin themes of sex and violence, tell the lurid pagan truth about life," says Camille Paglia, the feminist social critic who grew up reading, what else? *Confidential.*

Liz Smith, the most widely read gossip columnist around these days, takes a fizzier, funnier approach, quipping that, "Gossip is just news running ahead of itself in a red satin gown." But she credits Robert Harrison and *Confidential* with changing the entire landscape of celebrity press coverage.

"I remember that *Confidential* story about Rory Calhoun's felony prison record," says Janet Charlton, longtime columnist for the *Star* and a correspondent for "The Gossip Show," on E! "He was so sexy and *bad.* There I was, a little girl, just nine, and I'm thinking, I'll never miss another one of his movies. *Never.*" No one told her *Confidential* was off limits but somehow she just knew it was bad. "Sammy Davis, Jr. dating Ava Gardner! A Black man and a White woman! In the early '50s that was beyond shocking." The magazine was the spark that lit the way for Janet's future career, and she now collects and frames its vintage covers, using them to decorate her office walls.

Another veteran gossip columnist, Jack Martin, was a young P.R. assistant in Hollywood in the 1950s and he remembers feeling *Confidential's* tentacles everywhere, saying they reached into every nook and cranny of the town, terrifying everyone. Later he worked for Rona Barrett and had his own column in *The New York Post* and the *National Enquirer*, but he never considered himself to be in the same "vicious" business as *Confidential*, protesting that, "I never ever hurt anyone."

On every cover of *Confidential*, Robert Harrison swore to Tell the Facts and Name the Names. The tabloids called him "The Titan of Titter Tattle" and "The Sultan of Sleaze," with columnists breathlessly covering his nightclub tours, always with a blonde on his arm, always driving a white Cadillac, wearing a white alpaca coat, picking up the check for everybody.

Yet Bob Harrison didn't do it on his own. This is also the story of his niece, Marjorie Meade, a young newlywed living in Manhattan when her uncle launched *Confidential*. She was poised. Proper. But beneath her beautiful, movie star looks and bombshell figure, she had an active mind ready for new challenges. Think Barbara Stanwyck.

All she wanted was to get up, get out, and get something more out of life.

Uncle Bob sent Marjorie to Hollywood, hiring her to head up his new research organization. He hated the West Coast himself, *not enough nightlife*, but someone needed to control the hired help as well as the often indirect network of tipsters and private dicks trolling around for Tinseltown trash in the hopes of selling it to *Confidential*. Marjorie's assignment was to make sure everything was always on the up and up—that the magazine's lawyers had the ammunition to take on anyone who tried to sue. Hollywood Research, Inc. was formed as a "completely separate corporate entity from Confidential, Inc." That became an important issue in 1957 when the studios, California's Attorney General, and the L.A. District Attorney decided enough was enough.

Marjorie became the sensational centerpiece of The Trial of 100 Stars, then 200 Stars, facing prison time and fines for multiple felony counts of criminal conspiracy to commit libel and disseminate obscene material. The papers started calling her the "Flame-Haired Femme Fatale" and "The Most Feared Woman in Hollywood," sobriquets worthy of *Confidential's* own headline writers. It wasn't just the tabloids either. *The New York Times* and *The Washington Post* had plenty to say about her as well. It was the Trial of the Century, sparking a worldwide media frenzy not seen again until the trial of O.J. Simpson—or at least not until 1958 when Lana Turner's daughter accidentally stuck a knife into Johnny Stompanato's stomach. Trials of the Century tend to occur every year or two in Los Angeles.

Seven years after the trial, Tom Wolfe called *Confidential,* "The most scandalous scandal magazine in the history of the world." Its reputation has lingered somehow in the public consciousness, partly because of the success of the book "L.A. Confidential" and the film adaptation that followed, but also, rather inadvertently, because of the now-forgotten, third major character in this story: The goofball-popping, alcoholic, violent, Communist witch-hunter, Howard Rushmore. Here was a man so villainous, he wasn't just hated by the Left, not just loathed by the Middle, but after a stint working for J. Edgar Hoover, McCarthy, and Roy Cohn, the Right couldn't stand him either.

In the early *Confidential* days, Harrison relied on Rushmore for a crucial business contact, but soon Rushmore's flameouts and betrayals led to grisly coast-to-coast headlines and helped usher in the fall of an empire.

When he first went into the publishing business, Robert Harrison wanted little more than a lifetime membership in Café Society. Before it was over he would leave behind a legacy defined by accusations of murder, blackmail, suicide, and libel. Separating truth and fantasy would prove impossible, as his own life became more and more like a story in *Confidential.* Luckily, Harrison loved to laugh. Even if the joke was on him.

He created the monster, fed the beast, and nurtured it. In the end, the beast didn't just bite him in the ass, it swallowed him whole, then it put the meal on Harrison's tab and added a generous tip.

And me? I wish I could Live Large, Laugh Last, and Lust For Life too, just like Bob Harrison. My own journey into *Confidential* began with my curiosity about Robert Harrison, Howard Rushmore, and Marjorie Meade. Though Harrison and Rushmore are long dead, many people are still living who have vivid memories of them both, and several of the other major players are also very much alive. A few people I interviewed died soon after we spoke.

Was It Murder? Suicide?

That's an old *Confidential* trick: Ask the incendiary question, then answer in the negative. Dying of old age makes for a lousy headline.

The people I met who had known Robert Harrison generously opened doors into his life; his women, his obsessions, his personality tics, and how he played the big man about town and was a lifelong bachelor, but never spent a day without his two adoring older sisters at his side, always surrounded by family.

If my fascination with the characters involved took me to the very edge of the spider's web that was *Confidential*, the magazine itself grabbed hold of me and sealed the deal. I pored through every single issue published under Bob Harrison, and many later issues that weren't. Then I looked at the other scandal rags of the day: *Uncensored, Inside Story, On the QT, Hush-Hush, Exposed,* and *The Lowdown*. They didn't even come close to *Confidential's* creative approach to writing, reporting, and graphic design. *Confidential* didn't just capture the giddy, go-go 1950s, with its endless coverage of Marilyn, Lana, Ava, Elvis, Sinatra, Sammy Davis, Jr., and all the rest, but everything in it could be about Hollywood in the new millennium.

Substitute Paris Hilton for Zsa Zsa Gabor.

Britney Spears is Lana Turner (and music fans all over the world will probably cheer if the new baby grows up to one day stab Kevin Federline).

Jessica Simpson is this year's Marilyn; pretending to be as dumb as dirt, getting dumped on by her man, while using her baby-doll, bombshell body to hide her intelligence.

Who doesn't wonder if Tom Cruise and Katie Holmes are Rock Hudson, the icon with the vivid private life, and Phyllis Gates, Rock's hapless wife who later grew fangs and tried blackmail.

Brad Pitt and Jennifer Aniston are Eddie Fisher and Debbie Reynolds. And resurrecting herself in the public's affections through good works instead of near-death illnesses, Angelina Jolie plays other-woman Liz Taylor. This despite the fact that Liz has had a grand time happily playing herself, and will probably make headlines forever. At the grocery store checkout line in 2025: "Liz Besieged By Heavenly Ex-Husbands! Burton Threatens Exit to Hell!"

Michael Jackson? He's Elvis, Johnnie Ray, and Bobo the Chimp all rolled up into one media mega-monster. Bob Harrison must be turning in his grave at the thought of missing out on Jacko. He would have loved printing that weird police mug shot of the alleged child molester, the one where he looks eerily like Faye Dunaway playing Joan Crawford.

And Mel Gibson is the bizarre, conservative, papist evil twin of Orson Welles; endangering his stardom by engendering the most poisonous press coverage imaginable. All if it well-earned.

As I got deeper still into the world of Robert Harrison and *Confidential,* I wanted to know everything about him and about the magazine's stunning rise and fall. Why did Harrison succeed so brilliantly, and what caused the magazine's sudden flameout in the late '50s? Was it libel and bribery like everyone seems to think? Were there genuine First Amendment issues at stake? How did they manage for so long to avoid drowning in the avalanche of lawsuits launched against them? And in an era before the Internet and digital long-lens cameras, how did they get their gossip and stay on top of it all?

Hollywood has always been a town with not six, but two or three degrees of separation between people. I write this in late July, 2006, the day after my chiropractor happily revealed to me, as he was cracking my back, that it was his partner, Harvey Levin, who broke the inside story of Mel Gibson's anti-Semitic, Sugar-Tits tirade while recklessly resisting arrest for drunk driving. How did Levin dig up the real police record, only hours after it was buried? My chiropractor wouldn't tell me. But is that two degrees or one?

Never mind Mel, it turned out that before I even embarked on my journey into Bob Harrison's life and the story of his magazine, I had an unbelievably, impossibly coincidental connection to the story in my own life; a case of zero degrees of separation: Though I was completely unaware of it, I actually knew Marjorie Meade.

My very first point of entry into the *Confidential* universe was a 2003 Neal Gabler article in *Vanity Fair* about the magazine's "Reign of Terror." Robert Harrison, the libel and obscenity trial, and Marjorie Meade's arrest were all detailed. Always interested in old Hollywood, I mulled over the story, wondering if it might make an interesting movie or book. Then I got a breathless phone call from a friend of mine.

*Had I seen the story? Did I know that Marjorie
Meade is actually Marjorie Roth?*

As a matter of fact, no, I did not know that. Marjorie and I serve on a charitable foundation board together. After the death of her husband, veteran television and film writer Martin Roth, I had been asked to take over a screenwriting development and mentoring program for public high school students, something I continue to do today.

I didn't just know Marjorie, I had worked with her, eaten brunch with her, we had planned events together.

Shocking Tinseltown Twist of Fate!

Though at first Marjorie cooperated with the project that later became this book, she came to regret that decision, believing that what I have written casts her in a negative, inaccurate, and unfair light. I don't agree with her assessment, and have a good deal of respect and affection for her and for her achievements. I would like to state plainly, however, that she does not endorse the contents of this book. Marjorie's brother, Michael Tobias, and his wife Barbara answered endless questions. Attorney Arthur Crowley provided clarity and color about the libel and obscenity trial. More interviews followed with a number of Hollywood types who were affected by the magazine. Reliving the Fabulous '50s through their eyes and through the eyes of *Confidential* was a gas.

The New York Times and *The Washington Post* archives were vital to the process of recreating the 1957 libel and obscenity trial, since no copy of the transcripts seems to have survived anywhere, and tabloid accounts are riddled with mistakes and inconsistencies. Library searches and explorations of *The New York Post, The New York Daily News, The Los Angeles Mirror-News, Variety, The Hollywood Reporter,* and *The Los Angeles Times*, among many other publications, further helped me pin down the timeline of the events I explore here, and brought context to this journey through the rise and fall of Harrison and his magazine.

And then there were the Forces of Darkness to contend with, defined by James Ellroy and his brilliantly Twisted Tinseltown, by his "L.A. Confidential" world of corruption, malevolence, and masochism. Ellroy fingers *Confidential* and Bob Harrison as distinctly diabolical. Most articles and books on the '50s and Hollywood recycle the same stuff: *Vast underground rings of hungry informants; the impossible lengths Harrison went to not just to get a story but to create it; the bribes, the deaths, the suicides, and all the lies.*

Is that really how it went down?

Was Marjorie "The Most Feared Woman in Hollywood?"

Was Bob Harrison the Devil? He never thought so. On the one hand, as much as they existed outside the studio system, Harrison and his magazines ended up an inevitable part of the machine; with tipsters up and down the Hollywood food chain dishing dirt on the sly. Stars rise and fall on keeping themselves in the public eye—whatever the ways and means. On the other hand, Harrison ushered in a coarse sea change in what was considered print-worthy by the mainstream press. As a direct result of his efforts, celebrity journalism would soon make no distinction whatsoever between the public and private lives of the famous. Now anything is fair game.

> *Catch Sammy Davis, Jr. and Bob Harrison, laughing themselves silly as they crash the premiere of L.A. Confidential, invisible to the stars and screaming fans. Both of them love Kim Basinger. Davis sighs and asks, 'Think she would have gone for me?' Harrison looks over at his friend and laughs. 'If Ava Gardner could go for a one-eyed midget, why not Basinger?' But Danny Devito? That's another story. 'Talk about midgets. That little putz is supposed to be me?'*

Back in the day, Harrison printed so many stories about Sammy, he probably should have given his friend a cut of the profits. All those articles about the Black entertainer with White women... A few southern hotels canceled his gigs here and there, but Sammy was sufficiently nonplussed to give his pal Harrison a gold watch for his fiftieth birthday. They even double dated occasionally. And that's showbiz.

So no regrets. The idea of remorse or guilt over anything the magazine printed doesn't seem to enter into the equation for most of the people I spoke with. The prevailing attitude? The stars *Confidential* wrote about—the Marilyn Monroes, the Lana Turners, the Ava Gardners—these were basically trashy people anyway. So what did they expect?

—Samuel Bernstein
West Hollywood, California

PART ONE

PARTYBOY PUBLISHER

TAKES IT LIKE A MAN !

IT HAPPENED ONE NIGHT

CAUGHT
... Guy
Madison
Barbara
Payton's
Boudoir!

Guy used to see Barbara home from the studio,
but each time they kissed it was "goodnight."

TURN THE PAGE

MURDER,
TRAINED

THE
SHAH
did her
wrong.

When
he
was wrong
wife

LOWDOWN ON HIGH SOCIETY

...When a Vanderbilt
welshed on a
gambling debt!

tried to get
WALTER
WINC

The unpublished story of...

DORIS DUKE
and her
AFRICAN
PRINCE!

By GARRY PETERS

She's the richest girl in the world, and she
lives like a queen... But why did her ebony-
hued Prince Consort get the royal heave-ho?
Here's the story they kept in the dark...

FACTS AND N

AND THELMA BOARDED THE ILE DE FRANCE TO MAR

ORED AND OFF THE RECORD

When Joe Louis
Faced Murder Ra

PARTYBOY PUBLISHER
Takes It Like a Man

Spanking her wasn't the problem. She was game for it, the photo crew was ready, and the feel of her satin panties was certainly a sensual delight. But Bob Harrison couldn't stop laughing. It was all so silly. Why would anyone want to spank this gorgeous dame, when you could cuddle her, drape her in mink, and take her to dinner instead? Yet Harrison knew it would make a great magazine layout for *Titter*. It was fun, sexy, and just a little bit nutty. So he took the luscious model over his knee, smiled for the camera, and raised his hand.

Harrison was at home in this world. Literally. The photo shoot was taking place in his Manhattan Parc Vendome suite. Right there with him during the photo shoot was his two older sisters—Helen Studin; blonde, outgoing and quick to laugh— and Edith Tobias; dark-haired, seemingly shy, but quick to forcefully defend her loved ones—as well as Harrison's nephew and Edith's son, Michael Tobias; clean cut, respectful, but full of vivid fantasies. Nothing to be embarrassed about. It was all part of Harrison making a success with his magazines. Edith and Helen barely noticed the spanking. They were worried that Bob might be coming down with a cold and quietly discussed whether or not they should order chicken soup from the deli, or whether Edith had time to go home and make some.

Harrison's nephew Michael was stunned, his head swimming, as he tried to keep from staring at the beautiful, scantily dressed women. His high school classes were over for the day and he had come by Uncle Bob's to do odd jobs and make deliveries. He thought the photo shoot was the greatest thing since 7-Up. Michael would kick himself for years to come for being too embarrassed to ask any of the models out on a date. Of course that never stopped him from telling everyone at school that he did.

Michael loved his uncle's nine-room suite at the Parc Vendome. In one room, Harrison had built a stage area for snapping models in sexy tableaux for his growing family of girlie magazines. He had turned another room of the apartment into a miniature nightclub, complete with checkered cloth-covered tables, a bar, and zebra striped wallpaper that recalled El Morocco. For his bedroom, he bought a leopard print bedspread and mounted an enormous oil of a nude man and woman over the bed that was commissioned as art for one of his magazines. A large ceramic leopard took up residence with him too, and would stay on for the rest of Harrison's life.

But back to the spanking. Maybe if he could get more into it, lose himself a little, maybe play let's pretend... Maybe that would help him stop laughing and finish the photo session.

Have I been a bad boy? She looks up, her catlike eyes challenging, teasing, their fiery sparks setting off a combustible chain. She stamps her foot. He wants to kiss the razor-sharp tips of her five-inch stilettos, wants her to make him beg, make him suffer. Then in an instant his own desire for her dominance sends a white-hot bolt of anger up his spine. Who is she to take his manhood and chew on it? She's the bad one. She's the one who needs punishing...

Then he really got the giggles. Somehow he finished though, never quite managing to look like he was actually mad at the model, instead projecting a goofy air of innocent fun. Once the spanking session had drawn to a close, the models started to get dressed, and Bob got on the phone. He called a blonde, buxom, showgirl friend, Geene Courtney, and arranged a date for that night. Then he called his girlfriend, the also blonde and buxom, rather excitable June Frew, and told her he would come by her place after his other date. Both women knew the score. The showgirl date was just for publicity. June was for real. That didn't stop her from mad moments of jealousy, but this time she was fine with Bob having a P.R. date with another woman before coming over to her place. Of course, if Bob's sisters had anything to say about it, he wouldn't keep either appointment. He needed soup. And rest.

> *Do you want to get pneumonia? Do you want to go to the hospital? You could die!*

Michael watched, wishing he could go on both dates himself. The spanked model was dressed and ready to go home. She came over and gave Harrison a peck on the cheek. His smile to her was dazzling. He loved her. He loved all women. Before she could leave the apartment, Harrison made sure she had enough money, that her boyfriend was treating her right, and then he told Michael to escort her home.

Michael took her home in a cab, unsuccessfully trying to work up the courage to make a pass. Bob overruled his sisters and got ready to go out. After heated contemplation, Edith and Helen settled on matzo ball soup and made sure Bob ate every bite before going out on the town. Then for good measure, they joined him on his date, along with their husbands, Dan Studin and Charles Tobias, Michael, and Edith's daughter, the vivacious, shapely Marjorie; A couple of Harrison's attorneys and their wives joined them, and then what the heck, he called June and told her to come too. Two gorgeous blondes on his arms. Twice as many column mentions in next day's papers.

The spanking spread appeared with the headline "Babes Like It Rough" in a 1949 issue of *Titter*. In terms of public standards of decency, this was light years before Hugh Hefner, yet partly thanks to the pioneering nudie efforts of Harrison that began in 1941, it would be a scant three years more before that famous nude centerfold of Marilyn Monroe graced the very first issue of *Playboy*, published in December 1953. When Harrison started his girlie magazines, launching *Beauty Parade* in October 1941, it would have been unthinkable for a nationally distributed publication to feature a naked woman. Things changed quickly in the American magazine world of the late '40s to early '50s, mainly because of Bob Harrison.

Here's Big Bob in the "Babes Like It Rough!" photo spread, from the December 1949 issue of *Titter*. Harrison's guest starring role is bottom left. Using himself in the photo spreads may have started in order to save on modeling fees, but he continued happily taking part no matter how high sales soared or how much money he had.

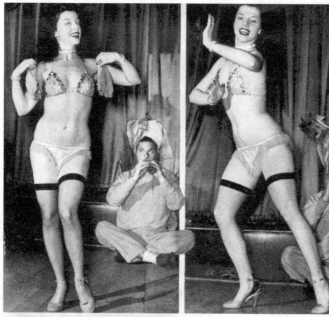

In the "Strip Ahoy Teasers!" hot spread of the December 1954 sizzling issue of *Wink*, Harrison's nephew, Michael Tobias, recently home from military service in Korea, played snake charmer to a cuddlesome cutie.

"Get Balmy Swami!" It was just another one of the fabulous fringe benefits of working for his Uncle Bob; though even by his early '20s, Michael still couldn't get up enough courage to ask one of the models out on a date.

As young as nine, Bob showed an early entrepreneurial flair by traveling out to Brooklyn and setting up shop at a subway exit to rent umbrellas during a rainstorm. His first magazine idea came like a bolt of lightning when he was 12 years old. He was fascinated by motorists, a new phenomenon, people who took road trips just for the fun of it. The problem was that their cars were always inconveniently running out of gas, no one knew where to get good, on-the-go grub, and there were no highway accessible motels since the highway itself had yet to be invented.

Little Bob had the truly bright idea to publish a guide to roadside inns and other services. He talked a printer into doing the project on spec, cagily reducing his upfront costs by offering a split of the profits. After all, how much start-up capital can a 12 year-old be expected to have on hand?

Bob hit the pavement, selling the guides on street corners, convincing neighborhood newsstand owners to sell it, and approaching anyone he knew with a car. The guide was such a hit that the printer stole it right out from under him, daring the pre-pubescent to prove the whole thing wasn't the printer's idea from the get-go.

The young publishing mogul was furious that he couldn't enjoy the spoils of his success, but there was an up-side. (In the Universe According to Bob there was *always* an up-side.) First of all he had learned to trust his instincts. He believed that he had a natural ability to sniff out what people wanted and needed, a sixth sense. Later that talent would serve him in ways he couldn't yet imagine. Secondly, the printer's treachery led to Harrison forming one of his strongest lifelong beliefs:

> *If you go into business with strangers they might betray you. But if you stick to family, you'll always be working with people you can trust.*

Even at 12, Bob knew he could trust each and every one of the members of his family unconditionally. Disloyalty was unimaginable.

The Harrison clan was intensely close.

Bob and his sisters remembered Benjamin and Paula Harrison, who had emigrated to America from Eastern Europe in the 1890s, as loving parents, and Bob inherited his father's sense of family. Though he didn't marry, or perhaps even because of it, Bob remained deeply immersed in the lives of his sisters, and of their husbands and children.

The Harrisons had three daughters in rapid succession, Helen, Gertrude, and then Ida, who everyone immediately started calling Edith, though no one now remembers why. Little Max, who later decided to call himself Robert, showed up on April 14, 1904, and he prospered in the household of five women who doted on him shamelessly, catering to his every whim. Surrounding himself with adoring women would become a lifelong habit.

Bob was not a scholar, and he lasted just two years at Stuyvesant High School, where he was good in English and lousy in math. His parents weren't particularly bothered by his dropping out of school. It was a commonplace thing at that time, when completing high school wasn't a given, and college was thought of as something for the privileged or for true intellectuals.

Harrison spent the next two decades in a series of advertising sales and journalism jobs, professions his father never really embraced, calling what his son did "air business."

A magazine, it gets thrown away. How can a person make a life from something that goes right in the trash?

Never mind the fact that to his critics, much of what Harrison would go on to publish didn't just get *thrown* in the trash, it *was* trash.

Benjamin Harrison felt that one should have a trade and stick to it, and that one should keep the station in life to which he was born. Harrison had a flair for selling, maybe even for writing, and he enjoyed it. His father wanted him to be a carpenter. Bob used to laugh about that since he couldn't even drive a nail straight.

One of Harrison's first stabs at writing was a story for *The New York Graphic* that certainly foreshadowed the *Confidential* era. It was a piece of the purest fluff, glorifying a chorine cutie he fancied who was hoofing it up in Florenz Ziegfeld's "Frolics," a midnight revue that featured girls clad entirely in balloons.

Balloons and Babes.

The Graphic tried to be to newspapers and Broadway what *Confidential* would later be to magazines and Hollywood. The afternoon paper was launched in 1924 by Bernard Adolphus Macfadden, an eccentric health faddist famous locally for walking to work barefoot, more than for being the publisher of *The Graphic, True Story,* and various other publications. It launched the careers of a young sports writer named Ed Sullivan and a Broadway columnist named Walter Winchell, and absolutely *scandalized* New York. Journalists of the day liked calling *The New York Graphic* the "Porno Graphic" what with its coverage of sex scandals, society divorces, and murders, and with its pioneering use of what Macfadden called "Composographs," heavily (if not particularly artfully) doctored photos that purported to show everything from Rudolph Valentino's arrival in Heaven to a society party featuring a naked girl in a bathtub. Even though its influence would last through the century, all the way to the fake *Weekly World News* photos of Batboy, aliens, and Virgin Mary appearances, *The Graphic* went bust in less than a year. Harrison loved the excitement of the publication, loved its slick language and fast pace. He didn't think of it as being trailblazing. He only wished the paper could have lasted.

> *So tell me the truth, am I right or am I right?*
> *Best Composograph we never got the chance to do,*
> *best ever, even better than Valentino? Would have*
> *been the Lindbergh kid. Terrific! A Must Read!*
> *'With his killer finally dead, the Beloved Baby*
> *finds final rest at last." We could have tricked out*

a picture of him with angel wings, a halo, the works. Marvelous! The best!

When *The Graphic* crashed and burned, Harrison did a variety of jobs, from writing copy for "Cook's Tour" brochures to selling song lyrics, all to middling success. He was doing okay but his dreams of becoming a big man were never out of his mind, and they never seemed out of reach, not to him anyway. In 1935 he landed work with Quigley Publishing Company, sewing up six years of stability and a handy dandy intro to the entertainment industry, the business that would power *Confidential's* heady rise to the top, as well as help ensure its headlong plunge to an untimely demise.

Even though he was based in New York, Martin J. Quigley, Harrison's boss, was a real Hollywood insider. After launching an early industry trade journal, the widely read and respected *Motion Picture Herald*, he became a confidante of Cecil B. de Mille, Howard Hughes, Samuel Goldwyn, Darryl F. Zanuck, Walt Disney, Louis B. Mayer, Irving Thalberg, Harry Cohn, and Jack and Harry Warner. Quigley became the creator of the Motion Picture Production Code, a complex and often conflicting set of rules and guidelines for movies. This would be the very Code that Harrison and *Confidential* would help shoot to smithereens in just another couple of decades. The Code was supposed to perform the Godly work of protecting the American family from immorality and obscenity on screen, and set nationalized standards so local censorship boards wouldn't be needed anymore. The Code's influence also extended to affecting how Hollywood was covered in the press throughout the country. Screenland ink was always frothy, its writers prone to going blind from the strain of maintaining a rose-colored view.

Not that there wasn't scandal.

But if you saw it in print it was usually because a studio head or a newspaper tycoon was wielding his power like a club, punishing some misbehaving star or other; maybe to get out of an inconvenient contract by charging a violation of the fabled Morals Clause; or maybe the publisher was angry at a star's refusal to give his paper an exclusive.

Really big scandals like Fatty Arbuckle's infamous (and quite fictional) Coke bottle orgy, the murder of William Desmond Taylor, Mary Astor's scorcher of a diary that named names with gleeful abandon; anything involving Errol Flynn or Charlie Chaplin—these were regrettable, unplanned detours into the public sector. Once a judge and jury got in the way of Hollywood's spinners of the quick fix it always ballooned out of control. But those were truly the exceptions. So much muck was routinely kept under wraps it's a wonder the whole town didn't collapse from the accumulated mold.

Harrison was sent on a trip to Hollywood by Quigley in 1935 and all the secret scandal aside, he quickly learned it wasn't a town for him.

Dullsville.

He was used to tearing through a dozen clubs in one night and watching the sun come up over the East River. Sure, Hollywood had a night life, *of sorts*, but try getting a pastrami sandwich at three in the morning after dropping your date back at her place.

The lack of a decent nightlife notwithstanding, Bob kept himself occupied. A rich supply of cheesecake photos flooded into the Hollywood offices of the magazine each week. Many were from legit studio public relations flaks, but by no means all. Some were barely removed from pornography by the standards of the day. Harrison started collecting them. At first it was just a hobby. After all, Harrison was a healthy, red-blooded American man, and there's nothing wrong with a guy wanting to look at beautiful girls.

Are you kidding me? These girls—hundreds of them, thousands—they sent us these pictures. Constantly! Amazing! Some of them practically in the buff—and all of it absolutely Free! It didn't take a genius to figure out they shouldn't go to waste…He could see the whole thing unfold right in front of him. In tableaux no less. Classy! The

red-hot redhead daintily prances through her
garden, wearing a sun-suit cut up to here, her long
legs made longer by four-inch heels, her delicate
pale skin protected by a large brimmed hat. But
then oops, she drops the hat. Watch her from the
rear as she leans over to pick it up off the ground,
not knowing that you can see practically up to her
whatsit. Then come up from behind and whisper
hello. She gasps in surprise then lets out a happy
squeal of joy. 'I knew you'd come!' Yeah, baby,
you can always count on me for that.

Harrison was thrilled to get back to New York and its superior nightlife. Quigley was paying him $70 a week, which was respectable coin in 1940, but ever the entrepreneur, Harrison began mocking up a concept for a new kind of magazine, something a guy like him would want to read, or at least look at. He decided he would call it *Beauty Parade*, and give it the slogan, "Girls, Gags & Giggles." On Christmas Eve, 1940, Old man Quigley heard about Harrison's plans for using pilfered pix from *The Motion Picture Herald* to launch his "smutty" enterprise and fired him on the spot.

Bob would later say he was depressed for one night after getting fired. But the next day brought a family holiday at Edith and her husband Charles' house—Edith was the only one in the family who cooked and entertained at home—and amid the fabulous dinner and seasonal celebration Bob announced his plans for the new magazine. His sisters, Edith and Helen, happily rallied around their baby brother.

Bob's going to start a magazine! We have to help
him! This is going to be big!

The fact of *Beauty Parade* being not far removed from pornography didn't bother the sisters in the least. All they knew was that it was a wonderfully exciting venture, that they hoped it would make a lot of money, and they vowed that they would back Bob no matter what. Their support was also driven by a sense of profound loss. Just five years earlier, their other sister, Gertrude, had died unexpectedly of pneumonia after going out one night with wet hair. Whether the wet hair had anything to do with it or not is debatable, but her death at the age of 32 hit the Harrison family hard. Two years before that they had lost their father to cancer. The deaths added fuel to their determination to stick together and help Bob at all costs.

Edith Tobias was the worrier who hated having her picture taken. Michael calls her fiercely loyal.

> *You could go to my mother and tell her you killed somebody and it wouldn't change how she felt about you.*

Highly sensitive, Edith was a bit of a bleeding heart. Not a Communist, certainly, but she often said how it's a wonderful idea that everybody should share, and there shouldn't be certain people that have millions and other people who couldn't get enough food to eat. Eating mattered a lot to this family. Dinner was something that almost always happened in restaurants. Lunch was usually ordered in and eaten at your desk, unless Bob felt like taking everyone to Lindy's. Edith never minded being the only one in the family who cooked, and she loved setting an elegant table—after all, since husband Charles owned an auction house, they had beautiful china, crystal, a gorgeous silver candelabra, the works.

Edith was devoted to her husband Charles and her two children, Marjorie and Michael, but her family became a satellite of her younger brother Bob's world, where his enthusiasms and activities set the agenda. No one minded. Going to the Jersey shore with him every weekend in the summer was fun. Constant dinners out and hanging around in glitzy nightclubs—it was the kind of life other people only dreamed about—with Earl Wilson from *The New York Post* usually there, Frank Farrell from *The World Telegram*, maybe Sammy Davis, Jr.—you just never knew who might show up.

Helen Studin was the opposite of Edith in terms of worrying. She never worried at all, or if she did, she tried hard not to show it. Not enough money? *Don't worry. Something will happen.* And nine times out of ten, it did. (In the late '50s, for instance, when she was in the process of divorcing Dan Studin, whose work for the magazines had always been haphazard, and whose own ambition seemed thwarted by a promised inheritance from his parents, Helen was really strapped for cash. The settlement wasn't good. He gave her two co-op apartments that he was convinced were losers. Out of the blue, though, the co-ops shot up in value and her financial security was taken care of almost immediately, like magic.)

See? Why worry?

At one point Helen became fixated on Gaylord Hauser, a food faddist of the time. She forced Edith to get a juicer and they made endless batches of carrot juice. Helen kept trying to influence Bob's eating habits, appealing to his sense of health, his vanity, anything. No dice.

Not in a million years! Crazy! Carrots are for bunny rabbits.

He may have nixed the rabbit food, but Bob was always a guy who liked to look good. Even before he could afford it, suits were made to order. Ties came from Sulka. And the shirts, always custom, sewn by a little man named Sy, were a production number unto themselves. Every collar had to fit perfectly, with not one wrinkle. Harrison demanded that the man redo shirt collars as often as ten times before they were considered truly wrinkle-free. And he insisted Helen and Edith be at every fitting, just to make sure everything came out right.

Bob starting a magazine was big news. Edith and Helen both contributed money, and this was also the beginning of Marjorie's involvement with her uncle's business ventures. She had received a $500 inheritance from her grandfather, and as far as she was concerned, she was *wealthy*. She had already spent $100 of it, but $400 remained. Her mother, Edith, came to Marjorie when she was still in high school, and asked her to contribute the $400 left from her inheritance to Uncle Bob's new publishing venture.

But Marjorie loved her handsome uncle. Brimming with brio, he was the kind of guy who, as the first one in their neighborhood to have a car with a rumble seat, took Marjorie out for a thrilling ride in it on her birthday. He was exciting, and more than that, always considerate and nice. She decided to give him her money. It was probably the smartest $400 Marjorie spent in her whole life. The story of her giving money to Uncle Bob became family lore. Little Marjorie helped her Uncle Bob start his magazine empire. No one made much of a fuss over the fact that Marjorie's brother Michael was also chipping in a few hundred bucks. He was used to his sister getting the attention. At the time it wasn't necessarily a matter for animosity. It was just how things were.

Edith and Helen could afford the investment. They were comfortable enough. Edith's husband, Charles Tobias was a chemical engineer turned auction house owner, and a Columbia graduate, while Helen's husband, Dan Studin, worked in radio.

Harrison's company was very much a family enterprise, in the beginning run completely out of the Parc Vendome apartment he shared at first with Helen and her husband, Dan, who gave up radio and tried his hand at becoming circulation director for the magazine. Edith worked every day at the apartment, and Marjorie sometimes sat in on editorial meetings after school, offering her own opinions whenever she was asked, and sometimes when she wasn't.

When planning *Beauty Parade*, Harrison looked for a new approach, and hit on the idea of applying a narrative structure to his pictorials. Truth to tell, his innovative photo "stories" had the barest of narratives. A typical one is "Trunk and Disorderly," in an early *Eyeful*, offering four pages of photos of a buxom blonde, wearing a chain-mesh and rubber brassiere and fishnet stockings, struggling oh-so-mightily to open and close a trunk. That's it. The whole "story."

Will she get the trunk open or not?

Wouldn't you know, the sheer *exertion* of the task brings her perilously closer to busting right out of that rubber bra in each and every picture.

For his covers Harrison utilized the talents of artists Peter Driben, Earl Moran, and Billy De Vors. These guys were at the top of the craft, and their cover art is highly collectible today. Models were plentiful, and favorites included the afore-mentioned Bettie Paige, worshiped now as something not far removed from a pagan goddess.

Driben's approach was typical: A girl is almost always posed to show as much leg as possible, against a bold background of red, yellow, blue, or green.

One important Harrison innovation was credited to Edythe Farrell, a Vassar graduate and former editor of *The Police Gazette*, a lurid newspaper launched in the early 1800s that celebrated the most gruesome crime details imaginable while maintaining that their only aim was to educate the public about the terrible danger lurking everywhere around them. Farrell was an intense woman, incredibly smart and forthright. Harrison hired her after meeting her at a cocktail party, and finding himself impressed with her fearless intelligence. She was the one who introduced him to Kraftt-Ebbing's "Psychopathis Sexualis," arguing that the sexual kinks it detailed, things like whips, chains, and six-inch spike heels, could outsell everything else in the sexy magazine marketplace.

Harrison never actually read the book. He wasn't one for spending quiet nights at home curled up in front of the fire with a good book. But his magazines took on a whole new look, with girls in bondage, girls wrestling, and girls chained by their evil slave masters, who, as with the spanking in *Titter*, often continued to be portrayed by Harrison himself, as much to save a buck on modeling fees as for the sheer, obvious fun of it. Maybe he was a bad boy after all. But Bob Harrison scoffed at the idea of searching for psychological roots in the material he published, telling anyone who asked:

I don't go for this psychiatry stuff.

Beauty Parade wasn't the homerun that *Confidential* would be 10 years later, but by mid-1942 it was a solid success, carving out its own niche in the publishing world. Before long Harrison launched his other girlie magazines: *Wink, Eyeful, Titter, Flirt,* and *Whisper.* Usually contributors and editors, including Harrison, used fake names on the mastheads, and often, photos would reappear with changed captions and storylines in all of the magazines.

Girlie mag success finally landed Harrison the luxuries he craved. He was ready for Café Society and no one around him thought it should be otherwise. He liked to project a playboy image in the media, and not just because it helped sell magazines. It was cool for everyone to think of him as a man-about-town, getting his snap in the *Journal* or the *Post* with the stripes behind him at El Morocco.

Most of the magazines stayed fairly consistent, but *Whisper* would go through three identities. At its launch in the early '40s, it was a recognizable cousin to *Beauty Parade*, mainly girlie shots with a few sexual deviance articles and fabricated Shocking True Stories like, "Girl Gangsters of the Waterfront," with plenty of models posed in sexy, violent scenes. As *Confidential* made its first appearance, *Whisper* got a little grittier, with gossip about famous sports and entertainment celebs joining the mix. At the height of *Confidential's* power and popularity in the mid '50s, *Whisper* morphed into a virtual clone, with Hollywood dirt its primary focus. Titillating painted covers of pinups gave way to cover photos of sexy deviant girls, who in turn made way for Ava, Lana, Marilyn, Judy, Sinatra, Crawford, Sammy, and the rest of the celebrity pack—often recycling photos and articles directly from *Confidential.*

Bob Harrison's very first issue of *Beauty Parade* published in October, 1941, featured cover art by Earl Moran and dozens of free photographs supplied by models, strippers, and starlets.

TOP ROW: Harrison launched Whisper as a Beauty Parade clone. MIDDLE: By the late '40s he morphed the magazine into a mix of outlandish sex and violence articles along with the girlie pictures. BOTTOM: When *Confidential* became a runaway success, Harrison quickly copied the same format for *Whisper*, frequently running slightly different versions of the same articles and pictures in both.

In this cartoon the nude woman is depicted washing at 8:00.

And dressing at 8:30. Quite racy stuff for the '40s and '50s.

As he grew more successful in the early '40s, Harrison wanted a signature style, something to clearly distinguish him from all the other swells hot-footing it into the high life. This is when he bought his first white Cadillac and started sporting the white alpaca coats.

It so happens I have three white polo coats. I love them! What the hell's wrong with that? Any guy with a little showmanship would go for it.

Nephew Michael idolized him. Whatever Uncle Bob wanted to do he did, once taking Michael and a troupe of girls in their panties and bras to a shoot on a New Jersey golf course, without permission, and being chased away by the cops. To Harrison it was all in fun; on to the next photo shoot; to the next sexual set-up of inspired silliness.

Marjorie thought her uncle published girlie magazines primarily because he knew they would sell. Today she laughs at the idea of him being interested in the kinkier scenes he staged, while heartily acknowledges his passionate interest in the female species.

But if all Harrison cared about was making money, there were plenty of ways to go about that without taking on the kinds of legal and financial battles he was forced to fight on behalf of his magazines. And to discount Harrison's passionate interest in depicting Taboos is to dismiss part of the very thing that made him a hit. He broke barriers and made an impact *because* of his own personal passions, not in spite them, which is perhaps the ultimate kind of "write what you know" life lesson, or in this case, publish what you know. Like Louisa May Alcott. But with naked people.

A happy sense of voyeurism, of peeking through keyholes (in fact, some covers of *Whisper* actually depicted cover girls seen through keyholes) clearly appealed to Harrison, providing a kind of motivating force for his whole empire. The brilliant thing he did was to take the perspective of the average Joe, even though he was far from average. Most of the male models in his girlie mags (apart from himself of course) were nerds, giving his readers a secure place in whatever fantasy or fetish was being explored. And once gossip became his true métier, he never lost that common touch, always asking what the reader would care about, what the reader would find interesting.

Beyond the business of publishing, he was keenly interested in reaching, amusing, and catering to his audience. It wasn't just about selling the magazines. He loved the process of creation; often staying late at night to work on layouts, asking anyone and everyone's opinions; the elevator man, a delivery boy, the models themselves, not to mention his family. And whether it was telling a story to friends and family or publishing his many magazines, Harrison relished communicating. It was the air he breathed.

*Maybe my father was right about it being
an "air business" after all.*

Bob often said he thought his dad would be shocked to see his son turning out to be such an important man. A story in *The New York Post* even credited an unidentified friend of Harrison's opining that Harrison's success was all about proving himself to his father.

*This is what makes Bob sweet and
pathetic. His entire drive is to show his
father he could be one of the rulers of the
world. When you hear a mature man
express this as often as he has, you realize
the significance. He wanted to tell his
father, 'Look at me, I can go anywhere
and be accepted anywhere.'*

Harrison laughed off the idea dismissively, like he did most of life's irritants; though he did take a moment to wonder darkly who was this "friend" saying this crap about him. Something as five-cent Freudian as a Father Fixation?

You think I got something to prove? Poppycock!
Ridiculous! I'm not trying to prove nothing to
anybody. And as for my Dad—he might not have
understood my work, but so what? He was an old
man with old ideas. Magazines are a young guy's
game.

To Harrison, his press clippings alone were enough to refute the idea that he was some kind of sad sack, trying to prove himself to his father, who with his old world notions might never have approved of what his son published.

There's Big Bob, stepping out of his Cadillac,
tipping his fedora as he slips some greenery to every
doorman and hatcheck girl in sight. On top of his
game and on top of the world with the fancy digs,
the dames flip for him, one after another, and
sometimes he shows up with one on each arm.

Coming off as a little bit of a lothario in the columns and behaving badly in real life are two different things, and Harrison was actually an old-school gentleman with the ladies. He treated them generously, both in sprit and financially, behaving respectfully and never forcing his attentions. He didn't have to. The women were usually after *him*.

He met Zsa Zsa Gabor at a party one night in the early '50s. One thing led to another and he liked the idea of dating her. *More publicity for the magazine, right?* He invited her out, thinking she was nice enough, but he wasn't seriously interested.

They were at El Morocco one night—she was really crazy about him by now—and she took out her bank book, showing him how her assets weren't limited to the anatomical. She had more than $400,000 saved up, which was real money back then. But Bob couldn't escape from her fast enough.

Hard cash is great, but getting serious about a Gabor? That's just insane. And who wants a dame with more dough than you, anyway? A girl should need a guy, depend on him.

It probably never occurred to Harrison that his whole life and career were dependent upon and based around women. Harrison lived in a house of women as a kid and relied on his sisters and niece to help put him in business; he built his first magazines around half-dressed girls; he would later find inspiration for *Confidential* largely from the testimony of Virginia Hill, Bugsy Siegel's girlfriend (or "moll" as the press usually called her) at the Kefauver Hearings in 1950-1951; and *Confidential* would gain its largest readership through its endless coverage of the Unholy Trinity of Lana Turner, Marilyn Monroe, and Ava Gardner, as well as so many other women in Hollywood. He certainly had more women working on his magazines than probably any other publisher of the day.

And yet...

Harrison remained a guy who thought women should need and depend on men. This despite the fact that all around him, powerful women contributed mightily to his success. Not that he didn't give credit where credit was due. His sisters were The Greatest! Marjorie was The Best! His models were Spectacular! Girlfriends were Gorgeous! But loving and trusting women didn't change his general ideas about a woman's place in the man's world of the 1950s.

Never mind that it was Marjorie who supposedly had so much pull in Hollywood that she was put on trial for it, and the influence of Harrison's sisters, Helen and Edith, was always strong. Bob was a guy who liked to ask everyone's opinion, even the shoe-shine boy, about a layout or about the cut of a new suit, but his sisters were always the last word. He never dreamed of going against their advice—except when Helen took up health food and tried to get him to cut back on red meat. She got nowhere with that idea.

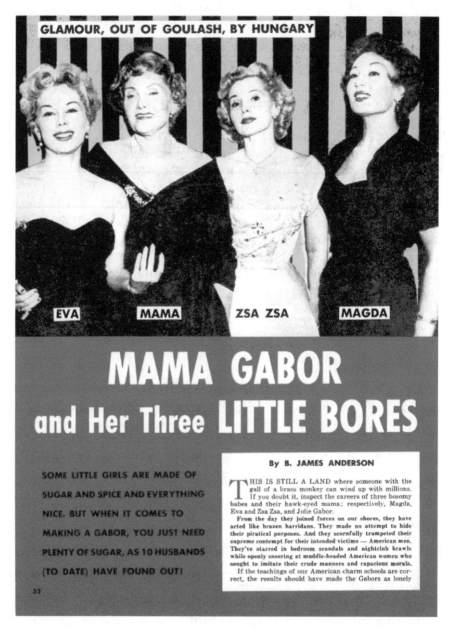

GLAMOUR, OUT OF GOULASH, BY HUNGARY

EVA   MAMA   ZSA ZSA   MAGDA

MAMA GABOR
and Her Three LITTLE BORES

By B. JAMES ANDERSON

SOME LITTLE GIRLS ARE MADE OF SUGAR AND SPICE AND EVERYTHING NICE. BUT WHEN IT COMES TO MAKING A GABOR, YOU JUST NEED PLENTY OF SUGAR, AS 10 HUSBANDS (TO DATE) HAVE FOUND OUT!

THIS IS STILL A LAND where someone with the gall of a brass monkey can wind up with millions. If you doubt it, inspect the careers of three bosomy babes and their hawk-eyed mama; respectively, Magda, Eva and Zsa Zsa, and Jolie Gabor.

From the day they joined forces on our shores, they have acted like brazen harridans. They made no attempt to hide their piratical purposes. And they scornfully trumpeted their supreme contempt for their intended victims — American men. They've starred in bedroom scandals and nightclub brawls while openly sneering at muddle-headed American women who sought to imitate their crude manners and rapacious morals.

If the teachings of our American charm schools are correct, the results should have made the Gabors as lonely

32

Despite (or perhaps because of) their affair never really getting off the ground, a piece about the "boring" Gabor women graced the November 1953 issue of *Confidential.*

Bob's ideas about women were hardly unusual for the time. Social, governmental, and religious forces in America increasingly pushed for a kind of mass myopia—perpetuating many myths about the low intelligence and erratic capabilities of women. Any evidence of the true presence of, and need for, women in the workplace was routinely ignored.

But day after day, until his death, for over 35 years, Edith and Helen were at his side. In a kind of metaphorical manic mood swing from his usual high spirits, Bob could be incredibly dramatic sometimes, and there were times he felt the whole world was conspiring against him. If it rained on a day he had a publication coming out at the newsstands, he would slouch into the office, wringing his hands, all tragedy and misery. He would call in Edith and Helen:

This is the end! I'm ruined! I can't take it anymore!

His sisters would get him back to his usual self, not by arguing him out of it, but by agreeing with him. Yes, the world was conspiring against him, it was totally unfair that it rained that day—going on until he started arguing with them, telling them to cheer up, that it would all work out and be Great! Fabulous! Stupendous! After all, what's a little rain?

It was a smart way of handling him. Their importance was about more than just being mother hens, though. Edith was sometimes credited on the masthead for doing research, and Helen was sometimes identified as a secretary, but that didn't even begin to describe their vital role in the whole Bob Harrison organization. They became the buffers; dealing with anyone who wanted to cause Bob trouble; from employees wanting more money, to firing employees Bob wanted to cut loose. Both sisters had families (though Helen would never have kids), but Helen and Edith were at the heart of Bob's trusted circle, and their time and passion for him and his magazines were limitless. They never got bored as editorial meetings went on for hours at a time, with Bob fussing over his bold layouts, trying to create as much action and excitement on the page as possible.

Do you like it this way? Do you like it that way? Should this be in red? This in black?

Because of Harrison's constant fiddling with the layouts, the proofs were never on time for the printer in Chicago. Michael Tobias, Marjorie's little brother, was drafted more than once to fly from New York to Chicago with the printer's offset boards in a portfolio case that his Uncle Bob insisted must be handcuffed to Michael's wrist at all times. Michael still laughs about it today.

What did he think? That someone would knock me over and run away with the printer's proofs?

Michael was also handy to have around in case Bob fought with one of his gal pals, since Bob's young nephew could be trusted to make sure the girl got home with no funny business—always much to Michael's regret. In between girlfriends Uncle Bob dated a lot of women at once, keeping them comfortable with allowances. Michael delivered weekly envelopes of cash from his uncle, never knowing who he might find behind the door when he knocked. Once it was Sherri Britton, a famous stripper of the day. Michael mumbled a few words to her before just handing her the envelope and rushing back outside.

Sherri Britton! I mean there she was—with those huge... They were so close you could touch 'em! Sherri Britton!

Britton used to get a lot of ink by saying Harrison once proposed to her and she turned him down—an idea Bob always pooh-poohed. He never wanted to get married, preferring a separate home life, but he usually acted the generous husband when it was time for splitsville. Upon breaking up, he once gave a woman an all-expenses paid trip to a ritzy resort full of brand new eligible guys, hoping to give her a leg-up in meeting someone else. The kicker is that it worked. She married a rich Romeo, and the situation worked out to be Harrison's favorite way for things to end up: Win-win.

Of the two major girlfriends that figured in his life, June Frew was the crazy one, always a little ready to fall off the deep end, futilely hoping for a wedding ring. Sometimes the papers actually called her Bob's wife, something she encouraged, but it wasn't true. Harrison once published a photo story he dreamed up with June as the semi-nude "White Queen of the Congo Tribe" which was about as close as she got to wearing white at a wedding. She was with him during the tail end of the girlie magazines and through most of the *Confidential* era.

Regi Ruta was the one who would be with him all the way from the early '60s to the end. She was much more even-tempered than June, and she seemed able to live with the idea of being with a man who wanted to nurture a public playboy image while secretly being a monogamist and even something of a moralist where his own home life was concerned.

Writer Tom Wolfe described Regi as:

> *More of an ensemble, a chorus, a tableau, an*
> *opulent colonial animal, than as one person...*
> *(with) great blonde bouffant hair, a coat of white*
> *fur whose locks fluff out wider than she is tall, and*
> *a dog, a toy greyhound named Tessie.*

For all the visual hoopla, Regi was a rather quiet girl with a gentle voice and manner. She came from Canada, where her family had fled after the war, and hit New York with hopes of an acting career. She was on a modeling go-see when she met Harrison. She knew immediately that she wasn't interested in the job, but that she was very much interested in the man.

The girls were part of the Big Man public image, but Harrison was one of the guys who really liked women, liked being around them, enjoyed their company. As far as girlfriends, they could only have him on loan from his true love, his magazines. The work he put into each issue drove some of his staffers to drink. Literally. Never mind. He stuck with the staffers he could trust. Having family work in non-editorial functions was a given. He liked being around them, and they worked as hard as he did. Win-win.

From the beginning of his girlie magazine success there were Post Office and censorship battles. Being a soft porn pioneer doesn't come without its difficulties. But in 1948 came a grave threat from the USPS to completely revoke the second class mailing permit for all his magazines. No magazines shipped, no money. No money, no Café Society.

Enter legal boy wonder: Albert DeStefano.

In his first case working on Harrison's behalf, the youthful, rather nebbishy DeStefano successfully argued that the United States Post Office was in violation of the recently passed Administrative Procedures Act, which required that federal agencies set up separate channels or procedures to adjudicate complaints brought by the agencies in their role as regulators.

The Post Office had not set up such a separate process or channel in Harrison's case, which left the same officials acting as both prosecutor and judge. DeStefano drafted a letter for Harrison demanding a hearing before the Post Office as required by the Act, and the Post Office dropped its complaint. Suddenly DeStefano, the "young genius," was Harrison's fair-haired boy. Then the Post Office reneged on its agreement, and started pulling Harrison's magazines from mail shipments again. They began another round of allegations that the publications were nothing but pornography, with no First Amendment protections whatsoever. DeStefano won again and again, but that didn't matter to the USPS. They kept finding new regulations that they claimed Harrison was breaking. DeStefano managed to keep the magazines in the mail, but he remained insistent that Harrison would have to tone down the content or risk being barred from the mails. But Harrison took one look at an issue of *Beauty Parade* clean enough for DeStefano and shook his head.

It may be mailable, but it ain't salable!

Robert Harrison in his New York offices in the mid '50s. Today, his nephew Michael laughs at this picture, one that Harrison most certainly staged and used for publicity, wondering as he shakes his head, "Why in the world would he ever wear his hat and a pair of sunglasses while talking on the phone?"

Marjorie Meade at the height of the *Confidential* era in Hollywood in the '50s. Newspaper reporters during her now-infamous libel trial variously referred to Meade as a *Flame-Haired Femme Fatale, The Duchess of Dirt*, as well as *The Most Feared Woman in Hollywood*.

In Tom Wolfe's 1964 Esquire article, Harrison described it like this:

A funny thing happened. One day my accountant calls up... to inform me I was broke. I think the thing was, we had six magazines, and if six magazines start losing money for a few months, you can lose hundreds of thousands of dollars and not even know what happened.

Now listen to this, I think this is a hell of a story. He told me I was busted, so I was looking for an idea. And that same week, I thought up 'Confidential.' That same week. I think this is a hell of a story because I'm not a rich man's son. I'm not one of these guys like Huntington Hartford who can start one thing, and if that flops, so what, start something else.

Actually, Harrison was working on the idea earlier than he admitted. Scandal was increasingly capturing the public's imagination in the early 1950s. Harrison dreamed up the concept of a magazine that would go behind the scenes, and tell the inside story, from watching a riveting television spectacle that transfixed the entire nation: The Kefauver Committee Senate hearings into organized crime.

The hearings were a fascinating revelation of the "enemy within," of criminals and their associates who formed a secret "government within a government." For eight days in New York City over 50 witnesses sang like birds about the highest-ranking mob syndicate in America, allegedly led by Frank Costello, who had taken over leadership from none other than Lucky Luciano himself. A special favorite was the tough-talking moll Virginia Hill, the mistress of rubbed-out Bugsy Siegel, and as rumor has it, a lady who stashed away millions by going through some of those famous Swiss Laundromats. (Her nickname was "Flamingo" which is how the famous Vegas hotel got its name.) Forty years later Annette Bening earned an Oscar nomination (and a walk down the aisle when she married her co-star) playing Hill opposite Warren Beatty as Bugsy.

> *Man walks into a bar. Harrison. Tries to get a drink. But can't get anyone's attention. He looks around. He starts noticing that it's weirdly quiet. Everyone in the place is staring at the television set behind the bar. Virginia Hill is testifying. Did she just use the word 'prostitute?!' Is she going to cop to spiriting away Bugsy Siegel's stash of blood money? Harrison knew it in an instant: If it hooks 'em on the idiot box, it'll hook 'em at the newsstand.*

Not everyone owned a television in 1951, but before the month was over, more sets were sold than in the entire 15-month period prior to the New York testimony. According to *Life Magazine:*

> *The week of March 12 will occupy a special place in history. . . people (gathered) into living rooms, taverns, and clubrooms, auditoriums and back-offices. There, in eerie half-light, looking at millions of small frosty screens, people sat as if charmed. Never before had the attention of the nation been riveted so completely on a single matter.*

Harrison saw the future and liked it. It sizzled. Felt new. Something he could really get his teeth into—and a magazine idea that would lend itself perfectly to the kind of bold graphics and eye catching layouts he favored—things with Pow! Stories that could wake readers up and make them laugh, or make them gasp, anything, as long as it was a strong reaction. He would reveal the secrets—the inside scoop—the truth behind the lie—everything that until now was kept *Confidential*. The name also came to him like a bolt from the blue.

This magazine would be special.

But before he started doing a mock-up, he wanted a unique insurance policy to help ensure the magazine's success, a way of making the publication stand out to the public. His girlie mags were for a somewhat specialized audience of readers (to say the least), not the general public, and certainly not women. The new rag would need to make a bigger, better splash—and capture both male and female readers, with a larger age range.

Two things occurred to him. First of all, Howard Rushmore, a reporter he knew casually at the right wing tabloid *Journal-American*, was really on the skids and needed money; and secondly, Rushmore and Walter Winchell were tighter than tight. Harrison set out to make Walter Winchell his Number One Fan.

Gruesome Twosome in Bare Banana Dance
Walter Winchell, Howard Rushmore, and Josephine Baker

In the media world of the mid-Twentieth Century you couldn't get any bigger than Walter Winchell—the most powerful journalist of the 20th Century. You could ask him yourself and he would tell you so, right to your face. In the Winchell world, he was always in the right, always had his facts straight, and was always, always, *always* on the side of Truth, Justice, and the American Way. The agile former Vaudevillian could probably even leap tall buildings, though keeping up a schedule like his, with a daily column in over 2,000 newspapers, weekly radio and television shows, and nightly Stork Club gabfests, was enough to make ordinary mortals too tired to leap anything higher than a wiener dog.

Winchell's colossal range of influence between the '30s and the '50s is unimaginable in the modern era of fractured digital audiences and Tivo. Bill O'Reilly? Chris Matthews? Anderson

Cooper? Larry King? Barbara Walters? Not even close. Compared to WW they have the audience reach of a couple of seventh graders writing in the school paper. At his zenith, over *50 MILLION* Americans, two-thirds of the entire adult population (at our current population level that would be around 200 million people) read WW's column or tuned their radios on Sunday nights to hear his signature hello:

> *Good evening Mr. and Mrs. North and South*
> *America, and all the ships at sea....*

His broadcasts were weirdly up-to-the-minute and choppy, like audio versions of the non-stop crawl that's now ubiquitous at the bottom of the screen on CNN and Fox News.

In one typical radio broadcast on a Sunday night in 1949, for instance, he raced through an astonishing 42 separate stories in 15 minutes. That was including two commercial breaks for sponsor Kaiser-Frazer. His staccato yet stentorian delivery was a little hard to understand (he was like a gangsta rapper on helium) as he used his own verbal shorthand to coin words and phrases that became part of everyday speech, like "scram," "pushover," and "belly laughs." When he started calling each show's nastiest news item the "Meow of the Week," his phrase was quickly added to "Webster's Third New International, Unabridged" to illustrate a new use for the word, "meow." That's influence.

Another 1949 broadcast: His news items included society births and divorces, Commie dangers, ambassadorial appointments, cancer miracle drugs, Broadway and Hollywood updates, striking union members in Philly, and several different stories about how right something or someone proved he had been about something or other. It was frenetic and pumped, except when he bizarrely paused around midpoint to give a maudlin, drawn out paean to Spring, in awkward, oh-so-flowery prose. His second longest piece was also told slowly, as he drew out each and every point with obvious pride, sentimentally launching into the shamelessly self-aggrandizing story of how his tireless fight against the Commie takeover of America (specifically, his on-air and print sponsoring of a boycott of an American and Soviet cultural exchange event at the Waldorf-Astoria Hotel in Manhattan) had resulted in him winning:

> *It's what you can call an important medal, pinned right on my chest by Russia. They say, 'The notorious open gangster and radio liar Walter Winchell tried to threaten participation, hinting to the American Legion they should picket the Waldorf-Astoria. And they did. Visas have now been refused to other cultural leaders.' There's what you call a real decoration, folks. The Russian government publicly denounces Walter Winchell.*

He loved referring to himself in the third-person, like Alice's Queen of Hearts, or Victoria, and he never shrank from chopping off the heads of his enemies, or sometimes even neutral parties. Famous sayings:

> *The way to become famous fast is to throw a brick at someone who is famous.*

> *Flash! Hollywood, California! The main reason why Ben Bernie, the alleged orchestra leader, can never be president, is because his head is too big to put on a three-cent stamp!*

> *The same thing happened today that happened yesterday, only to different people.*

> *I usually get my stuff from people who promised somebody else that they would keep it a secret.*

> *Gossip is the art of saying nothing in a way that leaves practically nothing unsaid.*

> *Remember that no one will ever get ahead of you*
> *as long as he is kicking you in the seat of the*
> *pants.*

Gossip columnist Liz Smith remembers Winchell reporting about Bette Davis coming down with cancer of the jaw in the mid-'50s, and some press agent or other saying:

> *Well, I don't know whether Davis has it or not,*
> *but if she doesn't have it, she'd better get it!*

Thirteen year-old Walter started his career in a Vaudeville troupe, leaving home in 1910.

> *I didn't want to be hungry, homeless, or*
> *anonymous.*

He did all right but was never really a hit on stage, and he migrated to journalism. His first big job was in 1924 as Broadway columnist and drama critic for a brand new tabloid, *The New York Evening Graphic.* Broadway news, puns, gossip, jokes; his beat was whatever he wanted it to be. Rumor and innuendo started to play a larger part in the column as he fancied himself a maverick, who broke journalism rules right and left, using blind and unverified sources. His popularity rose as he peeked behind closed doors and reported everything: Two-timers, thieves, bastard kids, botched abortions; all in carefully euphemistic terms of course. Anything was fair game.

The public loved him. The class structure was being smashed apart by one of their own, a smart guy who came from nothing and made himself into something. Even his targets, the rich and famous, ended up embracing him. Figuring if you can't beat him, join him, they co-opted him as one of their own, though just like the high and mighty friends of Truman Capote decades later, they often forgot that one is never really safe when a writer is in the room.

By the end of the '20s Winchell's column was syndicated nationally. He was only 31 years-old and already one of the most influential public figures around. When his weekly radio broadcasts began in the '30s he soon wielded more power with his voice and his pen than all the poor slobs whose only claim to fame was money, celebrity, looks, or political clout.

Democracy is where everybody can kick everybody else's ass, but you can't kick Winchell's.

The '30s and '40s were a rocket trip to the moon for Winchell. Recognizing the breadth of his influence, FDR invited him to the White House after his first inauguration. They were fast friends for the rest of the president's life. Winchell is usually remembered now for the petty squabbles, the Red Baiting, and the vengeance—that whole sinister *Sweet Smell of Success* atmosphere of maudlin self-torture and creepy mind games. That's a true part of the story. But WW was often bigger and sometimes even better than that in his heyday. FDR credited him with being a huge part of the war effort, raising morale and propping up America's resolve to enter the conflict in the first place. WW frequently gave generous plugs to show-biz has-beens or to beginners who desperately needed the boost. He tirelessly defended the poor and hungry during the Depression and regularly sided with the underdog afterwards, like in 1946 during A-Bomb tests, when he nearly caused out-and-out insubordination among the GI Joes in Bikini, who were listening to his broadcast on an old radio they set up at a Seabee camp onshore.

I've just learned from a reliable source, the forthcoming atomic bomb blast at Bikini, Operation Crossroads, might cause sterilization of all the men!

The GI grunts openly and angrily confronted their military superiors who hemmed and hawed but eventually made sure that none of them were anywhere near the blasts. It would be decades before anyone else seriously questioned the risks the

U.S. government subjected military personnel and the public to during the early era of atomic testing. Famously, the entire cast of *The Conqueror* would shoot most of the movie in radioactive dust in the Nevada desert in 1955, and just about every last one of them—John Wayne, Susan Hayward, Agnes Moorhead, director Dick Powell—all would die of the most gruesome cancers imaginable, riddled with metastasized illness. John Wayne's son Patrick visited his dad on the set for only a short time, and as an adult was diagnosed with breast cancer, a rare though not unheard of occurrence in men.

And who warned the public first about the dangers of all that testing? Winchell.

He also did a huge amount of work for the Damon Runyon Cancer Fund, an organization that often received plugs in *Confidential.*

Harrison had his eye on Winchell in the Spring of 1952. He hired Howard Rushmore as a freelancer for *Whisper* while developing *Confidential.* But the Winchell favorite's first assignment wasn't a story, it was a Florida vacation. Harrison knew Winchell would be taking a cabana on the Florida coast for an entire month. Harrison arranged for Rushmore to rent the cabana right next door. The two of them trooped down to Florida, families in tow, and spent every single day toasting and buttering WW like an English muffin.

In late Fall of 1951, Winchell got into a public dust-up that would provide one of Harrison's first full-length feature puff pieces on WW: "Walter Winchell Was Right About Josephine Baker!"

In the early '50s Josephine Baker, the sexy Black chanteuse and dancer, was still a big deal in Europe. The French had vivid memories of her sizzling shows way back in the '20s, where her signature stunt was the Banana Dance, appearing practically naked except for a strategically (or sometimes not-so-strategically) placed bunch of bananas. In 1951, still a looker, though middle-aged, she hoped to give her lackluster American show-biz career a shot of Dexadrine with a two-week stint at the Roxy.

The Tawny Temptress entered the Stork Club just before midnight on October 16, 1951, sparking titters and double takes throughout the room. It's the kind of rubbernecking you'd expect from the hoi and the polloi, not from hobnobbing highbrows in one of Café Society's swankiest supper spots. But the stir wasn't caused by a celeb being in their midst, it was all about a Black woman daring to break the color line.

Baker was with her husband and three friends, all White. The staff didn't technically refuse Baker service, they just never gave her any food. After a pissing match with management, Baker and company stormed out. The next day they met with the NAACP and several editors from the then-extremely liberal *New York Post*.

Baker was furious if not surprised that Sherman Billingsley, the owner of the Stork Club, would treat her so badly. Billingsley was pretty well-known to be adamantly against integration on any level. But Miss Baker was shocked that Winchell, oh-so-proud of his work to fight prejudice, was present during the incident at the Stork Club and did nothing, refusing to take on Billingsley, afraid, she charged publicly the next day, with wearing out his welcome at his favorite hang-out.

Legions of loudmouths who had been attacked by WW in past broadcasts screamed "Bigot!" and laughed themselves silly. His enemies exploited WW's purported hypocrisy, how he was trashing his own rep for racial tolerance by doing nothing to help the injured Baker. Winchell became a whirling dervish of an attack dog. Not enough to just challenge Baker's account of the Stork Club incident, no, according to WW, she was a liar, a Commie sympathizer, perilously close to being a fascist, and an anti-American whose decision to become a French citizen was an insult to every man, woman, and child in the nation. In the world. The universe. Infinity. *So there.*

Baker picked up and headed back to France immediately after her Roxy gig and that was the end of that romance. Winchell was absolutely delighted when the third issue of *Confidential*, June 1953, included a story backing up every single one of WW's assertions about the Red-loving, sex-crazy, lying miscegenationist. WW told his radio audience that week that *Confidential* was his new Pet Mag. *Meow.*

The *Confidential* WW articles piled up, trumpeting how his radio stock tip makes millions for his listeners, reprinting the whole Josephine Baker nonsense in 1956, patting WW on the back for saving a man from the Commie Kiss of Death, warning how the Red Menace marks a passel of prominent men for execution, including WW. The positive articles were endless. Winchell returned the favor, delivering no fewer than 16 plugs for the magazine to his millions of readers and listeners in its first six months of existence.

According to stories that would soon appear in *Confidential,* Winchell defended the nation from the Red Menace, exposed the degeneracy and hypocrisy of the rich and famous, and was the guardian and savior of pretty much everyone in America—maybe even a big part of the whole world. For the first two years of the magazine there was a story about him in just about *every* issue. People wondered if he had a financial interest in the magazine—he didn't—so relentlessly positive and incessant was coverage of his activities.

Various writers and freelancers worked on the WW showbiz and human interest stories, but only one man worked on the WW anti-Commie articles: Howard Rushmore.

Howard Rushmore was tall, gaunt, and one later news article referred to him as looking like Mephistopheles. He was certainly an unpleasant son of a bitch. That's the one element in the whole *Confidential* story that every single source, alive or dead, friend or foe, agrees on. The regular *Confidential* staff didn't much like him, and he returned the favor, spreading the word all over town that he was only slumming at Harrison's rag because he needed the money, biting the hand that fed him from the very start.

Marjorie found him unpleasant and argumentative, and she never liked the often badly documented Red Scare stories. Proof of the full horror of the McCarthy witch-hunts was yet to surface, and Marjorie wasn't against his ideas on political grounds—she just thought the story ideas would be boring and bad for the magazine—unlike Hollywood gossip. The fact that

Rushmore was playing fast and loose with the truth wasn't immediately apparent. An awful lot of his often factually dubious witch-hunt material found its way to print between 1952 and 1955. Rarely did any of it get the magazine in trouble, since the country was still in the grip of Red Scare, and story subjects rarely wanted to take the risk of publicly challenging Harrison, since it would bring even greater attention to the Commie accusations made against them. Occasionally someone sued anyway. Even more occasionally, someone walked away with a cash settlement after a cessation of court activities. There would be one serious lawsuit for a Howard Rushmore story that Harrison would have to settle, but for pennies on the dollar. Rushmore's influence at the magazine was overblown, according to Marjorie, trumpeted by Harrison to make a good impression on Winchell.

Mephistopheles? Howard never had that kind of power. Uncle Bob called him different things, maybe Managing Editor on one issue, National Editor on another... Whatever... He was just a writer... And so mean... I always stood up to him when he would propose these ugly, boring stories that I thought would be bad for the magazine. But not everybody wanted to stand up to him. He had such a temper, and he always got personal. If you didn't take his side you were a dummy. I can't for the life of me understand why Walter Winchell would have had anything to do with him. It's a complete mystery. But I guess there are some mysteries even Confidential couldn't have uncovered.

LEFT: Walter Winchell in the mid-'40s. TOP RIGHT: Howard Rushmore Names Names in Washington before the H.U.A.C. in Washington as a friendly witness. BOTTOM RIGHT: Frances and Howard Rushmore in a rare moment of calm at Walter Winchell's favorite New York hangout, the Stork Club. The savage end of their marriage in 1958 would inadvertently define the *Confidential* era forever.

By the '50s Walter Winchell's radio and television broadcasts reached an incredible 50 million listeners.

Harrison sweetened the pot early on for Rushmore, assigning him an exposé of *The New York Post's* extremely liberal editor, Jimmy Wechsler, who had once been a Young Communist League member years before. Wechsler and the *Post's* owner, Dorothy Schiff, were high on the list of supposed Commie-coddlers that McCarthy and J. Edgar Hoover were trying to torpedo, so Rushmore gleefully had at them, excusing himself for working at a gossip rag by rationalizing that *Confidential's* readers needed to know about the dangers of Communism too, the same as everyone else, and after all, it was a wider platform, with more readers, than any other job in his working life as a writer.

One of Rushmore's stories that got the most national attention was about J. Robert Oppenheimer, the "Father of the Atom Bomb" engaging in an illicit affair with a young psychiatrist who killed herself, leaving behind papers that were hastily burned, and whose funeral was attended by a group of mourners who included many Communist Party members. The story was classic Rushmore; gleeful about a Communist's bad end, unrepentant about accusing or exposing the famous, and factual enough to keep the magazine from being dragged into court.

With and without McCarthy, the hunt for hidden Reds was in full swing in America, thanks in part to the diligence of Congressman Frances Walter and his House Un-American Activities Committee. At an HUAC hearing on Communism in Hollywood back in 1947 Rushmore testified as an expert witness, identifying Alvah Bessie, John Howard Lawson, Clifford Odets, Dalton Trumbo, and John Garfield as party members. At further hearings in the Spring of 1952, Elia Kazan, a former Party member, famously switched sides and named names; an act so shocking it turned the honorary Oscar awarded to him 50 years later into a Hollywood war.

Like Kazan, Rushmore started his career as a Communist himself. His family had been desperately poor. Supporting a system that allowed everybody to get his or her fair share was a no-brainer. He started his work with the Party by publishing the Young Communist League newsletter and eventually became a reporter for the Communist Party's official newspaper. But whatever his share-and-share alike impulses, Rushmore bridled at the hands-on management style of his Commie bosses. The relationship was going South already, when in 1939 Rushmore quit in disgust, supposedly over the Party refusing to print his generally positive (though not uncritical) review of *Gone with the Wind,* a film the Party deemed racist and regressive. The whole brouhaha went public, even hitting *The New York Times,* and Rushmore self-righteously took a walk. Howard loved telling the story of why he resigned, because the wrongheaded insanity of the Party's position about this soon-to-be classic film was obvious to all, proving the rightness of his position. (Upon its original release, some in the African-American community bristled at the film's Mammy and Uncle Tom-like characters, organizing boycotts against it with limited success. Their opposition to the film, in agreement with the Party, went un-remarked upon by Rushmore.)

Rushmore and Walter Winchell were as unlike Harrison as any two people could be. Maybe Winchell and Harrison both loved Café Society, and certainly Harrison and Rushmore were both ambitious. But Winchell gleefully fed on the carcasses of his kills, and when a young teacher committed suicide after one of Rushmore's *Journal-American* stories exposed her as a Communist, he proudly boasted about it all over New York. Rushmore married two women whom he loved intensely, one with a deadly passion, while Harrison took a childlike delight in publicity about his playboy life; Rushmore had pretensions to rectitude, although he was a bigamist and wife-beater obsessed with guns. Harrison's public rep was as a hedonist, but family values were number one with him and he never embraced bitterness or vengeance. Life was too short. The city was too exciting.

The Truth About the Walter Winchell 'Retraction'
Writer: Howard Rushmore
Publisher: Robert Harrison

'The New York Post' screamed it was a victory for the truth. 'Time Magazine' called it an 'abject apology.' Communists, professional liberals and

pinko punks crowed that they had finally defeated the man who battled subversion of both left and right in all his adult life. This was the fanfare that greeted the news of a lawsuit settlement brought by the 'N.Y. Post,' a tabloid newspaper, against Walter Winchell. The 'retraction' was heard by millions of listeners over the American Broadcasting Company's TV-radio outlets last March and read in the hundreds of newspapers that carry the Winchell column.

But what the 'N.Y. Post,' 'Time Magazine,' Drew Pearson and others never printed was that Winchell to this day has never retracted his charge that James A. Wechsler, editor of the 'Post,' was a former official of the Young Communist League.

The controversy that shook the nation's press for two years began when the 'Post' printed a series on Winchell in 1951. At that time — as it is now — the 'Post' was the lowest ranking New York afternoon newspaper in terms of circulation; the use of Winchell's name on page one for two weeks was an obvious bid to pick up newsstand sales by attacking the columnist. During the Winchell series, this newspaper added 50,000 circulation on the strength of the columnist's name, but kept only 7,000 of this after the articles were concluded. Many readers claimed they were disappointed.

Winchell, seriously ill at the time the 'Post' aimed its blasts at his reputation, his family and his personal life, launched a hard-hitting counterattack when he regained his health and resumed his column. For the first time, his vast

*audience learned of the political background of the
'N.Y. Post' editor. But the 'Post,' which had
stopped at nothing in its series against Winchell,
couldn't take it. Both Wechsler and his newspaper
sued the noted commentator, the papers that
carried the Winchell column, and the ABC
Network. This didn't stop Winchell, whose
courage is a Broadway legend. He continued his
exposé of Wechsler… At no time did Winchell
take back a word of his original statements that
Wechsler had been a member and a leader of the
Young Communist League, an organization listed
as subversive by the Attorney General of the
United States… The case ragged on, with
Winchell insisting that it be fought out in the
American way — before a judge and jury…
(But) the insurance company retained by the ABC
Network to protect itself from libel suits negotiated
with the Post for a retraction. Under the contract,
if lawyers for the insurance company could settle
the case out of court with a retraction, ABC was
powerless to order these attorneys to insist on a
jury trial and still retain the benefits of insurance.
The network (where) Winchell has been a star for
25 years, had no choice… The retraction was
arranged. But the fact remains that Winchell has
never signed a statement or authorized one
repudiating his original declaration that Wechsler
at one time had been a Red who rubbed elbows
with men and women later convicted of conspiracy;
and that Wechsler admitted under oath that while
a Communist, he had slanted his writing to fit the
Party line; and that the 'New York Post' at one*

*time followed the Communist party line for 18
months. This magazine, in the interests of fair
play, gives its readers the story behind the story—
and it is that Winchell never retracted his
charge...*

Birth of a Sensation
The Legend Begins

Harrison fussed and fussed over the first issue, driving himself and everyone around him crazy with his constant changes of mind, the second-guessing over the tone of the stories, the layouts. Edith and Helen stood firmly behind him, going over details long into the night, well past the normal work day. He just knew he wanted to make it special. It wasn't only about making a buck or being successful. Sure, that mattered. White Cadillacs and alpaca coats don't come free unless you're a mistress or a gigolo. But he wanted it to soar.

*We put together the first issue. It must have taken
about six months to do it... But the truth is,
looking at it after the fact, it was lousy. I must
have ripped that thing apart three times before I
published it and it still wasn't right.*

Harrison finally launched *Confidential* as a quarterly in November 1952, with a press run of just 150,000 and a release date of December. His magazines always hit the newsstands a month early. If it's November, a magazine that says December will seem brand new for two whole months. The first issue's racy mix of stories included a feature on a gay wedding in Paris ("World's Queerest Wedding"), several "picture features" of women in their underwear ("Taboo!" "Too Hot To Handle"), a "hard-hitting" exposé ("I Was Tortured on a Chain Gang"), and a *serious* science story by a Manhattan psychiatrist revealing the long-suppressed truth that athletes are *lousy lovers*. The magazine trumpeted: NO FICTION—ALL FACT. If only. The wedding was staged and photographed in Harrison's New York

City apartment with friends and a few models, the chain gang story was so fictional it might as well have been from a comic book (and looked it) and the naughty underwear pix were retreads from Harrison's stable of girlie magazines. Harrison didn't yet have to embrace fact checking and affidavit gathering; activities that would become standard operating procedure all too soon. There really wasn't anything about Hollywood, just a pictorial on the racy sex scenes being shot in European films, which was really a series of unrelated girlie shots done by Harrison in his hotel suite.

Bob Harrison was completely unaware of how high the stakes were going to get in this new game. In those pre-computer days, even with going back and doing two more print runs, it would be a few months after publication before Harrison even knew the full extent of his magazine's success. But he had no doubt it was a hit in New York. A copy of that first issue surfaced the night before it was due to be on sale at newsstands, while he was at the Colony restaurant. This former mob hangout turned society enclave on East 61st Street attracted the likes of Dukes, Windsors, and Vanderbilts. To Harrison's enormous amusement and amazement, owner Gene Cavallaro was renting the magazine out at $1 a read to his curious and enthusiastic patrons, donating the money to charity. Harrison also spotted Café Society reading *Confidential* at El Morocco and "21." If that wasn't proof enough of the popularity of the issue, certainly the fact that Harrison had been at the Colony in the first place was one measure of how far this son of poor Jewish immigrants had himself traveled. Sherman Billingsley granted him entry to the Cub Room at the Stork Club, New York's most famous celebrity haunt.

For a minute or two there, it had seemed like the petering out of his girlie magazines might snatch the high life from Harrison's grasp before he had the chance to live it to the highest hilt. Nuts to that. Nertz. Harrison was going to be right up there with Winchell. You wait and see.

Big man, big plans…

▾

TOP LEFT: Bob Harrison's father Benjamin Harrison. TOP RIGHT: Edith Harrison and her attendants at her wedding to Charles Tobias, in dresses designed by sister Gertrude, standing to the right behind Edith. Helen is seated. ABOVE: Paula Harrison with grandchildren Michael and Marjorie Tobias.

Harrison's nephew Michael Tobias served in the Naval Reserve during the Korean War.

Marjorie and Michael's father Charles Tobias served in the Army during World War I.

TOP LEFT: Marjorie and Michael's father, Charles Tobias, in his Columbia graduation photo. TOP RIGHT: At a party in his honor, Tobias reads a phony gag newspaper. BOTTOM LEFT: Little Marjorie (center) with childhood friends Richard Katz and Eleanor Leaventhal. BOTTOM RIGHT: Marjorie's brother, Michael Tobias, in the late '50s.

TOP LEFT: Helen at sister Edith's house for the holidays; TOP RIGHT: Helen sunbathes at a beach club on the Jersey shore; BOTTOM LEFT: Gertrude, the middle sister who dies young; and BOTTOM RIGHT: Helen (left), an unidentified friend (middle), and Edith (right), sometime in the '20s after a tennis game.

RIGHT: Dan and Helen Studin out on the town in New York in the early 1950s. CENTER: The whole gang at Edith's for the holidays. Front row from left: Helen Studin, Robert Harrison, Marjorie Meade, Dan Studin; Middle row: Edith Tobias and Fred Meade; Back row: Charles Tobias, Michael Tobias, June Frew, and Robert Harrison's attorney Dan Ross. BELOW: A night on the town with Cafe Society. On the front row from left: Marjorie, Jules and Rhea Schlesinger (whose son James would later serve as U.S. Secretary of Defense); Back row from left: Fred Meade, Edith, Charles, and friends, Mr. and Mrs. Lloyd Clayton, an unidentified woman, and Helen and Dan Studin.

TOP LEFT: Fred Meade in Beverly Hills circa 1956. TOP RIGHT: Fred and Marjorie in New York City after his return from serving overseas in World War II. ABOVE: Marjorie after her marriage to Fred Meade, with the two sisters: Marjorie's Aunt Helen Studin, and mother Edith Tobias, at the Jersey Shore circa 1950.

Confidential publisher Robert Harrison at the height of his success in the mid-1950's

Robert Harrison on the town with a shapely subject featured in a cover story in the very first issue of his new magazine *Confidential*:

SHOWGIRL SELLS SHARES IN SELF!

Meet Geene Courtney Inc., whose obvious assets include blonde hair, hazel eyes, 37" bust, 23" waist, 36" hips—and a sexy voice!

.

Bob Harrison poolside with partygirls.

PART TWO

MOVIELAND MASSACRE
GUNPLAY GETS BIG BOB GUTTED

MOVIELAND MASSACRE
Gunplay Gets Big Bob Gutted

Big Bad Bob was well and truly tanked. He opened the unlocked door. The foyer was deserted but he could hear the raucous party going on within. From the high pitched chortles and unhinged laughter, he figured everyone inside was tanked too. God, it felt hot in there. He loosened his tie and undid his shirt. Then he started undoing his pants as he opened doors, hoping for a bathroom. Three closets, no john. So he pissed into a potted plant. *Christ, it really was hot.* Trickles of pungent, scotch-filled sweat poured out of him. As he shook his penis, an idea occurred to him. He let his pants fall to the floor and stepped out of them. Then he went in search of the kitchen.

*Ketchup? Mustard? Or both? What about
relish...Messy... Hot...*

It was Bob Mitchum. Not Bob Harrison. As "Robert Mitchum: The Nude Who Came to Dinner" appeared in *Confidential*, the story got so cleaned up it smelled from bleach. It opened with a digression on Napoleon, Churchill, and Caesar, before getting to the meat: Robert Mitchum, who apparently showed up drunk at a masquerade party thrown by Oscar-winning actor/director Charles Laughton and producer Paul Gregory, with whom he was shooting *Night of the Hunter*. According to the article, the he-man stripped to the buff, spattered his six-foot frame with catsup and shouted, "Well, it's a masquerade party, isn't it? I'm a hamburger!" Embarrassing? Sure. But for Mitchum, whose career had already weathered a 1948 stint "doing time in a Hollywood clink for flying too high with Marijuana Airlines," it was hardly earth-shattering or potentially damaging to his reputation.

Maybe the *true* story would have been.

According to several sources, Mitchum had actually squirted the catsup up and down his penis before waving it toward Laughton and the almost exclusively male group of guests, laughing lasciviously, and booming out, "Hey, which one of you fags wants to eat a hotdog?" The Homo Happy magazine was uncharacteristically timid about leaving the closeted Laughton and Gregory in the clear as far as the Lavender Luau goings-on that night at the beach house party. And mentioning Mitchum's penis—well, that would have been too crude for *Confidential*. Harrison liked articles to be thick with innuendo. Not thick with body parts. The hotdog even had to become a hamburger, since ostensibly, its shape alone would have given up the ghost.

It was vintage Harrison, who loved the idea of the pleasure seeking rascal, out of control, not giving a thought to conventional societal expectations. It took a big man to strip like that. Literally. It also came at a time when there was a shift for Harrison himself. He didn't just want to be a Man About Town in Café Society; he wanted to be thought of as cut from the same cloth as the guys he was covering, the hunky he-man stars themselves. The Mitchum story was the kind of thing that would make the magazine famous—or infamous— but increasingly, Bob Harrison wanted to be famous—or infamous—in his own right.

Hollywood stories didn't start dominating the content of *Confidential* until the third issue, August 1953. Harrison tried an experiment. The first two issues had sold well, but he felt in his bones that it could all go bigger. Bolder. He reasoned that if readers were fascinated by the inside dope on society figures and politicians, they would be even more interested in Hollywood stars. The trick was that he felt like he had to come up with a different approach—something readers couldn't get from movie fan magazines or the Louella/Hedda coverage of the day. Then he hit on it: Don't just say that such-and-such happened—let readers know why, let them get the inside scoop on how the business really worked. He stuck Marilyn on the August 1953 cover, her first of many for Robert Harrison, and then under the pricelessly silly pseudonym of Harrison L. Roberts:

Why Joe DiMaggio is Striking Out with Marilyn Monroe

He put the wood to the best fastballs ever served up in the American League, but 'Joltin' Joe' DiMaggio kept swinging at and missing those lovely curves in his world series of the heart—that gallant attempt to make Marilyn Monroe his wife.

Marilyn and the headline-conscious publicity department of 20th Century-Fox made a six-month riddle out of the question: 'Will or won't the wedding bells ring?'

Fans of Joe's and Marilyn's, who are still scratching their heads over this puzzle, can relax. The answer is Joe Schenck, an old artist at the fade-away pitch in the Hollywood league. Genial Joe (Schenck that is) said 'No dice,' when Marilyn went to him to confess palpitations of the heart over one of the best ball players since Babe Ruth. In effect, he told her 'Have fun, kid, but don't get serious.' That was enough to change a four-bagger into an easy out.

The uninitiated may well inquire how a balding, squat little gnome old enough to be her grandfather could exert such a strong influence over the beauteous Miss Monroe. Insiders will confess they, too, are often a little baffled over Joe's Rasputin-like powers. But none deny his abilities.

Schenck, they point out, occupies the role of a 'father' in Miss Monroe's life. He guides the luscious blonde's career, inspires her ambitions, lauds her triumphs and lulls her fears. He's always there with a paternal hug or a strong shoulder to cry on.

If Marilyn was ripe for such a relationship, there can be no argument that Schenck is a cum laude graduate of the university for 'Daddies, De Luxe.' This stubby Galahad has been a knight in a cream-colored convertible for years to gals from six to 36 (beyond that age bracket, a girl isn't supposed to need a pop).

If Hollywood needed alerting that Bob Harrison would take no prisoners, this was the wake-up call of all wake-up calls. No one with Harrison's circulation numbers had *ever* said anything this unflattering (or true) about a head honcho at a major studio. Maybe the public didn't know a Schenck from a Mayer, or a Zanuck from a Warner, but the show biz community certainly did; and they were shocked by the tone and more than a little nervous by what it might bode for the future. Schenck was incredibly powerful in Hollywood, but he could rave and rant all he wanted; Harrison was unconcerned. The story signaled to his readers that *Confidential* wasn't just another movie fan magazine. And it sold, pushing sales figures past movie fan magazine leader *Photoplay* into seven figure territory for the first time. Harrison knew that Hollywood would be his Holy Grail—which in no way implied that he wanted to be there himself. He had begun developing relationships there, but his attorney Al De Stefano strongly advised (demanded) that Harrison protect himself. At least two unrelated affidavits would have to be signed and in-hand before anything actionable could be printed—De Stefano knew that Harrison would have to be able to defend the information gathering. At first Harrison sent Howard Rushmore on trips to Hollywood to check-up on things, but by then Rushmore was taking more and more amphetamines, and his behavior was increasingly too unpredictable. Harrison worried that gathering the witness affidavits and fact-checking the more explosive stories wasn't being handled properly under Rushmore, and that someone else needed to be put in place permanently to oversee the investigative activities on behalf of the magazine.

You can always trust your family.

FLASH FORWARD:

Topless Tour of Tinseltown
Marjorie Makes Her Move

Getting out of the car at the swank Peninsula Hotel in Beverly Hills is tricky. Her rhinestone tiara could fall off at any moment. The parking valet does a double take before offering a helping hand. He bends forward in an unsteady bow, unsure whether she is royalty. Then, careful of the tiara, she sets her shoulders back, her head held high and very still. She thanks the valet for his help. With that, Baroness Marjorie von Rothbart of Vienna strides into the hotel lobby. The fake baubles look like the real thing, glittering atop her red bouffant hairdo, and she is soon happily in her element, surrounded by equally bejeweled friends.

The whole "Rothbart of Vienna" thing is a gag. Her name is Marjorie Roth. The occasion is a party for the Crown Jewels, a group of vivacious society women who like playing dress up. Most of them can well afford real tiaras but they all wear paste, giggling as they troop downtown on expeditions to the ethnic wholesale district, to the kinds of stores that cater mostly to young Latina coming out balls and confirmation parties, events where the array of tiaras and scepters is always staggering.

Marjorie is still a flame-haired femme fatale. Her curvy movie-star frame is evident, no matter the rather modest, tailored cut of her gown. Her posture is model-erect; her manner gracious and insouciant. Her voice is deeper now, throaty from the years of smoking. She lives very much in the present, keeping abreast of what's going on in Hollywood and Washington. Home is a chic, art-filled tenth floor condo facing the Hollywood Hills.

The day after the Crown Jewels party she drives down a West Hollywood street with the top down, carefully maneuvering her convertible, a classic Mercedes 560 SL. At a stop light she looks up to find a billboard of Paris Hilton, the current It Girl of the gossip pages and tabloids. Marjorie can't help rolling her eyes. *Paris Hilton?* The skinny hotel heiress can't hold a candle to the often notorious women who once occupied a privileged place at the center of Marjorie's Hollywood life. No foreign dignitary has showered Hilton with priceless jewels; she has no secret reform school past; she hasn't even gunned a lover down. Not yet anyway.

Marjorie is a Beverly Hills society matron now. Her tabloid magazine past isn't a secret to anyone who really knows her, it just seems very far away—the work she did, *Confidential*, the trial, the idea that newspapers had once called her "The Most Feared Woman in Hollywood."

> *That's ridiculous. No one thought of me like that.*
> *Or if they did they never said it to me.*

Paris Hilton can wait. The light changes and Marjorie keeps her eyes on the road. Her baby blues are almost completely concealed behind Chanel sunglasses. She's more careful with her kick-ass wheels now, and forget about driving at night.

SOFT FADE. FLASHBACK. 1955:

The red-hot redhead is a much more confident driver, tearing down the streets of a far swankier Hollywood. As she guns her topless pink Ford convertible she leaves a trail of Pall Mall butts stained with her signature coral lipstick. Marjorie Meade is on her way to lunch with a woman who's looking to make some much-needed cash from the kiss and tell on her very famous, very married, Hunky Hollywood He-Man.

Marjorie's Fab '50s Movieland was a land of romance, high stakes wish fulfillment, and adult pleasures. People still *dressed* for cocktails. They danced the night away in posh nightclubs, and cared so much about their appearance that a star like Fernando Lamas drove to parties naked from the waist down so he wouldn't crease his pants before making an entrance; and going commando so that underwear didn't spoil the line of his tight, custom-made trousers.

The wannabes lived in a different world. The single apartments on the eastern edge of Hollywood were cramped, chock full of the most beautiful girls and handsomest boys from all over America. They all just *knew* that fame was their fate. Whatever they did for money while they searched for the Big Break was usually a far cry from what they hoped to find. Varying levels of prostitution were easier for some of them than waiting on tables and pumping gas. So was selling tales to scandal magazines. The aspiring actresses stuffed their bras and swiveled over to Schwab's.

Maybe today I'll get discovered, just like Lana Turner!

Never mind the fact that it wasn't Schwab's, but some other drugstore counter where Lana's sexy sweater got her a part in a movie. But then, that's the thing about a world of make believe: Facts don't always count for much, not to most people, but facts *did* matter to Marjorie. Her life was centered around them as she dug down deep, tearing off the sheets to catch the nocturnal naughtiness of Tinseltown.

The move West had never been in Marjorie's plans, nor those of her husband Fred Meade. It certainly wasn't part of the future they saw for themselves when they first got married. In the postwar years, back in New York, as Uncle Bob was in the midst of his girlie magazine success, Marjorie wasn't unhappy. She loved her two sons and her husband, and enjoyed her extended family. But she was a little disengaged. It was hard for her to put her finger on, but she just knew she wanted something more, that the ordinary life of a housewife wasn't really satisfying her.

Fred had gone into the Air Force very young. As a lieutenant and a navigator sent over to Italy, he found himself in extremely active service. He was even shot down by the Germans, his plane riddled with bullet holes and shrapnel, yet all nine crewmen survived. At that time the Russians were advancing, but his plane crash-landed in Czechoslovakia, on the Russian side, and the Germans had to retreat. It was nine months before they could get back to their base in Italy. During that winter in Russia they drank vodka constantly. It was all they had to drink.

It was a time when it felt like anything could happen.

This was the backdrop of drama and intensity in the air when Fred Meade had returned to New York and married Marjorie in 1945. They settled down to an Upper West Side life of comparative ease, with Fred working in his dad's chinaware business. Yet neither of them were thrilled with their prospects as he looked to the coming years and saw his trajectory in a career with his father and she looked at the domestic scenes that would be her future.

Uncle Bob hit on the solution, sending Marjorie and Fred to establish a permanent California beachhead for *Confidential.*

The Meades had been to Los Angeles once before and had loved it. Relocating would also allow Fred to dabble some in his latest interest, real estate. They did a two-month trial run at the Beverly Hills Hotel before happily renting a swank house in the flats of Beverly Hills. They thought the move was a great thing for their two sons, Tony and Bruce, who would grow up and go to school in the clear sunshine.

Fred and Marjorie arrived in July 1955, and Hollywood Research, Inc. roared to life without either of them instigating much of anything. On their first day Mike Connolly, a powerful *Hollywood Reporter* columnist, called and took them out to Chasens and Mocambo. They started connecting with future contacts and sources immediately. The next day, an old friend of Marjorie's called—Eddie Le Baron—who had married Bernice Smith, the Smith-Corona Typewriter Heiress. He was one of Bob's friends, another playboy and man-about-town, who was well-known before moving to California as the bandleader at Manhattan's Rainbow Room, even though he couldn't play a single instrument. He had always told Bob and Marjorie that all he wanted was to marry a rich lady and he had, with Marjorie's parents, Edith and Charles Tobias, attending the wedding back in New York.

Eddie and Bernice had a Bel Air home now where they liked to entertain, and on the second day of the Meades' arrival, he called up and invited them to a dinner party. The Meades thought it would be a small, casual affair, but it was much more grand.

We pulled into this long driveway, and right when we got inside the front door, Eddie turned to us and introduced this woman. 'This is Queen Fazia of Egypt.' I'll never forget that. I'd never met a queen before. A queen! Imagine.

It was incredible, and all these people! Virginia Sinclair of the Sinclair Oil Company, Marion Davies... Eddie and Bernice had this great big black Doberman and it had pearls. Pearls! Around its neck! And they called the dog Negra. Black. I mean it was so exotic.

Marion Davies was with her fourth husband or something. Walda Winchell, Walter's daughter, was there. She didn't turn out so well, I think she died very young... And so this group was always calling us to go hither and yon, but we had just gotten there. We had just started!

It was a very, I won't use the word depraved, it wasn't depraved, but it was weird. It was a strange, weird crowd. They were like the decadent rich. You know, those people who are so wealthy. Like Bernice. Who was such a lovely girl really. Basically. She was very frail and fragile. And she had all these minks and all these sables and yet she would always bring this little faux fur coat with her. Crazy. They'd just do crazy things. And Virginia Sinclair? I think she was a lesbian. I do. And her husband, the phony Prince David Duvony. I mean, he was such a joke. Him and his gold digger brother. We used to call them the Gabor boys, because they were just like those Gabors. They were all a weird group, but very nice to us.

I also remember days later sitting in the Beverly Hills Hotel in the Polo lounge for eight hours, I swear, and I was on that phone all day, and people were coming in and seeing me, and coming in and seeing me, like I was holding court. This was maybe like my third day, and I mean word got around. They all wanted to see me and talk to me, tell me this or not tell me that… It was just incredible. Some were newspaper reporters, and some were publicity people who didn't come that time to have a story, but just to get to know you, or to try and get friendly. Later I thought maybe that was because they were hoping if we were friends then the magazine wouldn't do bad stories about them or about their clients.

It's funny. I didn't wake up one morning and go 'I want to go into the magazine business.' It was just this thing that kind of happened. But it changed the whole course of my life. If I hadn't gone out to California I wouldn't have done anything I did later. I would have stayed in New York, been a mother, a wife. It changed everything.

Marjorie and Fred may not have been welcomed by the studio heads, but they were more or less embraced by a wide array of Hollywood insiders. Mike Connolly of the *Hollywood Reporter* proved an important ally, helping them to connect to all the people they needed to know. Marjorie doesn't know why

Connolly was so helpful. She guesses it had something to so with him being gay, that perhaps he was afraid the magazine would do a story on him, and by helping the Meades he was protecting himself. His importance in town was monumental. In 1954, the year before the Meades arrived, Newsweek described him as, "Hollywood's unofficial arbiter, prosecutor, jury, talent scout, tend spotter, and social register." The fact that his column was so widely read made Hedda Hopper pea green with envy. She called him a "drunken faggot" as often as possible, to anyone who would listen.

By Fred Meade's estimate the couple received 750 leads for stories in the first year alone—without doing much of anything to find them. Minor stars wanted ink, and they were even willing to tell tales that didn't make them look so good, as long as they got themselves mentioned in the magazine.

Back in New York Bob was pleased as punch that his niece was getting on so well, and he constantly raised her salary, complimented her, and they both basked in the riches as sales soared higher and higher. They made for a good team. Marjorie thought of her uncle as brilliant, an extremely focused, single-minded person of relentless energy. She never really caught on to the fact that she had many of the same qualities. As her life changed, and the magazine demanded her focus, it became her whole world. She grew into every bit as much of a work-obsessed, savvy business person as her uncle—without actually realizing it. From being a young girl and a young newlywed who looked to others to determine the direction her life would take, she had become a woman in charge.

Marjorie was coming into her own.

Uncle Bob's spats with other publishers started to make news—even as these competitors often traded information on the sly with one another, understanding that public feuds only helped both parties involved.

What are Harrison and Wechsler in the 'Post' saying about each other today? Are Winchell and Harrison still friends?

A series of articles ran in *The New York Post* for an entire week, detailing every chapter in Harrison's life thus far. This was when his "friend" made the anonymous suggestion that all of Harrison's striving was based in a father fixation. Harrison's dates with glamorous women increased, much to girlfriend June's consternation, and she started making column headlines as well, staging public confrontations, complete with thrown drinks, meltdowns in night clubs, and hurled accusations in shops and restaurants. More than once, Michael was enlisted by his uncle to escort June back to her apartment while the perpetual party of Harrison's nightlife went on without her. It was all good publicity for him and for the magazine, which increasingly highlighted the bad boy behavior of Hollywood he-men.

To General Mills, Inc—Minneapolis, Minn.
May 1956

It may seem brash coming from an outsider, but you've been making one whale of a mistake in the way you plug Wheaties, boys. Big league ball players, boxers, ice skaters —so who cares whether they chew on the "Breakfast of Champions?"

You've been sitting on a gold mine, fellows, as you'll discover when you've finished reading this story. Then, if you're smart, you'll toddle around to Frank Sinatra's house and get that kid's endorsement on the dotted line.

Frank Sinatra, you say. What's he champ of? Plenty, men. Just ask the babes who know him.

He's had the nation's front-rank playboys dizzy for years trying to discover his secret. Ava Gardner, Lana Turner, Gloria Vanderbilt,

*Anita Ekberg—how does that skinny little guy
do it? Vitamin pills? No. Goat gland extract?
Nope.*

*Wheaties! That's the magic, gentlemen. Where
other Casanovas wilt under the pressure of a torrid
romance, Frankie boy just pours himself a big
bowl of crispy, crackly Wheaties and comes back
rarin' to go.*

*How he does it might have remained a mystery
forever, if it weren't for a curvy, dreamy-eyed little
pigeon who met "The Voice" on the coast just a
few months ago. When the bantamweight crooner
called up his new-found sweetie and invited her to
fly off with him in a chartered plane to spend the
week-end in his luxurious country house at Palm
Springs, the babe hopped at the opportunity—and
got practically no sleep at all for the next two days.
Why? Frankie was on Wheaties!*

The Sinatra-Wheaties article was one of Marjorie's stories;
and her all-time favorite that ever appeared in the magazine—it
was little more than cotton candy and a bright idea. She was
sitting having lunch with a girl who needed money and wanted
to sell a story about her weekend with Frank Sinatra. Sure,
there was sex involved, but nothing kinky, and Frank was
single then, so there was nothing special enough about the trip
to make it into an actual article. The girl really needed the
cash, though, and Marjorie liked her, so they put their heads
together trying to come up with something. Marjorie made her
go over every little detail of the weekend. The girl said Frank
ate his breakfast early.

What does he have for breakfast?

Marjorie was just fishing, with no real idea of where it might go. The girl shrugged.

> *Oh, Wheaties. He was always there in the*
> *kitchen eating bowl after bowl of Wheaties.*

That's it! Marjorie wrote it up in longhand, hubby Fred typed it up, and off it went to New York. Editor Al Govoni wrote the fizzy piece in his own distinctive style, and arranged for promotions in supermarkets, where stacks of the magazine were sold next to stacks of cereal. It was a big hit; one of Harrison's favorites as well; one he would later take credit in interviews for uncovering himself.

Frank was notorious his whole life for hating most of his press. The Tarzan story was no exception, and it was a point of personal pride for Govoni that Sinatra called him all the way from Australia to bitch about it.

Bob Harrison's friend Sammy Davis, Jr. bedded so many white women in the pages of *Confidential* it's a wonder he had time to sing. The star-as-lothario stories were a collected primer on How to Be a Big Man. Story after story appeared: "The Girl Who Made Greg Peck a Bad Boy," "Why Donald O'Connor Should Have Been Spanked," "What Made Bogart Run?" "Why Girls Call Sonny Tufts a Cannibal."

But it wasn't just the bad boys that propelled Confidential to its massive sales—it was the glamour girls. Marilyn. Lana Turner. Ava Gardner. Their affairs were legendary. They sometimes traded lovers back and forth. Frank Sinatra? *Been there, done that.* Frankie figures in all three of their bios. Artie Shaw? *You married him? Me too!* Together the frisky trio racked up an unlucky 13 renditions of the Wedding Bell Blues. Lana was the one who really skewed the curve.

> *I expected to have one husband and seven babies.*
> *Who knew it would turn out to be the other way*
> *around.*

Open Letter To General Mills:

HERE'S WHY FRANK SINATRA IS THE TARZAN OF THE BOUDOIR!

By BRAD SHORTELL

WHEATIES

WHEATIES

TURN THE PAGE

21

TOP: Robert Mitchum sued for millions but came up empty. The true story behind his nude barbecue was dirtier than *Confidential* dared print. BOTTOM: Sammy was Harrison's friend, but steamy "miscegenation" stories sold magazines.

Actually, Lana ended up finding God in the third act of her life, so perhaps that made her total *eight* husbands instead of seven.

History and sociology can be slippery little suckers when you look at the past and nostalgically imagine an innocence that never quite existed, or when you condemn an era for its supposed repression. We know all about the Frigid Fifties, when bullet-proof bras kept everyone's fetishes tightly bound. And the world today is supposedly a sexual free-for-all. If this is so, then why did the *National Enquirer* waste two years of cover space breathlessly tracking the optical illusion of Britney Spears' virginity? And how can one explain public acceptance in the '50s of the public flouting of conventions that saw Marilyn Monroe, Ava Gardner, and Lana Turner happily cavorting through such a "straitlaced" decade, with their gorgeous flesh spilling out of dresses so tight they sometimes had to be sewn into them, hopping on and off the mattresses of movie stars, matadors, tycoons, and athletes. JLo? Amateur Hour. The Unholy Trinity committed fully to making their screen sex queen images live and breathe in the real world. (Marilyn was even a Method Actress!) Elizabeth Taylor was merely their Novitiate at this point—her truly international stardom wouldn't come until after Harrison dumped the magazines. She popped up here and there in the magazine, but at *Confidential's* height she was only on her second marriage, and her real scandals were a few years ahead of her.

Confidential chronicled every move of its Unholy Trinity, celebrating the three stars endlessly. Harrison may have liked a girl who had to depend on him, but Marilyn, Ava, and Lana were women who took what they wanted, when they wanted it, and totally subverted any ideas about female submission in the process.

Ava Gardner—She Wows 'Em and Wrecks 'Em!
May 1954

> *'I'll kill you before I let you out that door,'*
> *Sinatra rasped, 'You can't get away with it.*

Damn it, you're supposed to be waiting to marry me.'

The most maddening mantrap Hollywood has ever known said nothing. But the green eyes bored holes in her lover boy's confidence. There followed an abrupt switch in his attack.

'I swear to God I'll kill myself if you leave,' he shouted, 'Please don't do this to me.'

In a few quick strides, he crossed the living room, dashed into the bedroom and shoved the door half shut. Twice the revolver cracked wickedly, then Sinatra waited. He had fired the gun harmlessly and expected Ava, at any moment, to come running into the room and throw her arms around him.

A small eternity passed and Frank's love-drugged mind came to a cruel conclusion. With the revolver now dangling from a limp hand, he reentered the living room to confirm something he really knew in advance. Ava Gardner, the love goddess who can't be bluffed at her own game, had coolly pranced off to keep a date with one of her former husbands, horn-tooter Artie Shaw. She had warned Frankie at the very beginning of his melodramatic outburst that she meant to keep the appointment and she had stuck to her guns, in spite of his.

Ava was always powerful and out of reach. The impossibility of taming her was the lure, setting up an emotional dichotomy existing as a sort of twin to the bondage and discipline fantasy world that still populated Harrison's popular girlie mags. When Ava "stole" Frank Sinatra from his wife she shrugged off her hate mail, addressed often to "Bitch-

Jezebel-Gardner, Hollywood, U.S.A."; she smoked pot with Robert Mitchum; compared notes with Lana Turner in the ladies room about their lovers; and made mincemeat of the high and mighty wherever she went. Howard Hughes going ballistic and yelling at her? She gave as good as she got.

When I lose my temper, honey, you can't find it anyplace.

Hughes tried to apologize, waiting outside her bedroom with a million-dollar box of the choicest carat-weight he could find; gold, diamonds, rubies; while Ava's sister Bappie tried to talk Ava into giving him a second chance. Ava's attitude was clear and to-the-point.

Tell him he can take the whole damned lot and stick it up his ass!

Lana was a girl whose private life was public property. Her specialty was love triangles, melodramatic misunderstandings, with gaga headlines like, "It Could Only Happen in Hollywood! When Lana Turner Shared a Lover with Ava Gardner!" "Topping Was in a Rage, and Lana was in the Den—with Billy Daniels!" "Too Hot To Print! What Lex Barker Never Told Lana Turner!" "Lana Turner: Why They Love Her and Leave Her," and "Lana Wanted Love...He Wanted Lunch!" In fact, *Confidential* printed less than they might have, soft pedaling her suicide attempts, ignoring the night Fernando Lamas beat the hell out of her, and, tragically, folding their tent in Hollywood before the grand opera of the Stompanato stabbing. People *still* wonder if Lana really did it and let her daughter, Cheryl Crane, take the rap, despite Cheryl's resolute insistence that she did indeed accidentally stab the abusive Stompanato. Thirty years later Woody Allen even based one of his most turgid dramas on the idea, with a sobbing, hysterical Mia Farrow in *September* playing the role of the betrayed daughter grown into an emotional basket case as an adult because of her mother forcing her to take the blame for the crime the mother actually committed.

Lana Turner was capricious and tempestuous, thinking nothing of shutting down a movie set when she felt insulted by her leading man, and then having him fired before lunch, or answering Hedda Hopper's question, "Why do you give exclusives to Louella and not to me?" by saying simply, "Because I don't like you." Of the three, her big box office survived the longest, from the sweater girl days of the mid-'40s clear to the early '60s. Improbably, she even earned an Oscar nomination for her smash hit *Peyton Place,* 1957's second highest grossing film, while her sumptuous ode to emotional masochism, *Imitation of Life,* was the fifth highest grosser of 1959, its glorious Technicolor breathtakingly showcasing Lana's over $1 million collection of jewelry and her lavish $78,000 Jean Louis wardrobe—34 costume changes at an average cost of $2,214.13 each. Now *that's* a star.

Then there was Marilyn. She was one of 20th Century Fox's most valuable properties, with the equivalent of over $200 million in box office a year in the early and mid-'50s, adjusted for inflation, and she reigned as *Confidential's* hottest honey.

The stormy saga of her courtship to Joe DiMaggio helped put the magazine closer to the million-seller circle in August 1953, and stories about the smash-up of their marriage in multiple issues published in 1955 rocketed sales figures past four million.

They were the Hollywood equivalents to the kinds of girls Robert Harrison liked to have on his arm when he went out on the town at night. As his magazine's popularity grew and his own publicity started becoming more important to him, Bob would up the ante and date even more exotic women, as he also started dreaming of bigger and better publicity stunts.
Guns, gals, and guts...

Marjorie kept busy with her sources. She came to be extremely friendly with Francesca de Scaffa, the Venezuelan beauty who also claimed Chinese, Hindu, French, and Egyptian ancestry; who allegedly spoke four languages; and called herself Countess Francesca di Bourbon y de Scaffa. Sometimes she gave herself a promotion to Princess Francesca de Scaffa. While married to actor Bruce Cabot she often referred to herself as Madame Pellissier de Bujac, after his old French-Indian family. Her highest rank, reserved for special occasions, was Queen Mother of Persia. She based her claim to the Peacock Throne on a "mystery son" from her well-publicized affair with His Imperial Majesty, the Shah of All Persians. Francesca was one of *Confidential's* chief informants. Other tabloids knew all about her influence; with *Revealed*, a *Confidential* rival, calling her "Miss Scandal of 1957." Marjorie hates it when people call de Scaffa an informant.

> *She was a* source. *And Francesca was a nice girl. Lovely.*

Who sold lurid information about former lovers. Marjorie doesn't bat an eyelash.

> *How else could Francesca support her elderly mother and young daughter?*

Desire and need justified anything, even as they obscured other possibilities. Maybe Countess de Scaffa could have become a nurse. A secretary. Or a stewardess. In a heady turn of fate, the kind of plot twist that seemed to happen regularly for this crowd, Francesca actually ended up married to the French Ambassador to Mexico in the early '60s. See? She really *was* a lovely girl. Maybe there were a few headlines about her "suicide attempts," her reckless flights from justice, her missing jewels, and her dubious royal liaisons, but lovely, really. Harrison had first made contact with her in 1954 when he was on a rare trip to Hollywood recruiting writers and sources. She gave him the scoop on Errol Flynn and his two-way mirror, where he could watch his friends have sex, she broke the Mitchum ketchup story, and one about Clark Gable being cheap with his first wife. De Scaffa was an unnamed source for those. But there were also several pieces about her adventures with Burt Lancaster, Orson Welles, and the Shah of Iran, where she was named and her photo was used.

Most of Francesca's stories were about her past adventures, and Marjorie swears that Francesca never gave them a story about a man she was currently seeing, but in *Vanity Fair*, Neal Gabler quoted Francesca as having told a *Confidential* editor, "If there are some secrets I don't know, I'll find them out, even if I have to have an affair with the man involved."

She was a determined girl. This former actress and ex-wife of Bruce Cabot knew the Hollywood scene intimately. Her flair for drama kept her in the headlines—including imbroglios involving the supposed theft of a $400,000 jewel from her hotel room, which had been given to her by the Shah. Of course, if she had a jewel worth that kind of money why would she be working for the Meades and Harrison?

Reports of the money she received during 1955 through 1957 range from $10,000 to $30,000 per year—huge money then. But she made it worth everyone's while. Issue after issue contained information from her used in the most sensational stories, but her reported exploits during the Trial of 100 Stars would be her most enduring press coverage.

There were other sources, far more notorious and lower on the food chain. Like Ronnie Quillan, whom newspapers called, "The Soiled Dove"—a madam and hooker who made no bones about what she was or what she did. Quillan's stories and tips, which Marjorie says never came to her but went directly to Harrison in New York, were just as important as de Scaffa's material, finding prominent placement month after month in both *Confidential* and *Whisper*. She even got a whole story to herself in the June 1955 issue of *Whisper*, calling her "Hollywood's No. 1 Madam."

Another source, who like Ronnie Quillan, reported directly to New York, was the now-forgotten star Barbara Payton. She was supposed to be the Next Big Thing Bombshell for awhile in the '50s, and after some lackluster movies started doing anything to get attention, including pasting temporary tattoos on her face. Selling her stories of affairs with Bob Hope and Guy Madison, among others, was probably more about keeping her name in the press than making a bit of cash. She wasn't that hard up—not yet anyway.

Payton's life made Francesca de Scaffa's look angelic. She even made the Soiled Dove seem sort of girlish, as the actress went from starring in "A" pictures to alcoholism, addiction, destitution, prostitution, and death. Along the way she found time to appear before a Federal Grand Jury in the shooting death of an FBI informant, to attempt blackmail, pass out during a theater performance, and lose custody of her son. There were knifings and beatings, porn films, homelessness, and arrests for passing bad checks, public drunkenness, shoplifting, drunk and disorderly conduct, and prostitution.

Marjorie does not say that Barbara Payton was a nice girl.

Still more sources included Dean Martin's governess, a bartender named Bob Tuton, who fed them stories on his exploits with Lana, Ava, and Joan Crawford, and the "Cannibal" actor Sonny Tufts' neighbor. Along with Francesca, Barbara, Tony Quinn's mistress, Mylee Andreason, and Ronnie Quillan, they were all part of a well-oiled machine that developed under the Meades, where stories could be generated and information vetted by detectives. Fact checking had to pass muster to the high degree demanded by Al DeStefano. By this point Harrison *always* deferred to him in matters of what could or could not be published safely.

The "vast network" of tipsters, informants, and detectives referred to whenever the magazine comes up in conversation or in articles, wasn't what that phrase suggests. There were many people ready, willing, and able to join that "vast network" on a strictly freelance, quite indirect basis. The entertainment industry is one where unemployment is chronic, and where people both Above and Below the Line frequently live much more hand to mouth than they ever let on. ("Above the Line" is the budget category for stars, directors, writers, and producers, and "Below the Line" is everyone and everything else. When budgeting a movie, most above the line costs are contractually fixed before going into pre-production, so they are relatively inviolate, while below the line expenses, in many cases, have yet to be incurred, and can be massaged much more to make the numbers work. Also, many of the below the line salaries are determined by union minimums.)

Whatever one's level on the food chain in Hollywood, finances can be rocky. Then there's the volatile, childlike love of emotional chaos that creative types and wannabes spread like cream cheese all over the place. Add to that a streak of anger in the oppressed. Movie sets are often horrible fiefdoms,

TOP LEFT: Mylee Andreason was a regular lunchtime girlfriend to Marjorie Meade. Andreason was also Anthony Quinn's mistress, and one of *Confidential's* regular sources for tales of Hollywood between the sheets. TOP RIGHT: The rather doomed and tragic Barbara Payton appeared many times in both *Confidential* and *Whisper,* supplying stories about herself in the hope of keeping her dimming star from fizzling out for good. It didn't really help. RIGHT: Ronnie Quillan was not the sort of girl Marjorie Meade liked to have lunch with. Quillan, a self-proclaimed madam and hooker, took her tawdry tips straight to Bob Harrison himself.

sometimes benevolent, but often dictatorial and even humiliating—people hold grudges. A lot of the "vast network" amounted to the mistreated making a buck every so often, acting out in moments of crisis, and/or anonymously getting back at higher-ups who pissed them off.

That's why it worked.

If all the worker bees in Hollywood were happy, well rested, and well fed, nobody would have had a reason to cooperate. But a kind of fear ruled the place, then as now, because of the terrifying uncertainty of jobs, endemic doubting of one's own abilities, and the fickle public. *That fear.* Lyle Stuart, an editor and publisher who would cross swords with both Harrison and Walter Winchell, called the fear:

> *A cancer that can only be beaten if you have guts enough to like yourself for who you are, instead of for what you do. That sort of emotional maturity could hardly be expected from people who have had to scrape, claw, and sacrifice to have any career at all—from people who are hopelessly devoted to making stories in their head come to life.*

The fear is inbred. It existed long before and long after Bob Harrison and the Meades, who lived their own lives blissfully unafraid, non-neurotic, and without significant financial worries.

Perhaps *Confidential* was an easy target. Hollywood could project its own anxiety and dread, give it form and voice as a way of avoiding deeper questions about fear and unhappiness—which is not in any way to say that the magazine didn't cut like a knife when it wanted to. It was a scandal rag. Its *raison d'être* was gossip. Gossip isn't usually the inside scoop on all the nice things being done by a bunch of sweet, upstanding citizens. It's dirt. And dirt can get people in trouble. When gossip mavens protest their own responsibility they always fall back on the fact that they aren't the ones misbehaving, it's the errant stars. If they didn't cheat, booze and dope it up, get arrested and what have you, there would be no stories. And while ordinary mortals usually are allowed to err in private, without public scrutiny, publicizing the foibles of the famous tends to make the objects of that press coverage even more famous. That's why the idea of gossip and celebrity being two sides of the same coin isn't just convenient metaphor. They exist hand in hand. Living a public life (which is what celebrity, as opposed to art, is all about) demands creative ways of keeping the spotlight. That's how you end up with poor Barbara Payton sticking tattoos on her mug and Britney Spears getting married and annulled all in the space of a weekend. Someone has to make your exploits known to the public. And the stars who put their mates and kids on display to secure positive press don't always like to acknowledge that doing so opens the door to any reporter who can prove they cheat on said mate or that they abuse said children. It's inevitable, if often a little gamey.

It is often suggested that before *Confidential,* the stars and studios held all the power. If a reporter wrote something they didn't like, they could freeze that reporter out of Hollywood. That is absolutely true. And the fact that *Confidential* had its own sources, that it didn't need or want the official access that only studio publicists could provide, certainly gave the magazine a freedom that no other publication with such a huge readership had ever had. But in framing the story as one where *Confidential* alone battles the stars and studios, the very phrase "stars and studios" is misleading, since it implies that all the studio heads had the same goals and desires as each other, as well as the same goals and desires of all the stars, and that the stars themselves were all of one mind. Life is messy. Hollywood is messy. Movies are extremely messy. Sometimes the studio heads had interests in common, but often they went behind one another's backs to gain an advantage; filtering information through the tabloid press when it suited them. They could punish a misbehaving star and not be directly fingered in the attack, or stick it to a rival when no one was looking. And stars have never, ever been some sort of monolithic group. They don't agree with each other, let alone with studio management. And the press—from scandal magazines to respected newspapers—has always been a convenient target, from the very dawn of the star system:

Florence Lawrence Lives!
Silent Star's Secret Revealed

She started out in Vaudeville as Baby Flo, the Child Wonder Whistler. By 1910 she had already worked her way up the ranks, starring for D.W. Griffith and under contract to the Vitagraph studios, an early leader in the flickers. She became a star just before the one-reelers began giving way to longer, more complex narratives. She may or may not have been the American cinema's very first Juliet—a cineaste controversy—though she was known chiefly for sweet comedies and dramas that highlighted her youth and naturalness, including the popular *Mr. and Mrs. Jones* comedies, usually cited as the first successful film series, where Florence played the pretty young wife to an older, bewildered husband, usually under the direction of D.W. Griffith, who was just a contract employee of the studio, and not yet the icon he would become.

Florence Lawrence would make almost 300 films, before killing herself out of loneliness and career frustration in 1938. Now that's a Hollywood career.

Until 1910, though, no one knew her name, and believe it or not, Florence Lawrence *was* her real name—sort of. Her mother, Lotta, also an actress, took the name Lawrence after splitting with Flo's father, and when Florence hit the boards, she used it too. In the early days of movies the studio heads zealously demanded that no actors be credited by name. Period. Creating a star system similar to live theater would only cost them money and give them grief. It suited most of the actors anyway, who were ashamed of slumming in films, and didn't want to hurt their real careers on stage. It was bound to change sooner or later, as films became more respectable, but Florence would be the first to go out a chorus girl and come back a star.

At the height of her popularity, Carl Laemmle of IMP, the Independent Motion Picture Company (later the founder of Universal) wooed Lawrence, the Biograph Girl, away from that studio. She would become the IMP Girl, at a hefty raise in pay. Florence liked the movies and saw the possibilities of stardom. At Biograph she had accidentally discovered discarded sacks of fan letters addressed to "The Biograph Girl," thrown away by the studio so she wouldn't get a sense of her own worth, and she learned that distributors and theater owners were demanding information about her—all without even knowing her name. Laemmle was fighting to gain recognition and market share for his company, which existed outside the Motion Picture Trust—the early film production monopoly controlled by Thomas Edison's company. Laemmle decided the time was ripe for a revolution.

He planted a heavily publicized rumor that the former Biograph Girl had been killed in a streetcar accident in St. Louis. Fan clubs grieved. A nation mourned. *And each and every obituary used her name, Florence Lawrence.* Then Laemmle issued heated denials of her death, calling the rumor a vicious smear from rival moviemakers. He staged a public appearance for her in St. Louis, advertising her by name. Florence Lawrence drew a crowd of over 25,000, far more than the 10,000 who came out to greet President Woodrow Wilson, who had visited the city a week earlier. Laemmle couldn't be blamed for using her name, since it was already public knowledge. The floodgates opened. Chaplin. Pickford. Fairbanks. Within months they were all making twice and three times as much as before. The star system was born and studio heads haven't stopped regretting it since. They *hate* the stars. Almost as much as they love them.

So the head of a studio defied industry norms and his own peers when he thought it was in his own best interests. He used the tabloid press and the gossip mavens to spread an untrue story that furthered his cause. An actress got her way by defying studio precedent and going along with a giant, gossip-driven publicity stunt.

And then they both blamed the press for printing scurrilous stories about innocent, hardworking members of the film community just minding their own business.

And that happened in 1910.

How much more sophisticated could the process become 40 years later when Oscar-winning producer Mike Todd and a pre-stardom Kim Novak decided to screw over Harry Cohn (after the thuggish Columbia head supposedly had his way with Novak). They got Novak a hefty pay raise from Cohn by pretending another offer for more money existed elsewhere. Then Todd revealed it all anonymously in *Confidential,* planting this so-called bad press. When the story appeared he loudly complained about it to any reporter who would listen, claiming *Confidential* was making up lies about him. Harrison thought the whole controversy was great. He admired Todd and thought what he was doing took balls.

A century after Florence Lawrence it's no different. The press is always a part of the entertainment industry. Not just for the Carmen Electras of the world, but for serious artists as well. Even someone like Sean Penn, an actor who truly hates the press, and who is as serious about his art as an artist can be, submits to the day-long press junkets to promote films he cares about.

> *What's it like working with Nicholson? Is he*
> *really as fun as they say? Give us a cute story*
> *about life on the set.*

One doesn't have to be publicity mad to need the media— after all, movies and television aren't solitary pursuits, and the business relies on finding audiences. It may be a troublesome, ugly process for some, who have little interest in being popular or in exploiting the mythology of stardom, but there's something about being on screen—about being lit, projected, digitized, broadcast. It super-sizes, taking the actor away from real life, no matter how realistic or serious the subject matter. Dogma filmmaking and its pledge to eschew anything non-natural notwithstanding, movies are *never* reality. Reality television isn't even reality. And stars exist in a world that can be privately real, but is rarely publicly so. Few think of Madonna as an artist for instance—not in her film career. But fewer still would call Meryl Streep a circus act. Yet the former is the latter and vice versa, while *both* are stars. Most famous players fall somewhere in the middle. The more childish or neurotic ones publicly misbehave in grand ways. The studios are supposedly more concerned with money alone, though the shenanigans of a lot of the studio heads, like the pissing contest several years ago between Harvey Weinstein and Stacey Snider, or the Disney board antics over Michael Eisner, leads one to think maybe the studio brass and errant stars have more in common than first imagined.

Sometimes the interest of the stars and the studios align, sometimes they are at cross-purposes. They all want and need press attention. They all blame the press when it suits their purposes.

Louella and Hedda have been done to death elsewhere and everywhere. It is generally agreed that they were loathsome women with too much power. As fun as it is to make it seem like their poisoned pens were governed solely by caprice and massive ego, both women served powerful studio and publishing interests. Whatever dirt they spread was almost always officially sanctioned, as the studios did their delicate dance of trying to keep the stars under their thumbs.

That put *Confidential* in an enviable position.

Robert Harrison was the only powerful interest involved. No one at the magazine answered to anyone else. Paramount couldn't bar them from the lot if they didn't like a story, because they were never welcome there anyway. They didn't need Lana or Marilyn or Mitchum or Gary Cooper to approve a cover shot or to cooperate—they already had signed affidavits from any number of sources.

A lot of people talked to *Confidential,* and Harrison's pockets were deep. Ezra Goodman, *Time's* Hollywood correspondent in the '50s said that even upper level studio personnel were often among the informants. Bob didn't spend money recklessly, but he never begrudged paying for a good story. Where he and the Meades also pioneered, though, was in their system of going behind the backs of many tipsters, and using private detectives to prove or disprove their stories. They were quite thorough. Far from exhibiting a reckless disregard for the truth, the staff of the magazine, from Harrison on down, was obsessed with getting enough proof to keep from getting sued. It was a constant refrain at the New York offices, and in the work the Meades did.

*Is it true? Can we get in trouble? Could
someone sue and win?*

There were never any printed retractions.

The New York Post did a puff piece on the supposed case of
the retraction of a story Harrison wrote exposing an unnamed
mobster. Never mind the fact that *Confidential's* heavily hyped
mob stories were almost never revelatory in the slightest. Bob
was incredibly careful about that.

*After all, who the hell do you think controls
magazine distribution?*

Harrison was quoted in the *Post* story, saying the mobster
visited him in his New York office and dangled him upside
down by his heels, out of the window, until he agreed to print
the retraction. No such retraction ever appeared. And Harrison
loved playing games with the press, building his own myth.

Marjorie busts a gut at the idea.

*My uncle held out a window by his heels? The
whole family would have been rushing in — I
mean, my mother and my aunt would have been
absolutely unstoppable. The real story would have
been 'Two Sisters Scream Bloody Murder Stab
Mobster to Death in Gotham!'*

Harrison also liked to tell a story about a group of
gangsters hustling him off one night, telling him over and over
that now he was going to get his, get what he deserved. The
quick-thinking publisher told them to go ahead with it, that
they would be doing him a favor since he had an inoperable
incurable cancer. The mob henchmen eased up and decided to
let him suffer.

I always had to use psychology with those guys.

Or there was the busty blonde who saved him from Izzy the Eel, a crook who, according to the tall tale, mistakenly believed Bob was a prison buddy in possession of a lot of stolen money. So Izzy the Eel got the bright idea to kidnap the publisher and hold him for ransom. The blonde was Izzy's girlfriend. She broke away from him long enough to whisper a telephone warning, choking back her tears. She had only met Bob once, but knew he was a gentleman, a straight-up guy who didn't deserve the kind of treatment her mobster boyfriend had planned. She was a nice touch in the story. Everybody liked a Whore with a Heart of Gold.

There was one story Harrison published about a mobster, though, that was light years ahead of its time. In the January 1954 issue (with Tallulah Bankhead on the cover guzzling booze out of her shoe) there was a piece about how New York boss Frank Costello went through a bad emotional patch and couldn't stop crying. So he went to a shrink. Just like Tony Soprano.

Harrison's own publicity stories aside, Al DeStefano's legal strategy was clear: Always have the facts to back up the story, never retract anything, never admit to doing wrong, and keep your nose as clean as possible.

Various detectives worked in Hollywood and New York on a freelance basis. H.L. von Wittenberg is often mentioned in stories about the Hollywood years, but the main *Confidential* private eye was always Fred Otash, the ex-cop blowhard who never told a story that didn't turn out with him being the hero. He got his start working Chief William Parker's vice unit, hassling and arresting gay men in "Vaseline Alley," the main walkway at Pershing Square in downtown Los Angeles. As he worked his way up through the force he was often at odds with Parker, who took a personal dislike to Otash. In one employment dispute, Otash won the day by showing up with his high-powered lawyer, none other than Art Crowley, and blowing Parker's case against him out of the water.

As he segued from police work to the P.I. beat, Otash operated with his own sense of right and wrong, gleefully telling tales on and off the record about his various deeds and misdeeds. It never seemed to occur to him that there might be something unwise about admitting in print to blackmailing an unnamed gay star to attempt a better settlement for his wife, or that the whole thing might have been a morally dubious enterprise. Author Sam Kashner, something of an authority on Hollywood in the '50s, claimed that the gay star was Rock Hudson in his divorce from Phyllis Gates. Liz Smith confirmed it recently, waiting for Gates to die before revealing the truth about the blackmail plot. And the attorney representing Gates against Hudson, once again, Art Crowley, also confirms it, though certainly not with the term "blackmail."

> *It was business. She was getting a divorce. Rock was trying to shortchange her. You use whatever you can to get your client a result.*

Today, Crowley's affection and respect for Fred Otash remain undimmed, over 20 years after the detective's death.

> *He was a great guy. Honest. A great guy. I did the eulogy at his funeral.*

Otash even admitted in his 1976 memoir "Investigation Hollywood!" (with a forward written by Crowley) to going against one of his client's own interests to force a financial payoff to a friend of his. He reveled in such situations, trusting in his own sense of rough justice.

Hollywood was and is a place with very little collective memory, and Otash operated with a Swiss sense of neutrality. He worked for attorney Jerry Giesler and for the studios as well, but saw nothing wrong in being the main man for Harrison—the enemy. They all knew each other. Otash stalked and staked out Walda Winchell, trapping her like a rat so he could serve her with divorce papers (from Hyatt Hotel heir Hyatt Von Dehn) yet a year later he was working for her. He worked for Harrison, but at Senate hearings was hired by Frank Sinatra to prove that the crooner wasn't where *Confidential* said he was, in a story that would have larger implications later on. Otash worked for Giesler even as the famous lawyer was gathering a horde of stars and studio heads to attack Harrison in court. It's like they were all little kids playing cops and robbers, happily switching roles and sides whenever the game got boring.

Art Crowley was also used to the shifting sands of Tinseltown. Pat Brown, his mortal enemy on the libel trial would later turn out to be a great friend and birthday party companion. Rory Calhoun ditto. Bob Mitchum. He met and befriended just about everyone in Hollywood, and among his innumerable other famous cases, Crowley served as co-counsel to Jerry Giesler, defending Lana Turner's daughter, Cheryl Crane, after the teenager killed Johnny Stompanato.

Fred Otash always did his best for Harrison, methodically putting together the evidence that would make a story stand up in court, or giving the thumbs down when a hungry tipster's tale couldn't be verified.

Whether his work got dirtier than that is open to speculation. He liked playing the big man. And he liked using the *Confidential* name as a billy club. It's not a huge leap to imagine him reassuring some ripe tomato in the wrong place at the wrong time that a scandal could go bye-bye for a little cash and maybe a quick cuddle. His own autobiography alludes to doing as much. Otash and someone as amoral as Ronnie Quillan could likely have come up with any number of disreputable schemes. Of course, just because something is possible doesn't mean it's likely. And even if it's likely, that doesn't mean it's true.

Rumors about near-constant Hollywood surveillance are still widespread. Gossip columnist Jack Martin remembers Elvis Presley and a girlfriend leaving his house for the airport. They weren't out the door two seconds before the phone rang. It was *Confidential*. They wanted to know if Elvis and his cuddlesome cutie were eloping. A pre-dawn call from Otash came on Christmas Day, making lewd insinuations about what must have happened at the Christmas Eve Jack Martin spent quietly the night before with Zsa Zsa—actually, with Zsa Zsa, her current husband, George Sanders, as well as the ex (or not so ex) love of her life, Profirio Rubirosa, the guy *Vanity Fair* fingered five decades later as having had a truly monster-sized penis that was supposedly a large part of his apparently devastatingly irresistible charm to women of all ages. Marjorie found the fact that *Vanity Fair* would report on a thing like that absolutely appalling.

I mean, come on. At least we never wrote about the size of anyone's genitals.

Martin's memories aside, no real evidence has surfaced in over 50 years to support the idea that *Confidential* set up an organized army of sinister informants—its own Stasi. Crowley adamantly insists his friend Otash would never have done such a thing, but even if he did get out of line, if it had been on the scale suggested by popular lore, someone would have had to have emerged in the half-century since to proudly acknowledge having been a part of it all. So does the whole dark reign come down to Fred getting laid and Ronnie Quillan being a loud-mouthed bitch? There was mud. There were tipsters. But what was the so-called "vast network" of informants really about?

This is where Harrison and the Meades were at best naïve and at worst irresponsible and unconcerned. They never figured that landing in town with a big bankroll and big ears might give people a little too much motivation to take a walk on the nefarious side. A community of the desperate quickly settled into place—desperate for fast money, desperate for attention, desperate for work. They weren't employees of the magazine, but that probably didn't stop them from saying they were once they got a quick fifty dollar bill for a lead here, a story idea there. And the idea that it could all turn ugly never seems to have occurred to Harrison. Never seems to have occurred to Marjorie. It was likely a failure of imagination more than anything else—hardly naivety. It just wasn't really in their DNA to put themselves in the shoes of other people—not the subjects of the magazine's articles, and not the sources they used to get them.

Marjorie was busy conquering a city.

Bob was busy becoming a star.

When Harrison published an article about Marilyn Monroe, Joe DiMaggio, Frank Sinatra and a "Wrong Door Raid," in the September 1955 issue of *Confidential,* it didn't seem all that different from most of the stories in the magazine. Juicy? Sure. A good story? Natch. Solid reporting, zingy style, big stars. But it ended up changing everything. *And his life would never be the same.* Just like in the movies.

The Real Reason for Marilyn Monroe's Divorce
September 1955

> *The Los Angeles private detective eased his car into the curb a few feet past 754 Kilkea Drive and took a drag on his cigarette as he watched the world's most famous set of curves wiggle up to an apartment house door and vanish inside. As he stepped from his car, a dark-colored convertible slid up and came to a stop behind him.*
>
> *Out stepped Joe DiMaggio, the famed Yankee Clipper and—as of that moment—the newly divorced ex-husband of the "Shape," luscious Marilyn Monroe. By the light of a corner street lamp, the detective could see Joe's face was set in hard, angry lines.*
>
> *"Well, where is she?" DiMaggio growled at the private eye. There was no need to identify "she."*
>
> *For weeks the dick had been tailing the nation's sexiest blonde. Time and time again the trail had led to this address and the apartment of Sheila Stewart, a little-known Hollywood bit player. Cocking a thumb at the now familiar door, the detective said, "She's in there again."*
>
> *"Who else is in there with them?" DiMaggio demanded.*

"I don't know," was the detective's reply, "I just got here when you drove up."

"Well, I'm not fooling around here any longer," Joe said, "Let's kick the door in and find out."

According to the article, the detective tries like hell to talk Joe out of it, but the jealous (and drunk) ballplayer was determined to go in there. Finally he agreed to call a friend for advice. That's how Sinatra got dragged into the escapade. Frank also tried to talk Joe out of the whole venture, but when Joe was immovable, Frankie stuck by him.

Picture it. Joe so jealous he couldn't pee straight, Marilyn spending the night at a girlfriend's apartment, Sinatra (of all people) playing the voice of reason, and two hapless detectives (one with a borrowed P.I. license—a fact that would figure importantly later on). No matter how much cooler heads tried to prevail, Joe would have none of it. DiMaggio was going to go in there, and show her she couldn't make a monkey out of him. He would catch her in the act! How this was supposed to convince her she couldn't make a fool of him was never explained. Sinatra did or did not stay in the car (depending on whose testimony, in which future court proceeding, you want to believe) as the group busted into the building and kicked in the door *...of the wrong apartment!*

The shock of their mistake was quickly driven home by Florence Kotz, the middle-aged occupant of the apartment, who screamed bloody murder at being invaded by this celebrity gang. DiMaggio sobered up in a split second, and they all high-tailed it the hell out of there. Marilyn, upstairs at her girlfriend Sheila Stewart's apartment, just like she said, was asleep—blissfully unaware of the commotion below, or probably of anything at all, since she was likely bombed out on sleeping pills. The L.A.P.D. labeled the case attempted burglary and closed the file. (There have been rumors since that Marilyn was actually having an affair with Sheila Stewart—a possibility that only adds to the dizzying silliness of the situation.)

Star-crossed love, heartbreak, jealousy, rage, coincidence, crime. It was a huge, huge story, and circulation exploded. It exposed the foibles of the famous in breathtaking specificity, while cloaking the whole event in a witty, well-written article that took the reader inside the minds and experiences of the people involved in the misadventure.

When Harrison published the Monroe-DiMaggio piece, he didn't give much thought to the impact he and his magazine were having on show biz, but the article would be a tipping point. Hollywood and law enforcement both had reputations to protect, and this article was deeply embarrassing to everyone involved. Tattling on this rather silly imbroglio would touch off state hearings, a unified plan among the studio heads to fight Harrison, and legal proceedings to try to shut the whole enterprise down. It would become an out-and-out war—a regular Movieland Massacre—as Hollywood rose up to ferociously defend the fable of its own morality.

The entertainment industry was (and is) an industry important as much for its economic might as for its powerful hold on the American imagination. Tinseltown is a funhouse mirror where the whole country can check its reflection. In the so-called Golden Age of Hollywood, that reflection was usually warm and reassuring, golden even, and more than a little warped. Gangs of publicists co-opted and compromised an often willfully unobservant press corps to create magazine and newspaper coverage that celebrated the myth that the real Hollywood was every bit as wholesome as the cinematic one. Probably no one much believed any of it—but most people tried to behave themselves, or at least pretend like they did. Talk to just about anyone alive at the time, and on the one hand they talk about how squeaky clean everything was, but on the other, they start remembering all the scandals—Errol Flynn, Chaplin, Lana, Mary Astor, Robert Mitchum—and they switch their stories, talking about how much fun the sizzle was, and how it never really hurt the stars' careers. People seemed to know the truth, but make believe they didn't.

The Motion Picture Production Code was to blame for a lot of the whitewashing, banning anything that might lower the moral standards of those who see it, explicitly forbidding all scenes presented in such a way as to arouse or excite the passions of the ordinary spectator, and stipulating moral retribution for every sin, including sex out of wedlock. Thanks to the Code's strictures, abortions and illicit drug seemed to be as rare on the screen as homosexuality and miscegenation—unless you looked between the lines—in which case, it could be seen virtually everywhere. Call a whore a "hostess" but the audience still knew what she was. Ironically, wholesome television housewife Donna Reed won a 1953 Oscar playing one of those hostess characters—a woman identified in the novel "From Here to Eternity" as a prostitute, who comes across in the film as one too, though the word is never uttered. You can ban anything overt, but still get Cary Grant in a women's robe saying he's gone gay, not to mention Franklin Pangborn, Clifton Webb, and dozens of others mincing across movie screens. Even miscegenation was often dealt with in stories where Blacks tried to "pass," from *Showboat* to *Pinky* to *Imitation of Life*. Of course, movie moguls (and Southern audiences) were a lot happier with Ava Gardner pretending to be "colored," than with the idea of Lena Horne (who had almost done *Showboat*, and had even recorded the score, until MGM chickened out) pretending within the confines of a fictional story to be lily white and singing about a white man. And in 1949's *Beyond the Forest*, which Bette Davis believed to have been her worst screen performance, she induced a home abortion and fatal Peritonitis by throwing herself over a cliff.

The Code was always a sham. The powerful could figure out ways around it, on and off screen, while using it to cloak themselves in respectability. Movies of earlier eras absolutely reflected a more sexually modest society (modest, not innocent) but things were changing fast, and the Code could barely keep up. Still, it was a great device for deflecting attacks from the Catholic Legion of Decency and various state censorship boards, and it appeased federal legislators. The Code and Morals Clauses also reassured good people everywhere were shocked, shocked, shocked by the movie colony's drug and sex scandals of preceding decades.

The affluent, mostly Jewish immigrants who ran the studios wanted their films to reflect the America of their dreams—which is how these middle-aged Jews ended up shaping most of WASP America's own vision of itself. People who lived 50 years ago wouldn't have thought to name things the way we do, and there were many things that weren't discussed in polite society, but that didn't mean readers and moviegoers were fooled into accepting Hollywood propaganda as fact. They may have tended to still believe their President, go to church, and try like hell not to get divorced—for the sake of all their children who were destined to grow up and turn cynical in the '60s and '70s—but that didn't mean they swallowed all the fluff. Few were blind enough to believe that Liberace was just looking for the right girl. Even the gaggles of middle-aged women in fan clubs for old Kittenish on the Keys, who eagerly exchanged hopes that this or that romance might lead to his marriage—deep down probably understood it was unlikely—like they knew about their own sons and daughters who were "different." It was a strange kind of knowing, certainly, embedded with lots of denial, and genuine as well as slightly feigned ignorance. But trafficking in the myths of Hollywood, reading about them and exchanging stories, helped take one's mind off life's inconsistencies.

People in the '50s enjoyed believing in Rita Hayworth's skills as a mother, in June Allyson's wholesomeness, in Rock Hudson's heterosexual virility. It is entirely possible to lose oneself in the fantasy of idealized belief while still knowing deep down that the essential truth of that belief is about as sturdy as Jello.

There was also a revolution going on in Hollywood that had nothing whatsoever to do with morality or *Confidential*. Television. As movie audience levels plummeted there was a panic in the air not seen since the advent of sound. Everyone knew things were going to change, but no one could tell exactly what the changes would be, or how said changes might affect them *personally*. There's a saying among the Tribe whenever anything significant in the world happens: "Is it good for the Jews?" That's a short-hand phrase sometimes co-opted in Hollywood by Jews and non-Jews alike, when contemplating change—and it has nothing whatsoever to do with Judaism or being Jewish. *Is that lousy black and white box good for the Jews? Probably not.*

The smart ones in town, like Lew Wasserman at M.C.A., were already hedging their bets by diversifying heavily into television packaging, a term that hadn't yet been invented, that applied to a large agency putting together the entire show. They would own the whole talent pool, behind and before the cameras, getting individual commissions on the participants, and then charging an overall commission on top of that. Whole empires appeared from out of the sand and the balance of power shifted. Yet for the most part, in 1955, the studios were doing what they always do when the winds are about to shift in a major way: They were sticking their heads in the sand and hoping it all would blow over.

Three Cheers For Queers!
Lavender Lads and Baritone Babes Sell Magazines

It was into this atmosphere of fear, if not outright despair, that the roof fell in at the Universal Studios flack farm. Rumors swirled around the press offices that a monumentally damaging story was going to break in *Confidential*—Rock Hudson, the he-man of the studio, star of their smash hit *Magnificent Obsession*, and their great white hope, would be revealed as a Swish. Rock wasn't on the Quigley Top Ten list of box offices stars yet—that happened in 1957 when he debuted in the first place position—but his fan mail count, movie magazine covers, and the breathless sighs of women (and men) in the dark all over the country whenever he stripped off his shirt, pointed to the fact that Hudson would be a major, major star. Once he made the list he stayed on it for eight years, coming in first twice, and in second place three times. He topped Doris Day on two occasions and played bottom to her top in four different years.

Legend has it that in 1955 "The Studio"—it's always "The Studio," never an actual, named person—made a desperate deal with Bob Harrison: Kill any story about Rock Hudson's late night lavender life and The Studio would offer up another star as a sacrificial lamb. That's supposed to be the skinny on how Rory Calhoun's mug shots made it to the cover of the May 1955 issue, complete with the macho star's arrest and prison record. Some say Henry Willson, agent for both Hudson and Calhoun, as well as Tab Hunter and Guy Madison, was the one who brokered the deal.

When the legend is repeated it almost always involves Lew Wasserman, later the powerful head of Universal for decades. But Wasserman was still years away from having anything to do with Universal. Milton Rackmil was then the president of both Universal and Decca Records, which had bought the studio in 1952. Rackmil would have known a thing or two about playing hardball. Not only did he come from the music business, an industry that has always made Hollywood seem squeaky clean, but he dated Joan Crawford, casting her in *Female on the Beach* in 1955, ostensibly instead of buying her jewelry. But Rackmil never went on record about *Confidential* or Rock. The top-secret, Studio-crafted betrayal of Calhoun is a story that has gained underground currency in Hollywood over the years, yet everyone who was there is dead or not talking. Not exactly the kind of thing people leave a paper trail about. Marjorie can't confirm the story either, except to say if it happened, it was something that went directly to her uncle and had nothing to do with her or Fred Meade. (In truth, she says that a lot when you bring up anything ugly or controversial about the magazine.) But she does remember something...

> *There was this call we got once from someone very important in the industry—bigger than we ever heard from otherwise. And it went right to my uncle. It was about a big story and I remember we didn't do it after the call...I think that was probably it... Because Rock Hudson—that would have been some story...*

By any measure it is astonishing that Rock was never mentioned in the magazine. By the standards of the day, his sexuality was known openly around town and he was a guy who really liked to sleep around *a lot*. He was a hunk, in his 20s, horny as hell, so why not? It isn't a value judgment. But documentation would have been ridiculously easy. All it would have taken was sending Fred Otash to follow Rock around for a few nights at best.

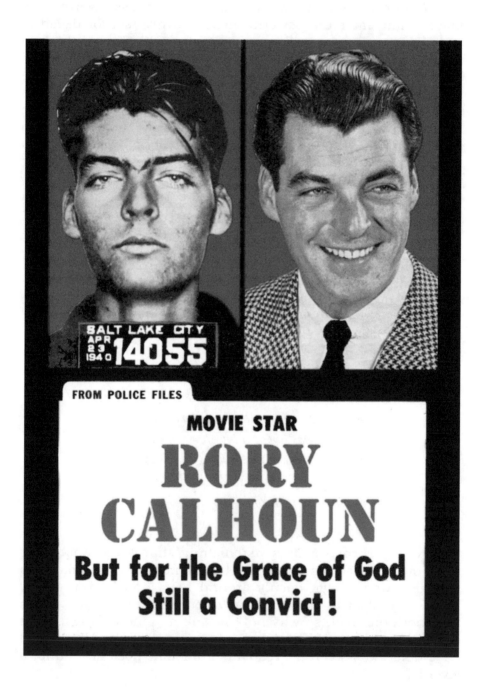

FROM POLICE FILES

MOVIE STAR

RORY CALHOUN

**But for the Grace of God
Still a Convict!**

No surprise that other mainstream publications wouldn't touch the story since they never ran anything about the hidden lives of gay stars anyway. But *Confidential* did—and routinely at that. Rock tried to be covert sometimes. He and friends like George Nader and his boyfriend Jack Navaar tended to go out in threes since two seemed like a couple and four seemed like double dating. His 1955 marriage to Phyllis Gates, Henry Willson's secretary, only lasted a year before imploding. The divorce was messy and ugly, with blackmail threats on both sides. Rock's camp still claims she was a lesbian who knew the score. Phyllis' defenders say otherwise. Whatever. Logically, Rock was a front page scoop waiting to happen. Add the fact that the Rory Calhoun story was one of the biggest honest-to-God scoops *Confidential* ever had; sales figures soared by almost a million copies around then. *Something* extraordinary happened to put the Calhoun story in Harrison's hands, and it was equally extraordinary how the magazine kept mum about Hudson.

Decades later it was revealed that J. Edgar Hoover's F.B.I. tried rather clumsily to keep tabs on everyone in Hollywood. He had a file on Rock Hudson, like he did on many stars. So even the F.B.I. had a file on Hudson, but *Confidential* had nothing? An *Esquire* article in November 1956 did the math and came up with the same answer—without naming names of course— the story that has since been whispered about forever: Universal sold out Calhoun to save Hudson. *Confidential* editor Al Govoni's son, Steve, agrees, saying his dad told him about the deal, and he quotes his father on the whole subject of homosexuals in the magazine:

Harrison would try anything. And when it came to proving so-and-so actor or politician was a homosexual—a curious preoccupation of his— Harrison would spend thousands of dollars, if necessary, to check facts and line up witnesses.

The Calhoun story raised a great outcry, but it had a curiously positive boomerang effect. A priest involved in the story sent a glowing letter to Govoni commending him since the article showed that juvenile delinquents could have a future. Even Calhoun himself seemed to take it in stride, later telling *Newsweek* that it was a relief since now he didn't have to worry about blackmail threats, and his career was going great guns. In a *Post* interview Harrison said he wasn't concerned about any of it:

> *Sure they're scared in Hollywood. I feel for those guys. You take a producer. He makes a star out of some guy and then he finds out the guy is a queer. That producer stands to make a million bucks off of this queer. But it's all overblown. In the end, who cares? Maybe people don't even believe it. It keeps the guy in the news. They go see his movies, wondering, Is he? Isn't he? It brings people to the theaters. It sells tickets.*

So *Confidential* never got a piece of the Rock.

Never mind. The magazine had a gay or lesbian exposé in just about every single issue. And a lot of people noticed, begetting that whole "queer for queers" reputation for Harrison and the stories that interested him.

A number of gay men who bravely picketed the White House demanding civil rights for the first time were disappointed that no mainstream press covered their efforts, but they were thrilled that *Confidential* did—even including the address of the picketers new magazine, *Mattachine*, in the article. The nationwide exposure sent subscriptions to their pioneering gay publication skyrocketing.

There was never a lack of homosexual content. *Confidential* articles took readers everywhere—to a succession of Liberace's hotel suites where the campy pianist relentlessly (hysterically, famously) tried to put the moves on a public relations underling; to auto scion Walter Chrysler Jr.'s quarters at a Florida Navy base where he allegedly seduced many a young seaman; to disgraced Under-Secretary of State Sumner Welles' bedroom, fit for a queen, in Washington, D.C. Van Johnson,

Marlene Dietrich, Tab Hunter, Lizabeth Scott, singing sensation Johnnie Ray, Dan Dailey, an entire Harvard University dorm, the King of Sweden, famous bank robber Willie Sutton, a Vanderbilt heir—the whole gang's there, in issue after issue. There were even a couple of (staged) gay weddings. Harrison drew the line at an Eleanor Roosevelt bombshell from Howard Rushmore, who wanted to expose the former first lady's affair with a female journalist (generally considered by many now to be true). Not content with the gay angle, Rushmore also wanted to accuse Roosevelt of sleeping with a Black, male chauffeur.

Liberace was in a class by himself.

Why Liberace's Theme Song Should Be Mad About the Boy
July 1957

The handsome press agent thought his job was just to boost Liberace's concert. The sour note came when the Kandelabra Kid tried to turn public relations into private relations... The pudgy pianist's many faithful fans would have popped their girdles if they had witnessed their idol in action last year in an offstage *production that saw old Kittenish on the Keys play one sour note after another in his clumsy efforts to make beautiful music with a handsome but highly reluctant young publicity man.*

In one of the zaniest plots in theatrical history, this comedy of errors rang up the curtain in Akron, Ohio, played a crazy Act Two in Los Angeles, and closed in Dallas, Texas, with the wildest finale since "Helzapoppin'." The show had everything: unrequited love... conflict... mob scenes... low comedy. And through it all throbbed the theme song, "Mad About the Boy."

Ironically this article led to one of the very few times the magazine actually paid out a settlement to keep from going to court. Almost every modern article or book that mentions *Confidential,* recycles the fiction that Harrison paid out millions in settlements, that they were besieged by lawsuits. It is true that there were many lawsuits, but almost all of them were either thrown out of court or withdrawn. How could Robert Mitchum successfully sue for "The Nude Who Came to Dinner," when the magazine had signed witness affidavits attesting not just to the general accuracy of the story, but to the fact that the real truth was so much more vivid and lewd. And Harrison was also a master manipulator at getting press. In every interview he gave a different figure for how much money he was being sued for. Like the changing numbers bellowed out in the first version of *The Manchurian Candidate*—if you keep switching the numbers, people don't ask *whether* there are Communists (lawsuits) threatening, but *How many are there?* A lot of the time there were no lawsuits pending at all, but that didn't make good copy.

The 1957 Liberace article screwed up on one date. *Confidential* attorney Al DeStefano had the signed affidavit of the press agent, and of other witnesses, but Liberace could prove he was in London at the time the article said he was supposed to be in one of the three cities where the alleged man-on-man incomplete passes took place. To avoid the headache and cost of the trial, Harrison paid out $40,000—a far cry from the $2 million Liberace wanted—and not the sort of money that would have hurt the coffers of the magazine. That was also in an era when proving one small part of a story inaccurate could lead to successful libel prosecution. Today it is far different. A plaintiff must prove malice or reckless disregard for the truth, charges that would not have applied in any of the *Confidential* cases. There were always affidavits on file. Supporting evidence was always gathered. The only way to prove malice would have been to show Harrison had a personal axe to grind. He didn't. Proving reckless disregard for the truth would have had to come down to Harrison knowing a demonstrably damaging story was false, him printing it anyway, and the subject of the story proving financial or emotional harm.

These elements were arguably never present in any of the stories that sparked celebrities to pursue cases against *Confidential*. The facts lined up. In terms of harm, the gay stories were an area where career damage might reasonably be anticipated—yet most gay celebrities mentioned in the magazine went on to bigger and better things. Far from libel, it's Theater of the Absurd. Liberace's paid settlements technically involved Robert Harrison having to say that perhaps Liberace wasn't gay after all—though he never retracted the original story in print.

And nothing *Confidential* ever said was as bad as the kind of venom that was printed in the London tabloids, where Liberace would sue and win some serious recompense. In a column in *The London Daily Mirror*, "Cassandra" (William Connor) showed no pity:

> *He is the summit of sex—the pinnacle of masculine, feminine, and neuter. Everything that he, she, and it can ever want... He reeks with emetic language that can only make grown men long for a quiet corner... Without a doubt he is the biggest sentimental vomit of all time. Slobbering over his mother, winking at his brother, and counting the cash of every second, this superb piece of calculating candy-floss has an answer for every situation.*

There were some other settlements of lawsuits against the magazine. A January 1954 Howard Rushmore *Confidential* article about Lyle Stuart, editor of a liberal publication called *Expose*, alleged that Stuart was "an admitted extortioner (sic), a hate peddler, and a coddler of Communists." Harrison settled Stuart's $250,000 libel suit for just $9,000. Stuart died in 2006 soon after being interviewed for this book. He confirmed the small amount of the settlement but held it up as a major victory. He thought Harrison was a blowhard.

Harrison was like a big kid with a train set. Maybe he didn't care when he hurt people. More likely he didn't notice. He was happy living his life, what did he care?

Lawsuits didn't ruffle Harrison's feathers since he knew he could win, and since they were common in Hollywood anyway, with *The New York Times* reporting that in September 1954 alone, Twentieth Century-Fox was suing Frank Sinatra for $1 million for walking out of *Carousel*, Ring Lardner, Jr. was suing Fox for $20,000 in back salary, Columbia was suing Rita Hayworth in a $175,000 contract dispute, and Joseph L. Mankiewicz was being sued for $50,000 damages for plagiarism.

It could certainly be said that Harrison and his staff showed a reckless disregard for the *consequences* of their stories. Though of course that's what journalism is supposed to do, and Bob was usually quite upset if negative consequences to a story were brought to his attention. Until his death he remained completely naïve about how people react to bad press. He liked being written about so much he just couldn't conceive of a world where others didn't.

It's easy today, after *Brokeback*, *Will & Grace*, *Queer Eye*, and all the rest, to look back in wonder at what the big deal was about being gay. We're given to understand that in the '50s the worst thing you could do was suggest someone was a homosexual. It wasn't just that it was abnormal. It was unimaginable. At least that's now the impression given by the numerous articles, books, interviews, and documentaries made about the era. But assumptions about the era's black and white rigidity about homosexuality are thrown completely out of whack by a 1954 *Confidential* story about Van Johnson, exposing his gay past. The story itself is kind of preposterous in its own hysterical terms, all about homosexuality keeping Van Johnson out of the army and then how either the love of a good woman or a car crash or *something or other* miraculously helped him change his ways, turning him into the happily married man he was at the time the story ran. This story was read by millions and millions of people—many of whom must have believed it. Van Johnson was never exactly a pin-up hunk, but he was certainly one of MGM's more popular leading men, who two years later was still starring in "A" pictures opposite Elizabeth Taylor, among other stars.

The studio said nothing. Van Johnson remained a star. Nobody really cared; at least not publicly. How could this be? If the '50s were as unforgiving and straight-laced as we are given to understand, there should have been a hue and cry, picketing American Legionnaires, newspaper editorials, and angry denunciations in the Hollywood trades.

None of that happened.

Is Van Johnson gay? Just about everyone who knew him at the height of his stardom is dead or now quite elderly. Johnson maintains a very low profile in New York, exhibiting no interest in resuming a public life. But it's one of those things where when you bring it up, everyone in Hollywood nods and says, *Oh of course, I knew that about Van Johnson.* Like they knew about Rock. Or *know* about today's supposedly closeted stars. What we hope to gain by knowing is a murkier business, and if Anne Heche taught us anything at all, "for sure," is a relative concept. Of course, sometimes rumors are true. A television producer named Bob Chmiel remembers working as a bellman and delivery boy at the Beverly Wilshire in the '70s and delivering a package to Van Johnson.

> *There were clouds of perfume, and Johnson arrived at the door wearing these fantastic flowing robes. I don't know if he was wearing make-up, but he was definitely, well, kind of... Queenly. He was really nice, and kind of happy with himself, totally uninhibited in the best way, just floating around the room in a good mood. And no, he didn't make a pass at me, thank you for asking...*

EXCLUSIVE!

THE TOUGHEST DECISION OF HIS LIFE...

THE UNTOLD STORY OF
Van Johnson

For the famed star with the boyish grin, his girl friends represented not love, but a triumph over himself. Now — for the first time — the hush-hush story of Van Johnson can be told!

After auto accident in which he suffered fractured skull, Johnson went to home of best friend, actor Keenan Wynn (left), to recuperate. There he fell in love with Wynn's wife, Eve, married her after she won a divorce.

By BRUCE CORY

VAN JOHNSON came to Hollywood in 1941 and his slow, boyish smile sent millions of bobby-soxers screaming in juvenile ecstasy.

But there was a mask of tragedy behind that smile and the wide, innocent face of the Newport, Rhode Island lad who hoofed his way into the big time . . . Tragedy and heartbreak, because Van realized that there was another inner self that completely refuted the he-man husky he portrayed on the screen.

For the idol of the nation's gals of all ages during World War II was an admitted homosexual.

Perhaps that's why Van winced when he read in the Hollywood columns that Esther Williams had said, after playing opposite him in "The Thrill of a Romance": "The ones who got a charge out of Sinatra just wanted to 'take care of him,' but the kids who're nuts about Van figure he'll wait for them to grow up so they can marry him."

And often during those years when the Johnson star was blazing a trail of gold across Beverly Hills, Van sat in his room and sobbed. The virile hero of the big muscles and the fierce embrace was a scared, lonesome boy locked in his secret, whimpering and afraid.

Only a psychiatrist could explain the reasons that caused Van Johnson's abnormality, and certainly the men who study the mind would take into account his early boyhood. Van's father and mother separated when he was a youngster and he was raised by relatives.

The loneliness must have started then.

He found an outlet in singing and dancing and starred in high school plays and musical shows. Then came several years of a hand-to-mouth existence as a struggling young hoofer in the small towns and one-night stands.

Van has never revealed, except to the FBI, how his trouble started. Among the other chorus boys with whom he worked, he might have found a friend to compensate for the father he had missed during his boyhood.

He first came to public notice in "New Faces" when producers noticed his dancing ability and, above all, his grin, plus what Hollywood calls the "all-American" face. He got his first big chance in the Broadway musical "Pal Joey," dancing with June Havoc. The critics raved and Warner Brothers signed him to a $500-a-week motion picture contract. Van went to Hollywood.

Showed He Had Plenty of Courage

But before he went, Johnson had come face to face with a decision that was the toughest of his life. In March, 1941, he was called for induction. He was young, husky and passed his physical with flying colors.

During the war, men cursed with sexual abnormality looked forward to a career in the armed services. Many of them saw a future that might cleanse them of their unhappiness; others were ashamed to make such an admission to Selective Service officials.

There is nothing in Van's life to show that he lacks courage. Indeed, the decision he made when he was called for induction took plenty of old-fashioned guts. Exactly what Van told his draft board is still a secret, but a few days later, Selective Service called the FBI.

Under the direction of J. Edgar Hoover, the G-men in war time are assigned all investigations dealing with the draft. This included checking on whether self-admitted homosexuals were telling a lie to escape military service.

In the course of their careers, FBI men deal with crim-

14

inals, subversives, and the weird characters that haunt the periphery of the underworld. But G-Men seldom had heard a stranger story than Van Johnson told them.

It was a story of both truth and pathos.

Van told the FBI he didn't want to be a homosexual. And he added that he was making a desperate effort to return to normal living.

In one of the most unusual "kiss and tell" stories in the history of the FBI, Van gave a full account of his relations with women. He gave them a list of the ladies with whom he had physical relations, including a well-known musical comedy star.

These secrets are the kind the average man carries with him to his grave. But Johnson was baring his soul in an effort to prove to the FBI that he was making a supreme effort to return from the world of shadows to the clean light of mental health.

When Van went to Hollywood and the press agents started beating the drums, the FBI continued their silent work of investigation. Johnson reported to the Los Angeles field office of the FBI that he was continuing his desperate effort to rid himself of his abnormality. . . . But it took another tragedy in Van Johnson' life before he succeeded.

Spent Months in Hospital after Accident

In March, 1943, Van Johnson was driving to his studio. His car rammed into another and Van's auto whirled through the air with a crash of steel and bone. He was dragged out, half-alive, with a fractured skull.

He spent months in a Hollywood hospital. Surgeons inserted a silver plate in his head and finally he was discharged, wan and underweight.

Van went from the hospital to Lake Arrowhead to recuperate. And then to the home of his good friend, Keenan Wynn, son of famous comedian Ed Wynn. Keenan's pretty wife, Eve, a former actress, helped nurse Johnson back to health.

Perhaps Van's helplessness, and that slow, boyish smile that caused the formation of a New York fan club of 25,000 bobby-soxers, won Eve's heart. The Wynns were divorced and Johnson married Eve.

Then Van took another step along what he hoped would be the road to complete recovery. He made a trip back to New York and asked to be reclassified on the grounds of physical disability.

Johnson often wears uniforms in film roles which cast him as hard-bitten GI. In real life he escaped service in last war with shocking confession to draft board.

Pete Martin, writing in the *Saturday Evening Post* in 1945, said: "The skull fracture Van suffered in the accident, the several major operations that patched him together again, and the long convalescence that followed resulted in his being turned down for military service, although prior to the smash-up he had been awaiting induction." Martin apparently did not know that Van's rejection four years before was for different reasons. But Johnson, in February, 1945, returned to New York and asked for re-examination.

Head Injury Changed His Classification to 4-F

The draft board's doctors said Van was physically unfit because of the head injury. The FBI did not intervene because whether Van was a homosexual was no longer important. No matter what his abnormality, the silver plate under the blond Johnson hair would prevent his donning a uniform.

The simple classification of "4-F" put a finis to the story of a man's fight against himself.

The locked files of the FBI, which no one outside the FBI has ever seen, hold the names of the women whom Johnson knew in his struggle to return to a normal world. The public will never learn their identity.

Since that time Van has made many movies and to the few who know his triumph over tragedy, he seems almost a new man, filled with a vibrant confidence.

Perhaps this confidence has grown out of his greatest victory. He is a father now and a solid citizen of his community. Those things, it is true, are average for millions of Americans, yet for Van Johnson his new place in society was achieved through the kind of battle few men have ever won.

Johnson's greatest role was never played on the screen. He will never get the Academy Award for this performance, yet no actor in the history of the movies ever worked harder or deserved it more.

It's Van Johnson's story, played by himself. ▲▲▲

Few glamour gals who enjoyed Johnson's company, like Roz Russell, here shown dancing with him, ever knew of bitter struggle Van had to wage against himself.

15

A couple of years after the *Confidential* story Johnson starred in the turgid 1956 box-office bomb *Slander,* with Steve Cochran and Ann Blyth. It was MGM's only public response to Harrison's "attack" on their star. In it, Steve Cochran played a scandal magazine publisher who tried to use Van Johnson, a rising kid television show performer, to get the dirt on a bigger star who happened to have been a childhood friend of Johnson's. It all hinged on whether Van Johnson would sell out his childhood friend to keep the magazine from publishing a story about how Johnson once did four years for armed robbery. A story that will *ruin his career forever!*

As the publisher, Cochran was one-note evil incarnate, endlessly dismissive of his ashamed mother who drank to get over the pain of what her son did for a living. Van Johnson did the brave thing and refused to rat out his friend. The armed robbery story ran. Johnson got fired from his television show. His son was then taunted at school and while trying to escape his tormentors got hit by a car and *died.* When the publisher's mom found out the kid died because of her son's magazine she picked up a gun and shot her son dead in cold blood. The end.

They even named the lawyer for the publisher "Mr. Crowley," after Art Crowley, who not only worked for Harrison, but remained a lifelong friend thereafter. The film was eighty-one endless minutes of abject hysteria, rooted in the idea of Harrison as the Devil, using any means necessary to dig up the dirt. It's interesting to note, however, that in *Slander* the fictitious magazine's stories were all true. The publisher was evil. But no libel was involved.

Tales are rife about Harrison's tools for verifying the gay articles, including a Ronnie Quillan tale told at trial in 1957 of Marjorie and Fred Meade supplying her with a wristwatch that concealed a microphone and ordering her to make a pass at actress Lizabeth Scott. The story today still makes Marjorie furious. It also makes her laugh.

Not our style at all. Fred couldn't figure out how to set an alarm clock and I could barely make toast!

Otash's methods were mostly straightforward private dick stuff like tailing in cars, guys with cameras outside windows and inside closets, and digging through police records, which is where the Lizabeth Scott story came from—it was right there in the files of the Los Angeles Police Department, where an address book of call girls' customers included Lizabeth Scott's name along with those of George Jessel and George Raft.

Confidential claimed the cops never questioned Scott. If they had, the magazine said, "...they would have learned that Liz was a strange girl, even for Hollywood, from the moment she arrived in the cinema city. She never married, never even got close to the altar....Liz, according to the grapevine buzz, was taking up almost exclusively with Hollywood's weird society of Baritone Babes."

Rumors about Lizabeth Scott were already rife at the time, with some not only swearing that Anne Baxter's character in *All About Eve* was based on Scott, who had understudied Tallulah Bankhead in "Skin of Our Teeth" on Broadway, but that she had also had an affair with the pansexual Miss Bankhead. No hard evidence exists to support either story. Or to disprove them. Scott sued *Confidential* over the September 1955 story, in one of the series of suits orchestrated by hotshot attorney Jerry Giesler. Like almost all the other suits announced or filed against *Confidential*, Scott's was dropped, in this case on the technicality that since the magazine was based in New York she couldn't bring suit in California. But she and Giesler declined to file a suit in New York.

There was almost always enough truth to these stories to scare the stars and their attorneys from ever giving open testimony in court. If you attacked the magazine's honesty, then it would be fair play for the magazine's lawyers to force you to testify under oath as to the validity of each and every rumor, supposition, or fact that had ever appeared in the magazine about you—which is exactly the strategy the magazine's defense lawyers would employ, to varying degrees of success, at the 1957 trial.

A Tab Hunter gay story was also pulled from old police files, exposing a raid at a gay party that occurred well before Tab became famous, back when his name was still Arthur

Andrew Gelien. It detailed his 1951 arrest and conviction for disorderly conduct after his attendance at "a limp-wrist pajama party—strictly for boys." Tab Hunter was a major new star on the block in September 1955, when the story ran, and he would go on to even bigger success. There were heated denials. *He wandered in to ask directions. He didn't know it was a fag party.* And as with Van Johnson, the story seemed to do little or no real harm. Today Hunter doesn't single out *Confidential* as any better or worse than other publications, lumping them all together as being nightmarish.

Sometimes the fun was in bringing up a rumor only to quash it, like *Confidential* did in August 1953 with a story that luridly detailed each and every homosexual accusation against Adlai Stevenson before revealing the allegations to be scurrilous lies. The technique is still popular. One of the juiciest sections in the relatively new and increasingly hot gossip magazine *In Touch*, is its column that brings up Hollywood rumors, and then pronounces them true or false. The really lurid ones are almost always false, but the format allows the magazine to print the original accusation in all its sensational sizzle anyway. Fool-proof because there's no chance of libel.

Other stories, like a July 1955 piece about Marlene Dietrich in 1930s Paris making a spectacle of herself with a notorious lesbian gal-pal and currently enjoying the company of a close lesbian heiress friend, were less specific about the love that dared not speak its name. And as with a Willie Sutton article, about a famous bank robber who had a few love affairs with other men in prison, these were stories that were really old news, repackaged as new scoops. Everyone knew about Sutton already, and Dietrich was, well, she was Dietrich—a force of nature that no one expected to be confined or defined by anything as boring as her gender. There were stories about possible "cures" for homosexuality, a few Howard Rushmore smears of gay people in government (Rushmore's articles, unlike others in the magazine, tended to be mean-spirited and disparaging in tone), and exposés about the horrors of the gay life. But there was also one rather non-judgmental story about innocent men being caught up in overly rigorous sting operations in public bathrooms, and like the Van Johnson article, it exhibited a curious air of tolerance.

The overriding tone remained rather gee-whiz, without significant gay-bashing, at least not in relative terms. Compare that to an issue of a cheap porn and gossip magazine called *Hollywood Confidential* published in 1956, which promised to forward fan mail from readers to any of the stars mentioned in the issue except, "No fan mail will be forwarded for Tab Hunter, Liberace, Johnny Ray, or Van Johnson, a line must be drawn somewhere." Harrison would never have printed anything like that.

One fact emerges again and again. Liberace, Johnson, Dietrich, Hunter: very few of the famous people tarred with the scandal of homosexuality in the pages of *Confidential* suffered any significant career harm as a result. The arguable exception is Lizabeth Scott, but she had never reached full-fledged stardom and she was on something of a downward spiral at the box office anyway. Gay, a studio could accept, failing at the box office? Unforgivable.

That's not to say that it didn't cause a lot of private grief. There's no way around the fact that anyone caught in the web of a gay accusation was terrified then, as they can sometimes still be now. Yet the whole uproar, the terrible fear of disaster seems to have been as overblown then as it just may be now.

Even in the '50s, how disapproving could anyone really be in Hollywood? It was a town where Vincent Minnelli showed up to direct on movie sets wearing full eye make-up, where Joan Crawford's very best friend was the gay former leading man-turned top designer Billy Haines (Box Office Top Ten in 1930) who famously told L.B. Mayer to "go fuck himself" when the studio head ordered him to give up his boyfriend; where Cary Grant lived with Randolph Scott seemingly more happily than he ever did with any of his wives; and where Louella Parson's own daughter, Harriet, became a successful producer of such hits as *I Remember Mama* and *The Enchanted Cottage* while living a comparatively open life as a lesbian.

A freeform relativism and sense of experimentation is hardly surprising in a community of creative people. That's one of the things about artists: From the beginning of time they have been, and continue to be, freer spirits. It's just the nature of the beast, which isn't to say anything as ridiculous as all actors are gay, but rather that actors are a lot more likely to try anything once, at least more likely than their civilian counterparts. Their stock in trade is trying on personalities and experiences.

Forget the '50s for a moment. Remember the train wreck that was Anne and Ellen. While horrified *Oprah* viewers tried mightily to make heads or tails out of the scary and terrifying idea that a straight person could turn gay overnight, Hollywood watched with a different kind of horror. Ellen was well-liked and no one wanted to see her get hurt, but she forgot that above all else, Anne Heche was (and is) an actress—a deeply committed, talented, Methodist type. Sure, her love was genuine and deep. *In the moment.* For that scene, that movie, that month. Tomorrow would bring another passion. And it did. And that's what actors do. Or in the immortal words of Joan Crawford: *If you want the girl next door, go next door*—a line Sharon Stone could have coined if Joan hadn't gotten there first.

That freedom of expression and experience among creative people is part of what made Hollywood coverage in *Confidential* possible, not just with the gay material, but with most of the stories. Voracious stars and starlets, race mixers, two-timers— these were people who didn't care to live by society's conventions, and often didn't really care who knew it. That made them main course material for the magazine. Even today, Marjorie talks about how she never really wanted to be just a regular person with an ordinary life. She wanted more. Hollywood was and is full of a whole lot of people who want more. John Patrick Shanley in his play, "Four Dogs and a Bone," came up with the Theory of the Un-licked Cub, which paraphrases out as a mother bear gives birth to a bunch of baby bears. She cleans and licks all but one of them when she is shot and killed by a hunter. That last bear cub is left unclean, i.e. un-mothered, un-nurtured. That baby bear, the un-licked cub, is the one who goes to Hollywood.

The public gasps when they hear tales of celebs misbehaving, but what do they think? That people who struggle against the impossible odds of Hollywood, who lay it on the line and risk anything and everything, not just to get what they want, but merely to be able to do the work that makes them tick—that these people are just plain folks? It's an idiotic, almost demented expectation. Harrison knew that. That's where the joyful, zingy, upbeat feel of the magazine came from. He had no interest in being just plain folks either, so even as he covered the stars, getting the story behind the story, naming the names, telling the facts, and all the rest of it, he was at once identifying with his subjects while acknowledging that he was taking average people to places they could never otherwise go, and revealing a whole other world in the process.

Harrison celebrated being out of the mainstream. He elevated what most people of the day considered deviance to a kind of art form, refusing to get involved in being the judge and jury over the "transgressions" of people out to have a good time.

The lack of puritanical zeal in tone was obviously a choice on Harrison's part. An immensely popular non-fiction book series of the early '50s, written by Jack Lait and Lee Mortimer, started with "New York Confidential," moved on to "Chicago Confidential," "Washington Confidential," and finally, "U.S.A. Confidential." The books promised to give readers "the full-scale, full-bodied, uncensored, unafraid account of the shockingly corrupt underlife of America..." One of the co-writers of the books, Lee Mortimer, was a gossip columnist for *The New York Daily Mirror* who wrote articles that regularly attacked Bob Harrison and *Confidential*. Privately the two men were actually on friendly terms, with both handing off tips to one another via pay phone to keep their public feud going, keeping their names in print as much as possible.

Jack Lait and Lee Mortimer's writing was incredibly, aggressively mean-spirited though. And they went after gay men with an Inquisitional vengeance:

Original captions from these two photos that accompanied the Marlene Dietrich lesbian story:

BELOW: "Famous men were chasing Marlene all over the world in 1936, when she met Frede, a slim, 20-year-old-brunette. Their 'friendship' was the talk of sophisticated Paris."

RIGHT: "Another baritone babe who's been linked with Marlene is the multi-millionairess Jo Carstairs, whose huge yacht took them on crazy weekends."

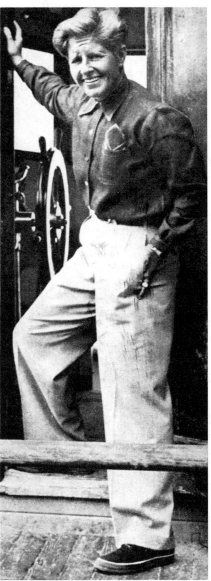

> *America is becoming a land of manicured hermaphrodites, going the way of Rome... the entire nation is going queer! Young men are being infected with the virus of an epidemic which was old when Spartans believed he-men and warriors should love each other. The Prussian military caste thought along similar lines, and depravity became official among many in Nazi Germany. See what happened to Sparta and Germany.*

They were also nasty about women, lesbians, people of color, union members and bosses, and politicians. But a whole chapter in the last book was devoted to how sick and disgusting it is that men have sex with other men, and how it would destroy the nation and the entire world if allowed to continue. The tone was hateful and emblematic of popular discussion in the "respectable" mainstream media of "the other" who might be living next door.

Harrison was miles away from any of that. He had no sense of hostility toward any particular group—not gays—and certainly not the "Race Mixers" who crossed the color line.

Salt and Pepper Sundaes
Black + White Is Beautiful

There's a luridly mesmerizing moment in 1994's *That's Entertainment! III*. It is a compilation film, following late in the footsteps of its two earlier siblings, utilizing all too familiar footage from classic musicals. But suddenly time stops for a segment on a Cyd Charisse number that was dubbed by India Adams and cut from *The Band Wagon*. The number got shoehorned into a 1953 MGM turkey called *Torch Song*—famously summed up by Otis L. Guernsey, Jr. in *The New York Herald Tribune* as:

> *Joan Crawford, all over the screen, in command, in love, and in color!*

Crawford played an aging, brittle Broadway musical comedy star, falling in love with an obviously embarrassed Michael Wilding, gamely doing his best as a *blind* rehearsal pianist. Her big song in the show-within-a-show was the above recycled Cyd Charisse/India Adams song with a title of tragically unintentional irony: "Two-Faced Woman." It was a huge production number that opened with Joan's appearance in what was then euphemistically called Tropical Make-Up.

It was blackface. Joan Crawford was in blackface.

There she stood, all steely shoulders and evil stare, stomping and glaring her way down the stairs and across the pretend Broadway boards (as always, shot on a humongous soundstage that's larger than any theater stage in the world)...

IN BLACKFACE.

It reportedly made the few audiences that actually saw *That's Entertainment! III* gasp out loud with shock. One could hear the collective sharp intake of air at the horror of it all. Not that it should be surprising. The great Hollywood musicals were full of blackface, from Mickey and Judy, to Fred Astaire, and just about everyone who did show-within-show sequences, or ever took part in depicting the all-hallowed Vaudeville of Yesteryear—a nostalgic, happy, colorful side of show business that most available research shows never actually existed. Mostly, we forget, regardless of our race, because it's so unpleasant. Or we excuse it.

It was the times they lived in. Everyone did it. No one thought anything about it.

Much more revealing is watching the final few minutes of Spike Lee's 2000 film *Bamboozled,* where the horrifying scope of the racist footage he edited together from old films, television shows, commercials, and trailers is heartbreaking and numbing all at the same time—almost obliterating the impact of the whole movie that precedes it—because of the awful power of seeing the mean-spirited, water-melon infused cartoons of the '30s, the hateful film depictions of lazy, deceitful, and imbecilic behavior, and even the "nice," "tolerant," portraits, where Mammy never had a life of her own, but thought only of Vivian Leigh, of Jean Harlow, Bette, Colbert, Hepburn, or, for that matter, Joan Crawford, Miss Two-Faced Woman herself; and where Bojangles' entire world (and career) evolved around a tap dancing little white girl in movie after movie. Don't even talk about Step'n Fetchit.

It's against that history that *Confidential's* breathless stories about race mixing have to be measured—and the magazine's artfully silly use of language judged. From Harrison's very first issue, December 1952, with "They Pass For White!" to one of his very last, the April 1958 "Negroes Can Elect the Next President!" *Confidential* was always filled with stories about race, but mainly about *mixing* races—going on about white women breaking up Billy Daniels' various marriages, Ronnie Quillan trying to kill Daniels for dating other white women, Orson Welles and his Chocolate Bon Bon making merry with a Whoopsy Waiter, Brando and his Tan Tootsie, Sammy Davis Jr., Eartha Kitt, Billy Eckstine, Joe Lewis, Willie Mays, Sugar Ray, Jackie Robinson, Floyd Patterson, there's even a Lana Turner story about her attentions to Billy Daniels enraging her current husband at the time, Bob Topping.

Of course, Harrison's friend Sammy was always a particular favorite.

What Makes Ava Gardner Run For Sammy Davis Jr.? *March 1955*

> *Bellhops at the Warwick Hotel are still prattling about her sassy trips to Davis' quarters in suite 2409. And a pal who dropped in at Ava's diggings in the Drake remarked, "They were the chummiest." Said Sammy after his meeting with Ava, "We just dug each other, that's all."*

> *But dark skinned gents have been proving their powerful fascination for Ava for years.... When colored crooner Herb Jeffries was palsy-walsy with*

Ava, his career began to zoom... Back in the late forties, the copper skinned crooner from Detroit was strictly a nickel–and–dime warbler. Things changed dramatically when Ava's green eyes started smiling at him a few years ago. Hollywood still remembers this torrid duet....

Ava hopped on the bandstand with Dizzy Gillespie. Between numbers they put on a show that the "hepcats" liked better than music... Dizzy ranked her company "the most" and used to tell his Negro friends that Ava was the "greatest ofay" he'd ever known. No one has ever asked Ava whether she enjoys such distinctions. On the record, though, she seems to be collecting them. As the lady herself says, they really "send" her.

That was from one of two major stories in *Confidential* about Sammy and Ava, and it was one of many stories Harrison printed in both *Confidential* and *Whisper* about Sammy Davis Jr. dating fair-skinned women.

Sammy was his friend. They hung out together a lot in New York. There are some reports that Davis was terrified of the publicity, that he was fearful and resentful of the magazines and of their coverage of him, but that doesn't jibe with his continued socializing with Harrison throughout the decade, his presence at Bob's 50th birthday celebration with a cake and gold watch, or with the fact that the entertainer continued to appear in the public eye accompanied by white women, not only dating Kim Novak, but marrying the blonde, Nordic Mai Britt to an enormous avalanche of publicity well after Bob Harrison had left the scene.

Interestingly, the same March 1955 issue contained an exposé about how the Bermuda tourism industry unfairly discriminated against Blacks by using coded language to alert other establishments on the island when a traveler wasn't white. An earlier story in the January 1954 issue angrily accused the Yankees of using Jim Crow tactics to keep the team White Only. The decidedly forward-thinking nature of those stories notwithstanding, there is still plenty to be offended about in the Ava and Sammy story. The leering sense of miscegenation being such a taboo is obvious, and some of the descriptions of Davis' physical appearance are pretty insulting, though perhaps not actually in a racial way, only seeking to marvel at how a funny looking short guy got all those statuesque beauties to chase after him—perhaps echoing Harrison's Average Joes in the girlie magazines.

But as with the gay stories, there was a lack of righteousness in the race mixing articles, a complete absence of horror or appalled approbation. Readers of the time may well have come away unpleasantly shocked—and as detailed earlier, there were short-term career repercussions for both Ava and Sammy, as some southern theaters pulled her movies and he lost club dates in Miami. But the storm died down pretty quickly and their show biz stock stayed stellar. Reading the material now, there's the sense that the magazine thought Ava was a bad girl—but in an unmistakably admiring way. The Black men are considered lucky. She is just being Ava. Raised eyebrows and disapproving looks figure everywhere, but never once is a stand taken against her.

In relative terms, that was rather progressive.

Eartha Kitt was featured in more than a couple of stories, mostly for dating white men and being what the magazine characterized as a sexual and social aggressor. The language was worse here—and yet somehow it all got turned around.

Eartha Kitt and Her Santa Baby, Arthur Loew, Jr.
January 1955

> *His family lined up half a dozen finishing-school fillies for Junior, but he brushed them all in favor of a Negro sharecropper's daughter with a velvet*

*voice and a wriggle like a panther. Here's what
the gossip columns have only whispered about...*

*When the sly sepia singer croons, "Santa Baby.. I
want a diamond ring, yachts and things... so
hurry down my chimney tonight..." she's not
thinking of any gent in a red suit and whiskers.*

*She's got her cute, ambitious mind on a real life
Santa with a million bucks in his jeans... (His
family) quivered and quaked when Junior started
dating the bronze baby but hoped for the best.
Their shock was far worse when cultured members
of the family began getting a strange and husky
voice on the telephone when they called Art.*

*It sounded as though Arthur and Eartha had
taken up light and dark housekeeping. The family
demanded an immediate check-up of Eartha's
background, the results of which satisfied
practically no one.*

Loew's choice to be with Kitt was not ridiculed. It was considered a given that any man would want to be with the sexy minx. A lot of the "Santa Baby" and "landing a millionaire" jargon is reductive, but frankly, that whole "My Heart Belongs to Daddy" trip was her own shtick. *Confidential* just took the idea and ran with it. Kitt may have been embarrassed by some of the tone of her coverage in the magazine, but she really couldn't logically quibble with being portrayed as something of an ambitious gold digger. It's how she has portrayed herself in just about every song she has sung during her entire half-century career. And that's part of what people love about her, without ever imagining it to be a true revelation of her essential inner self.

That the wealthy Loew family might not have been thrilled with Eartha Kitt as a match for their pampered prince goes without saying. By their standards she had a lot going against her, even beyond the race issue. She certainly wouldn't have been what they had in mind for young Arthur, which unfortunately probably isn't so very different today for a lot of wealthy white families. The real difference now is that no one smart would ever publicly acknowledge race as *the* issue, or as being any issue at all. If they did, they would risk losing their corporate board seats, or senate majority leader positions, or what have you.

Eartha's family's possible reaction to the idea of having a white, Jewish son-in-law, however rich, was not explored. Maybe the magazine staff knew she had no real family to speak of, and had come from a truly Dickensian childhood, or maybe they just didn't think to ask. Nor was the point ever made that the Loews and Adolph Zukor (Arthur's maternal grandfather), however wealthy and influential in the entertainment industry, were in no way considered by High Society to be High Society.

But look again at the Kitt/Loew article. This is from a section going into her background, and chronicling her move to France after leaving the Katherine Dunham dance troupe:

> *Negroes—especially entertainers—are fondly accepted in Paris and for the first time Miss Kitt got a taste of real living, real success. She began singing her naughty songs in intimate bistros and became the darling of the sophisticates.*

Her wish to be free and successful was taken just as seriously as any white person's would be. It's self-evident that she would like being in Paris, where her options would be wider. But it was also an overt acknowledgment that current American attitudes about race were inherently unfair. Subtle, maybe even a little unintentional, but the piece took her a lot more at face value than other publications of the era would have done, where "negroes" are often treated as "the other," as beings without the "normal" desires or expectations of "regular" people—i.e. whites. The phrase, "The Negro Problem," loomed large in the media. *Confidential* always loved the whole alliterative Copper Cutie business, but in fairness, they did that about everything and *everyone*. Reducing the lives of celebrities to vignettes of wordplay and innuendo was truly a color-blind business for Harrison. (In the end, Kitt would consider Loew one of the great loves of her life, but his mother's edict that he would marry her over her own dead body stood—preventing their marriage.)

This is not to imply or impose after the fact some sort of liberal mission on the part of Harrison in his coverage of performers of color. A far more entertaining Eartha Kitt story that appeared in March 1954 detailed how Orson Welles got mad once and bit her. So much for serious sociology.

One of the stories that figured later at the 1957 libel and obscenity trial was a silly and rather sweet Mae West article from November 1955 called "Mae West's Open Door Policy." It depicted her fascination with muscle men of all races, and her particular shine for a Black boxer named Chalky Wright, whom she briefly employed as a chauffeur while enjoying his romantic attentions. The story came from Wright himself, who was down at heels at the time and needed the money, but there was never any proof that anything in it was untrue. In it, the race issue is hardly raised at all. West comes off as kind of nice, if a little daffy, in her support of Chalky through some of his various troubles, and the only negative issue raised is that Miss West was apparently quite cheap, and systemically averse to paying most of the brawny men in her employ. They usually had to wait until going to the fights, when she would give them a few hundred bucks to make bets with. You could skim off that kind of dough and do all right. The story was bright and cheerful—and downright respectful toward Chalky.

Of course, when it was sexy, Harrison wasn't above using the racism of the day to his advantage. If "Negroes" were slightly less than human in some Americans' eyes, then African tribal women were deemed so subhuman that you could even show their bare breasts in print. With nipples. Which he did at least once in most of the magazines he published.

Bob Harrison was not a revolutionary person in a social sense. Often his sense of family and of male and female roles was very old-fashioned. But without thinking much about it, or pondering the social repercussions, more often than not, his magazines tended to support the idea of inclusion and fair play. He was like Walter Winchell in being publicly supportive of the underdog—which in the case of African-Americans then, included just about everyone. He even dated Dorothy Dandridge.

> *The columns are bored with the blondes. Even Zsa Zsa is old news. I bet Dorothy would get some ink. And heck, she's one of the most beautiful women in the world. Gorgeous! The Ripest Tomato in Town! He wonders what it would be like—touching her tawny skin—his own white hand traveling up her legs, exploring what he can only imagine is the dusky, musky scent of her. Any man who isn't a queer would want her. Any man... Me...?*

Dandridge was singing at a nightclub called The Flame and Bob took her out one night after the show. He brought her back to a restaurant for drinks and they wouldn't let her in. Marjorie remembers him being absolutely shocked.

> *To be perfectly honest, I don't think that Bob had any particular causes that he was terribly involved in—not really in any shape or form. If he thought it made good copy, he would do it. That's where it was at. And then he wanted to see people get a fair shake. He was quite upset though about the Dorothy Dandridge thing. He told me about it because I was in Miami at the time. But really, you know, he was quite shaken up, I guess he just didn't expect that. She was famous! An Oscar nominee! How could they not let her in? She was*

*so beautiful. And famous! I mean, she was a
famous woman!*

An odd kind of equal opportunity mindset, but nondiscriminatory all the same: Fame should cross any color line. Then came a May 1957 *Confidential* story titled "Only the Birds and the Bees Saw What Dorothy Dandridge Did in the Woods," which actually had almost no element of race in it. Dandridge's unnamed amorous partner at a Lake Tahoe resort where she was the featured headliner wasn't identified specifically as white, but as having "pale, nightclub pallor," when, while sunbathing, Miss Dandridge happened to walk by. The article wasn't particularly coy about painting a picture of the singer and her new friend having sex in the woods. This was one of the stories where Harrison ended up making an out-of-court payout. Dandridge held that there was no way the story could have happened. Tahoe was completely restricted. As a negro she could never have walked anywhere on the premises. She described spending every moment between shows in her room, a virtual prisoner. It's not clear whether Harrison paid out because the article wasn't true, or whether he did it out of shame. He was mortified that Dandridge was so upset by the article. He really didn't see anything wrong with it—figuring it was all part of building up her sexy public image. But she seemed genuinely hurt, and he regretted causing his onetime friend any grief. His naiveté and his loyalty probably had as much to do with him approving a $10,000 settlement check as any concern about having gotten the story wrong, or facing legal sanctions. The settlement was well below the seven figures she announced she would sue for, and no printed retraction was offered or specified.

The Dorothy Dandridge incident remained one of the few regrets Bob Harrison ever had about any of the stories in his magazines. Of course if the story was completely true, it's kind of sweet revenge. Dorothy Dandridge was a brilliantly talented singer and actress whose tabloid travails and eventual overdose were heavily influenced by the depressing lack of opportunity she faced. Even with an Oscar nomination under her belt, the overt racism of the day guaranteed a dearth of film roles for a Black leading lady. If the *Confidential* story was true, but she was able to turn the segregation and bigotry of Lake Tahoe into a weapon for her own defense, there's a kind of rough justice to that. Harrison always loved irony anyway.

Who cares? First of all, ten grand is pocket change. Peanuts! And if it made her happy... Nothing worse than a woman upset. Hate to see it. The worst! But there was nothing... That story... First of all, it was true—affidavits, eyewitnesses, the works—but secondly, who the hell would find anything wrong with it? Dorothy in the sun... Naked... Beautiful. Truth is I loved 'em all. Lana, Ava, Marilyn, Liz, Rita Hayworth... Hell, I even loved Lizabeth Scott. Who cares if she was a dyke? She was a looker. And I never printed anything that would hurt any of them. Never.

Harrison truly believed that he never wrote anything that could have really hurt anyone, so ostensibly, Rita Hayworth should have been unconcerned about being called an unfit, uncaring mother, whose children were wallowing in dirt and garbage.

EXCLUSIVE PHOTOS!

...How Rita Hayworth's Children Were Neglected!

"Justified in full" was what the judge said about charges that Rita's children had been neglected. Here are on-the-spot pictures and an eyewitness report confirming his verdict!

By JAY BREEN

Unretouched photos on this page show Yasmin in littered kitchen of her "foster home." Above, she plays in sink filled with dirty dishes, pots, pans.

Far left, Moslem Princess digs in malodorous bushel basket of garbage and trash; in other photo, heiress to millions attempts to "sweep" shabby floor.

SEE NEXT PAGE

Yasmin and half-sister Rebecca (left) were unguarded on dingy porch, despite threats on younger child's life.

In glaring contrast to daughters' surroundings, Rita and new husband, Dick Haymes, wined and dined selves in such expensive nightspots as El Morocco (above).

Rita Hayworth (continued)

IT WAS A SHOCKED and disbelieving nation that picked up its newspapers late this spring to read the incredible story of Rita Hayworth's children. The new Mrs. Haymes immediately cried "foul," and set off a nationwide debate as to whether she was being persecuted or whether the little girls had, in fact, been neglected.

Spread before you on these pages are authentic pictures which settle that argument for all time. They tell, better than words, exactly how Yasmin—four-year-old daughter of a Moslem prince and heir to a $500,000,000 fortune— was living in White Plains, New York, with nine-year-old Rebecca. These are pictures a whole world who discussed the case never got to see and this is a report never before put in print.

Judge Said Complaint Was Fully Justified

Judge George W. Smyth wrapped a tight cloak of official secrecy around his courtroom last April, when Rita appeared before him to answer charges of neglect. He, himself, will be seeing these pictures for the first time in this magazine.

But he received other evidence confirming the story you are now reading—evidence which prompted him to rule that, while Rita had not been directly guilty, her children had suffered neglect. He said the complaint, brought by the Westchester County Society for the Prevention of Cruelty to Children had been "fully justified." And he

Children occasionally played in vacant lot across busy highway from house (arrow) where they were boarded out.

Dowdy bathroom was typical of conditions in foster-home where Yasmin slept in bedroom jammed with boxes.

With unconscious irony, Yasmin asked photographer "Are you taking pictures of me just like they do Mommy?"

ordered Rita to sign papers stipulating that both her daughters were to remain in the jurisdiction of his court for 90 days, while their mother proved she could eliminate the shabby conditions under which they were being raised.

Any day now, Rita and Dick will be entering Judge Smyth's court once more. In the meantime, here's this reporter's eyewitness story of how Yasmin and Rebecca were being cared for at least two months before their situation made national headlines.

Tipped off by angry neighbors, I went to White Plains to investigate this modern Cinderella story last March 18th. Perhaps they were the same neighbors who later protested to the Westchester Children's Society; I do not know. But there was no doubt that I had found a million-dollar baby —literally—among the ash cans of White Plains.

Asked Lensmen Not to Photograph Yasmin

Little Yasmin and her half-sister Rebecca had been living — off and on — in the seedy, rundown home of an antiques and second-hand-furniture dealer ever since Rita, Dick and the two children were tossed out of a Greenwich, Conn., mansion Haymes had rented. Newspaper reports at the time quoted Dick's landlord as claiming he was owed $675 in back rent, plus another $4,000 for damage to his property while the four had lived there.

Rita, Dick and the little girls swept off to the swank Madison Hotel, one of Manhattan's best hostelries, and Mrs. Haymes maternally told the press, "the children are going to stay with us from now on." She emphasized her mother's role by asking photographers not to snap pictures of Yasmin, explaining that she was still nervous over letters she had received threatening the child's life.

Less than 48 hours later, however, the little girls were dumped in the custody of an aging matron whose strongest claim to her right to care for the youngsters was the fact that she'd known Dick for five years.

I arrived at the combination shop-and-home of Mrs. Dorothy Chambers, to find Yasmin in a trash-littered back-yard, playing among an assortment of loaded ash cans. What added to the irony of (Continued on page 46)

WAS COUNTESS DOTTY DiFRASSO MURDERED?

Continued from page 9

he was marked for elimination and told her the names of the men who he'd learned were on his particular firing squad.

When everything he feared (and told Dotty) came true, the gossip-peddling society queen just couldn't keep her inside story to herself. Time and time again she whispered the facts in the ears of society blue-bloods, movie stars and just plain no-bodies. She had one small inkling of good sense in that she never mentioned the names of the assassins. But as Dorothy got older and hit that bottle harder, nervous Mob chieftains began to wonder what should be done with her.

Their alarm was doubled when, some three or four months before her end, Dotty announced she was considering writing the story of her life. Her increasing poverty, she told friends, was one reason for the project. As it turned out, there's evidence the Countess wasn't lying on this point. Latest reports on her still un-probated will indicate there may not be enough left to pay some $75,000 in

bequests — that's from a fortune once estimated at $15,000,000.

If Dorothy thought the news of her writing project might scare the underworld into buying the book in unpublished form, she was mortally incorrect. For her wagging tongue had also provided The Mob with the perfect set-up for murder. Anyone who knew her for more than half a day soon learned all about Dotty's heart and the vital pills she needed to ward off a fatal seizure. They knew that without them, one attack would mean the end — and that Dorothy frequently took as many as 10 and 15 pills a day.

The world knows she died in a train. It never knew till now that she must have awakened with a savage grab of pain in her chest, only to probe in the darkness for pills that weren't there. Was it the clever work of the underworld — a clean and safe killing like the boys who once used tommy guns now prefer? Those in the know say it was and offer the reasons you've just read to explain why Bugsy Siegel's titled girl friend had to follow him in death. ▲▲▲

HOW HAYWORTH'S CHILDREN WERE NEGLECTED

Continued from page 43

the picture she presented was that afternoon newspapers of that very day were headlining a statement to the effect that Prince Aly Khan was on the verge of settling $1,000,000 on the little girl, plus a maintenance income of $7,000 per year. As I watched her play and talked to her, she looked like she'd have traded the whole thing for a cup of hot soup and a friendly lap to sit on.

Mrs. Chambers, whom Rita had publicly identified as the "governess" for her children, welcomed me as a prospective renter of her dilapidated house. She waved me into the kitchen,

offered me a jigger of Scotch out of a bottle from which she and another woman were drinking. It stood on a small table, crowded with assorted bottles and boxes of food and the greasy dishes from several meals.

Mrs. Chambers had never set eyes on me in her life, but identified the million-dollar babies less than a minute after I stepped into the house, pointing out the kitchen window to Yasmin, playing in the yard, and Rebecca, who was sitting on a back porch heaped with trash, reading a book.

I walked out and opened a conversation with Rebecca, who seemed delighted to have someone to talk with. I asked her if her storybook was exciting. She picked out a paragraph and read it for me, haltingly, with obvious difficulty. I commented that learning to read was a pretty hard job.

"I'm not as good as I should be," she said, with a quick smile. "But I'd read better if I could go to school, like the other kids."

Yasmin Wandered to Basement

I stepped off the porch and walked to a warped outside door leading to a dank, almost pitch-dark basement. Mrs. Chambers had invited me to inspect the aged coal furnace which heated the place. Yasmin clambered after me. Mrs. Chambers turned and shuffled back into the house, completely at ease, apparently, and undisturbed over what might happen to her tiny ward.

When I returned to the festivities in the kitchen, she launched a glowing account of the antiques business in White Plains. She said she'd never have considered leaving, had she not received an offer from Rita and Dick to accompany them, first to Key West, Fla., and then to Europe. She made no secret of her plans to cash in on the junket.

"I'm supposed to be Rita's secretary," she said, "but actually my job will be keeping an eye on these kids. It won't take all my time, though. I'll be watching for some good deals in antiques."

She went on to describe how the children were living while we made an inspection of the house's upstairs rooms. As it turned out, the little girls were even deprived of the comfort of sleeping in the same house at night. Rebecca was bundled off to a next-door neighbor at nightfall. Yasmin slept in a room so littered with boxes of clothing that she had to climb over some of them to reach her bed. It was 5:00 p.m. the evening Mrs. Chambers showed me around her premises, but not a bed in the house had been made. She herself wore a faded, soiled wrapper and casually remarked she'd just "never gotten 'round to even getting dressed" that day.

Didn't Worry about Traffic

Anyone who witnessed the afternoon's events—including this reporter—couldn't have helped thinking of how Yasmin's parents lived. Aly Khan, for instance, has estimated the cost of caring for his polo ponies and race horses at upwards of $100,000 a year.

After completing a preliminary inspection tour of the house, I left, promising to return the next day. When I arrived at about noon, I again found Mrs. Chambers in the same
(Continued on next page)

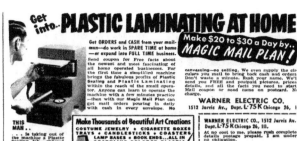

wrapper; the children were once more playing in the backyard, among the ash cans. I called their governess' attention to the busy street which runs in front of her house—at 307 Central Ave.—a major highway serving New York City traffic—and asked whether it didn't worry her that Yasmin and Rebecca might wander out into the road, since there were no fences or guards to prevent them.

"Oh, I never give it a second thought," was her jaunty and undoubtedly accurate answer, "but if you'd worry about your children, you could always put a fence up."

Kids Could Have Strayed

Across the street was a marshy dump, heaped with huge boulders and choked with seven-foot high weeds.

"It would bother me that children might be tempted to play over in that dump there," I said.

"I gave Yasmin and Rebecca strict orders never to go over there unless I took them across the street," Mrs. Chambers said. "They sometimes climb around those boulders, but they're safe when I'm watching them."

As we talked, a photographer who had accompanied me on the second trip was snapping pictures of Yasmin and Rebecca in the trash-covered kitchen and littered backyard. For all Mrs. Chambers knew, they could have been miles away by the time we walked to the backyard.

The kind of protection the children were getting was in pathetic contrast to what their mother had promised they'd receive. When Rita re-

ceived letters threatening the lives of herself and little Yasmin, she said no money would be spared to keep both Yasmin and Rebecca "safe and unmolested."

Yet the two girls had absolutely no protection at the White Plains house. There were no guards to watch over them—not even fences to make an intruder's job difficult. It was plainly obvious that Rita talked a better game of parenthood than she played.

Her new husband also has made continued protestations of how much he loves Rita's children. But there are indications that it might be better to be Dick Haymes' dog than his stepdaughter.

While the two girls were living in the sordid circumstances pictured on these pages, he and Rita were not only enjoying the luxury of New York's Madison Hotel, but spending their money freely on other extravagances.

$5 to Baby-sit Their Dog

During that same period, Broadway columnist Dorothy Kilgallen reported that the two lovers dropped in for lunch at Maud Chez Elle, one of the most expensive restaurants in Manhattan. Dick tipped the doorman $5 to "baby-sit" his blue-ribbon boxer, while he and his bride sampled the excellent fare. Since they were honeymooning, it might have been considered unkind to inquire why the two children couldn't have come along and at least stayed with the dog.

Were Rita Hayworth's children neglected? You've seen the pictures, you've read the facts. Now, you be the judge! ▲▲▲

regarding certain mercenary dates she'd been keeping and—as we said before, Peggy had gone off to see the land of the midnight sun.

By this time, you might say that Julie had developed a grudge against men. She now had two daily reminders to keep her from forgetting, a little boy, as well as the aforementioned Lynn.

She decided that since none of the men she met seemed willing to go to court, she would. Six months ago, she slapped Mr. Bedford III with a paternity suit naming him as the father of

the boy. Just about the time you're reading this, Mr. Lex Thompson will be getting his summons to appear before a judge and explain what, if anything, he had to do with siring Lynn.

The gentlemen in this rather involved case cannot, however, take the attitude that fate is picking on them alone.

As we said earlier, the finger of fatherhood is stabbing the playboys right and left. As this was being written, a famed movie actor was being given the bad news, and one of the nation's most adored crooners was anx-

Society Swells & Belles
Silver Spoon Set Swivels and Sizzles

It wasn't just the children of Hollywood wallowing in mud.

Children of America's best families, as well as their parents and grandparents, were busily getting themselves in just as much trouble as their West Coast counterparts. A logical modern successor to the kind of society dish *Confidential* favored are the *Vanity Fair* articles of Dominick Dunne. He can tell you the pedigrees of anyone, and seems to know where each and every skeleton is buried, even before the spade hits the dirt. Yet as plugged-in as he is to the world of the Bright and Beautiful, he is far more focused on crime than *Confidential* was, with High Society figuring in when they become part of a crime story or a particular injustice. He writes a kind of deeply felt non-fiction literature. The overwhelming tragedy of his own daughter's murder and her killer's subsequent slap on the wrist gives his writing an urgency and a sense of moral outrage that *Confidential* never attempted, or indeed contemplated. *Confidential* was just in it for the sex, drugs, and lawlessness. The fun.

Still, so many *Confidential* stories could be pieces in *Vanity Fair* today. Woolworth family heir Jimmy Donohue was fingered as one of the ringleaders in a gay gang-rape scandal; later, Donohue, on assignment for Harrison, examined the genitals of the transsexual Christine Jorgensen; a Vanderbilt heir also dated Jorgensen, Gloria Vanderbilt shacked up with Stowkowski, other Vanderbilt women reneged on their gambling debts; the gay Vanderbilt; Jack Astor and his dishy dice girl; the merry wife of Windsor; Bobo Rockefeller flew the coop; why the Mob protected Bobo Rockefeller; Rockefeller payoffs; Elsa Maxwell exposed as an unpleasant and obese busybody; J. Paul Getty agreed that Maxwell was an unpleasant and obese busybody; society ex-wives keeping their former husbands' sex lives out of the divorce court in exchange for more dough; how Lady Ashley used her trick pelvis to get her man; bulimia pioneer Brenda Frazier's secret hospital trysts with her Latin Lover; the alcoholic, sex-mad Dodge heir; Peggy Joyce's big switch from being the gold digger to getting fleeced by a gigolo; Batista's $8 million divorce; Doris Duke and her African prince; Anne Gould, skid row heiress; judge's peek at Biddle birthmark; Horace Dodge's angry tantrum; Barbara Hutton's son and his naughty nymph; the same son with a mail-order sex queen; Nicky Hilton's preference for liquor over sex; high society call girls; Lord Rothschild's slut of a daughter; The debt and domestic discord-driven suicide of Winston Churchill's son-in-law; and on and on...

The banner year for High Society stories was 1954, when each issue of the magazine contained at least two or three, if not more. The November 1954 issue alone gave readers Vanderbilt, Astor, Peggy Joyce, Batista, and a Biddle—plus a Churchill story. By 1955 the stories became more and more Hollywood oriented. Only really big High Society scandals made the grade, with the lesser ones falling by the wayside. The tone of the articles was usually reminiscent of Winchell's populist edge—going for the cheap thrill of making the reader feel morally superior to the rich and powerful. Not too hard, when the Socials in question were alcoholic, gambling, debt-ridden, sex-starved or sexless, free spending or tight-fisted—total, irrevocable twerps.

Few pieces made any allegations of real wrong-doing—at least not in a legal sense—which made a particular story published in July 1954 about Jimmy Donohue remarkable. Donohue was one of the 20th Century's most chronicled highborn ne'er-do-wells, a sort of gay court jester to the high and mighty, but with a bad-boy edge of the rapscallion. Recently *Vanity Fair* breathlessly chronicled Donohue's famous friendship with the Duchess of Windsor, which they assert may or may not have been heterosexually inclined, or, for that matter, may or may not have been *homosexually* inclined, since rumors about the Duchess being a man, or at least a hermaphrodite, dogged her relentlessly, all the days of her life.

At any rate, *Confidential's* article "Jimmy Donohue's Hush-Hush Secret," written by Hewitt Van Horn—a fake name if there ever was one—starts off with the story of a wellborn Harvard grad named Peter Williams, now a wallpaper salesman of all things, found naked and a bloody mess on a Long Island City street. Then the backstory: It pieced together Donohue's privileged, if a tad overly colorful, upbringing, and filled in the bios of his three pals on this excursion, Billy Livingston of Knickerbocker ancestry, Duke Fulco di Verdura, and Argentine playboy Pancho Muratore. Their upbringings and social positions were snidely and endlessly described, taking readers to the fateful meeting of the drunken quartet with the article's hapless hero, who accompanied them to the Italian duke's apartment, along with some "rough trade" the four men picked up along the way.

A nightmarish scene followed, as Williams mysteriously took leave of his senses, and was only dimly aware of the wide variety of abuses he was subjected to. At first the article offered mainly innuendo—as if the dirty deed itself might not even be named. But then this:

> *St. John's hospital attendants said Williams was treated for scalp lacerations, the disfigurement of an ear which was seriously bitten "apparently through mayhem," and injuries from "other kinds of mistreatment." Neither the hospital, police, or Williams himself ever clarified "other kinds of mistreatment" but it was commonly rumored in society circles and along Broadway that the party at the Italian duke's had some aspects of a sadistic Roman orgy... Sometimes a companion mentions the Peter Williams affair and it gives Jimmy a good laugh. "Oh, that guy!" he says, "He just wasn't a good sport!"*

The whole legal history of the case never making it to court and Williams refusing to testify in order to save his honor was giddily chronicled, along with information about his then current employment in a chi-chi design store with a male partner and a poodle. The end of the story offered Donohue's sick joke about Williams not being a good sport, tying up the story with a sort of wink.

This was printed in the supposedly straight, uptight '50s. A national magazine with an increasingly large readership made the outright allegation that a member of High Society's smartest set committed homosexual rape and assault. No one sued. No one really cared. There was no outcry. Donohue even went on a year later to pen a story himself for *Confidential*—the piece where he inspected Christine Jorgensen to report to readers whether or not her sexual organs looked like the real thing (they did). It was a truly bizarre turn of events. What could possibly make someone write for a publication that had accused him a year earlier of being a gay rapist? Maybe it was some sort of desperate, demented attempt to make it look like he was always in on the joke—*a good sport*—a highly valued personal attribute among the upper classes. Maybe Donohue played it all as a big joke because his social circle allowed him to. They laughed. He laughed. And everybody had a cocktail.

Then there was the fabulous tale of a reform school graduate who briefly became Mrs. Cornelius Vanderbilt, Jr., which ran in September 1954. It had everything—sex, a broken home, the barest hint of a lesbian women-in-prison kind of thing, big money, disapproving elders, squabbling rich siblings, and a rags-to-riches saga that readers could envy. The Meow of the Week tone was the same as in the Donohue story—but the content was all froth and Turkish Delight.

Harrison's vaunted sense of truth notwithstanding, the article got almost all the literal details right and most of the human story wrong. Cornelius Vanderbilt, Jr., was a person of far more substance than the magazine suggested, and he had a lot less money than they presumed. They did get Patricia's zany helplessness right. When she squatted in the Vanderbilt townhouse with no electricity or water, and showed up in a mink coat to plead destitution, the judge reportedly laughed out loud. Vanderbilt always acknowledged his own marital failures, allowing that women were usually attracted to him for his name and presumed wealth, but after marriage were turned off by the fact that he had a real job, real interests, and far less cash than they thought. Yet he also took responsibility on the record for not only making foolish choices himself, but for often being a distant, preoccupied person of a changeable nature.

...What Society Never Knew—

Mrs. Cornelius Vanderbilt— Reform School Graduate!

By HEWITT VAN HORN

ON JANUARY 4, 1939, in Ventura, California, a beauteous 18-year-old blonde slipped out of her ill-fitting uniform and poured her curves into a cheap but fetching cotton dress that was supplied her as a "coming out" gown. As she left the exclusive precincts of the Ventura School for Girls, a motherly "faculty member" gave her advice as sound as any ever offered a debutante: "Keep out of trouble, dear, and earn a good name for yourself."

Patricia Murphy took the reformatory matron's counsel to heart — in spades. Nine years later she acquired a name as solid as Tiffany sterling when she became Mrs. Cornelius Vanderbilt Jr., heiress-apparent to THE Mrs. Vanderbilt who had reigned as unquestioned Sultana of American society since the turn of the century.

Had to Create a Legend of Her Own

The dowager Mrs. Vanderbilt was never one to forget the past. Hers had been gloriously crowded with emperors and kings who had accepted her as the American equivalent of royalty. But Patricia Murphy Vanderbilt, who started her early life in an institution for juvenile delinquents, had to create her own untarnished legend. This she did, and so successfully that — until the publication of this article — society never knew its hereditary Crown Prince conferred the Vanderbilt moniker on a reform school alumna.

When Pat married Neil on Sept. 7, 1948, the front page stories in newspapers across the nation described her this way:

"The socially prominent, 28-year-old bride was born in Honolulu, where her father, Eugene Murphy, was a banker. Her parents died in an auto accident. She lived with an aunt in Los Angeles and attended convent schools there. She is a niece of screen star Jeanette MacDonald."

Actually, Pat is a product of society's basement and her only claim to exotic Hawaiian origins is a visit she once made to her grandmother and uncle who lived there. She grew up in the melting pot of Los Angeles County slums. Papa Murphy rarely saw the inside of a bank, since his employment record was sketchy and his pay envelopes

Pat talked her reform school supervisor into putting up $2,400 so she could learn to be a lady. It helped her snag a Vanderbilt, but she's never paid the money back.

24

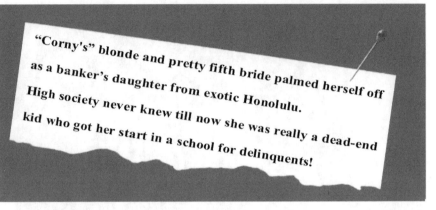

"Corny's" blonde and pretty fifth bride palmed herself off as a banker's daughter from exotic Honolulu. High society never knew till now she was really a dead-end kid who got her start in a school for delinquents!

slim. When Pat was two-years-old, Murphy deserted his wife, leaving her to fend for a hungry passel of little Murphys and very little time to keep tabs on her daughter who grew into a trim five-foot, four-inch, 105-pound filly with a 31-inch bust.

When Pat was sweet 16 and the whistle bait of her neighborhood, Los Angeles County authorities filed charges against Mrs. Murphy for lack of parental supervision. Pat was taken into custody by juvenile authorities who placed her under lock and key in the county's El Retiro School for Girls for vocational training and rehabilitation, and her brothers were placed in foster homes.

El Retiro records show that Pat didn't "adjust" to strict institutional life. She was such a problem case that she was brought before Superior Court Judge Robert H. Scott who committed her, on June 4, 1937, to the state reform school for "felons, misdemeanants and juvenile court commitments" at Ventura. The company was rough there, and Pat made up her mind to get out as soon as possible. She won the confidence and maternal interest of a brilliant and highly educated state parole supervisor for delinquent girls. Linda Schroeder. It was Miss Schroeder who became Pat's fairy godmother.

Life as a Common Domestic Galled Her

When Pat finally paroled from Ventura on Jan. 4, 1939, Miss Schroeder got her a job as a maid in a private home in Los Angeles. But life as a common domestic galled Pat. She was quickly fired by three housewives in succession, with Miss Schroeder always coming to the rescue. Pat had mulled over enough movie magazines to know that the world was wider than a kitchen sink. She wanted to pack up her troubles in her battered luggage and dump them in the nearest kidney-shaped Hollywood swimming pool. But instead, the parole board was suggesting that she be packed up and returned to Ventura "for further social adjustment."

Miss Murphy managed to convince Miss Schroeder in the nick of time that she could well be Eleanor Powell and Bette Davis all rolled into one, if she had the proper schooling. Miss Schroeder earned only $150 a month, but she shouldered the full responsibility of Pat's parole. She took Pat into her home and enrolled her at a dancing

school for lessons in ballet, tap, ballroom dancing and the hula. Then she sent to the Bliss-Hayden Dramatic School where she mastered the essential grins and grimaces of Hollywood acting style.

Finally Pat persuaded the big-hearted parole officer to send her to Mme. Mario Ouspenskaya's star factory for the finishing touches. (Continued on page 62)

Though Neil's grandmother claimed she could "spot a phony at 40 paces," she and entire Vanderbilt clan were fooled by his 'wrong-side-of-the-tracks' bride.

She came out a typical Ouspenskaya product—an actress with the manner of a lady. She was on her way to becoming a Vanderbilt.

Pat faithfully promised to repay Miss Schroeder for board, room and tuition when her training paid odd in long green. Unfortunately for her patron, the closest Pat ever got to employment was an unsuccessful tryout for a Little Theater group. However, she readily found another sort of casting—as an adornment at filmland parties where there is an insatiable demand for honey blondes of her proportions.

At one pool-side pleasure dome she met strapping Earl K. Wallace, a movie photographer. Wallace had one major asset to offer Pat. He was the nephew of celluloid songstress Jeanette MacDonald, who was then at the pinnacle of her career. After a quickie courtship, Pat became Wallace's June bride in 1940. Thereafter Pat always referred to herself as "Miss Mac-Donald's niece."

Threatened with Lawsuits

The following year, when the Wallaces were settled in their own home in El Centro, Calif., where Wallace worked as a border guard, Miss Schroeder threatened to sue Pat for the $2,464.79 it had cost to launch her as a useful member of society. Pat persuaded her to layoff by pleading poverty and pregnancy, adding that her husband had spent all their savings on a new car. Her daughter, Nanette, was born in 1941. The Wallaces were divorced three years later.

Pat soon returned to the screen colony's social whirl and tried her hand at interior decorating. In the spring of 1947, one of her wealthy clients introduced her to a celebrated Hollywood visitor whose name rang bells like a cash register.

The visitor, who jocularly described himself as "America's foremost vagabond," was 27 years older than Pat, more than a little grey, just short of portly, and had a record of four marital busts. But his name was a good name, and Patricia Murphy remembered Miss Schroeder's words.

Before Cornelius Vanderbilt Jr., the great-great-grandson of the original Commodore Vanderbilt, left Hollywood for his sixty-eighth trip to Europe, our girl had won his notoriously susceptible heart. Little Nanette was a big help to Mummy by innocently asking Neil daily if she could have him for a father. The childless Vanderbilt scion, a pushover for tots, loved it.

Pat and the 55-year-old Vanderbilt were married on his return from abroad. After a midnight ceremony at the Pickwick Arms Hotel in Greenwich, Conn., Neil took his bride to New York to meet his ailing, octogenarian mother at the 40-room family mansion on Fifth Avenue at 86th Street. Pat must have needed all her courage and acting talent for the ordeal of facing the old dragon who claimed she could scent a phony at 40 paces.

Grace Vanderbilt had been such a bloodhound for bloodlines in her heyday that she checked each of the 10,000 guests she entertained annually in the collection of Social Regi-sters, Peerages and Almanachs de Gotha she kept in her bedroom. But now the old dowager's sight and hearing were failing. Pat was correctly deferential and her charm and beauty won the day. "Her grace" rolled out her moth eaten red rug for Pat, and society had no choice but to pay its respects to her as one of the charmed circle of Vanderbilts. Neil's sister, Mrs. Robert L. Stevens, said she thought Pat would work out better than any of her predecessors.

Mrs. Vanderbilt had in mind the first Mrs. Vanderbilt Jr. who left Neil after he sank $3,000,000 of the family's railroad fortune in a chain of unsuccessful newspapers; and the second, who divorced him to marry a trumpeter in a Reno nightclub. Then there was Neil's third wife, who was so fascinated by airplanes that she jettisoned him for an airlines pres-ident. By the time he took a fourth wife, Neil had developed a passion for roving the world in an aluminum trailer to hunt royal highnesses and hottentots with his movie camera. She divorced him when he refused to settle in New York so she could understudy his mother in the role of society leader.

Neil gave Pat small chance to lord it over the 400 with her new Cadillac, diamond bracelets and rings, and Breath of Spring mink coat. After a summer in the social sun at Mrs. Vanderbilt's monstrous Newport "cottage," Pat dutifully took to the road with her itchy-footed husband and his travel films. They toured 179 whistle stops on the ladies' club lecture circuit, then settled down for a while in film star Dennis O'Keefe's house in Hollywood which Neil leased for 800 smackeroos a month. For the first time in her life, Pat had a maid of her own. But she barely had time to try the magic of the Vanderbilt name on her old filmland friends when she and Neil were off to Europe in search of fresh travelogue material.

While they were visiting the Grand Duchess Charlotte in Luxembourg in August, 1951, Neil's trailer got smacked by the junior-sized nation's only train. The trailer was demolished and it was soon obvious that it was ditto with the Vanderbilt's marriage.

Charge and Counter-charge

Neil claimed Pat received neck and spine injuries in the collision. Pat counter-charged that she received the injuries on the return trip home when he tossed her into a bathtub during a shipboard argument.

After they separated, Pat turned up in a Santa Monica, California hospital with her neck in a traction brace. Neil said she was putting on an "act" and claimed that to prove it, he had pictures of Pat wriggling a mean hula at a binge given by a famed silent film star a few days before.

While on this visit to California, Neil learned for the first time of Pat's record as an inmate in two reform schools. Naturally, Neil never told his mother, whose last days already were saddened by the knowledge that her son's fifth try at marriage was a flop.

In May, 1952, Pat obtained a nonsupport warrant for Neil's arrest in New York. Claiming that she was impoverished, she even tried camping in her husband's suite in the Vanderbilt mansion where light and heat had been turned off since Grace Vanderbilt's death. She finally applied for city relief—a fact that caused the entire Vanderbilt clan to blush collectively. Miss Schroeder finally got around to suing her, but had to settle for $500, which Pat has never paid.

To top her troubles, after the New York Supreme Court threw out Pat's suit for separation and $1,500 weekly maintenance because she wasn't a resident of the state, Neil established residence in Reno and got a divorce in July, 1953. Pat sat tight for a year in Manhattan and filed a second separation suit on the ground that the Nevada divorce was worthless.

She has been living quietly with Nanette in the moderately expensive Barbizon Hotel for Women on the smart East Side, and although she claims to have hocked even her engagement ring, she is still the best dressed and coiffed pauper in the city.

Neil even foiled the warrant she obtained for his arrest by slipping into New York last May 7th for six hours before sailing on the Swedish liner *Kungsholm* for Europe, where he will make films for a multi-millionaire publisher friend, Ed Parker, at $100,000 a year for five years. It's a sure bet that Neil won't return to these shores with a pile of loot as long as Pat keeps the legal mills grinding.

In fact, the foremost graduate of the Ventura School for Girls might adopt an eccentric fashion which was her late mother-in-law's trademark. THE Mrs. Vanderbilt used to wrap a swatch of gold lamé around her blue-white curls on important occasions and call it a headache band.

Pat could use a drawerful. ▲▲▲

WHAT ENDED
DARCEL–"MR.B."
ROMANCE?
ntinued from page 19

night, Mr. B. says with what is probably no understatement, "Man, it was real crazy!" To most American girls, such escapades might have seemed mighty daring. Not to Denise. She's on record as considering our customs puritanical and most of our males on the infantile side. Of her

two marriages, to actor Bill Shaw, and Washington socialite Peter Crosby, she says, "What can you do with a baby for a husband?" Crosby lost out when in Feb. 1951 he jealously doused Denise with what newspapers reported was a quart of champagne (Continued on next page)

63

Vanderbilt's work for F.D.R., his going against his family's wishes to become a respected journalist and publisher, his vast charitable endeavors, and the numerous books he wrote weren't part of the picture *Confidential* chose to paint. Instead, he was just a Richie Rich giving a Glam Gal the business.

On the other hand, Corny's own take on the situation tended to leave out his bitter tenacity, or the fact that he tried to swindle Patricia by moving to Nevada so he could divorce her there, since in Nevada no alimony would be required. Patricia established New York residency and sued for support there. They fought it out all the way to the Supreme Court— where the technical issue of whether she had standing to sue for alimony in New York (which had granted it) when Nevada (a state where she never lived, and which did not have jurisdiction over her) had already dissolved the marriage and left her nothing. The case was decided in her favor in 1957 and she won her spousal support.

The *Confidential* story missed the Constitutional law angle and tarred them both with a lot of dirt. But again, no one sued. There was no outcry. Corny and Pat got on with their lives. And so it went. Donohue met the Duchess for drinks. Vanderbilt remarried again. Everyone got richer—except the ones who Lost Everything, Went Broke, or were Down to Their Last Nickel. And High Society survived to face another issue of *Confidential*.

Harrison wasn't as personally turned on by the Society stories as he was the Hollywood articles. He saw himself in the stars—thought of himself as one of them, in a way, certainly equally newsworthy. The upper classes were something else. They didn't earn their place in Café Society through smarts, hard work, or moxie. It was all given to them. Watching them throw it all away was highly satisfying, both to Harrison and to his readers.

His perversely bad boy sense of humor was tickled pink by another kind of story though, a genre that he began publishing first in *Whisper*, and kept printing throughout the heady days of *Confidential's* success.

Kinks & Kicks That Kill
Nympho Pill Poppers & Guys with Guns

Hot Springs, Arkansas. Who knew?

> *Confidentially speaking, the lid is off! The bunk is going to be debunked! Confidential will open your eyes and make them pop. It pulls the curtain aside and takes you behind the scenes, giving the facts, naming names and revealing what the front pages often try to conceal!*

Merry Christmas. It was December 1952 and Robert Harrison, in his very first issue of *Confidential* took on the dangerous responsibility of warning America's unsuspecting John and Mary Q. Public that sleepy little Hot Springs, Arkansas, with its restorative waters, was, in actuality, a "Retreat of Racketeers!—a Hoodlum's Paradise!" This piece of purple prose was attributed to Hugh V. Haddock, newspaperman and "crime authority."

According to the article, there wasn't a mobster or public enemy in the country, dead or alive, who didn't make Hot Springs his Hideout Home Away From Home: Lucky Luciano, Al Capone, Frank Costello, Joe Adonis, Jake "Greasy Thumb" Guzik, Frank Nitti, Alvin Karpis, Harry Campbell, Adam Richetti, Rocco Fischetto, Owney Madden, and Pretty Boy Floyd. The exposé went on for a mind-boggling 4,000 words, detailing the writer's every step, every sip of coffee, and practically, every trip to the bathroom. Yet it's bizarrely tame, almost a puff piece, which is how Harrison liked his stories about gangsters. There wasn't anything in the story about any (living) hoodlum that could get him in trouble.

Though the article claimed to give an historical perspective on mobsters in Hot Springs, they failed to mention a rather spectacular, if unsuccessful, F.B.I. raid on Hot Springs in 1936, when they attempted to apprehend one of America's Ten Most Wanted, Alvin Karpis. The F.B.I. was apparently led there by a tip-off that a Karpis accomplice frequented mineral wells and health resorts in Hot Springs because he was afflicted with gonorrheal rheumatism. That was the big Arkansas crime link for real. Gonorrhea. How in the world did Harrison miss out on that?

Other tough guys mentioned in the story had certainly checked into various establishments in Hot Springs on occasion, but one could just as easily say that the Plaza Hotel in New York was a hotbed of hoodlums, since just about everyone mentioned in the story probably had lunch or a drink there at least once in his life too.

That first issue of *Confidential* also had a first-person tell-all about being tortured on a Southern chain-gang. Such things were still going on in the rural South (as they once again do today) and prison reform was and is an important issue. You wouldn't know that from reading "I Was Tortured on a Chain Gang!" The pictures are fabulously fake, with one of the Black actor-prisoners doing a picture-perfect, eye-popping grimace directly to camera, like Step'n Fetchit, and a long shot of a whole chain-gang that must have come from a 20-year-old Warner Bros. Ripped-From-the-Headlines crime drama.

The hard journalism in the magazine was neither hard nor particularly journalistic, and cheap shots are a good goof, but in revisiting the non-celebrity news pieces, you can't help but notice something fresh and interesting about the look of them, and about the voice the magazine was finding. Even though both stories were largely fictional, they read now as definite (if slightly demented) precursors of the New Journalism that Nora Ephron, Joan Didion, and Harrison's 1964 *Esquire* profiler Tom Wolfe, among others, would popularize in the '60s and '70s—a kind of first-person, you-are-there narrative that draws people in, taking them as deep into the world of the story as possible. The style is very filmic, and is arguably the most influential force still felt today in non-fiction writing. Glimmers of future fashions in journalism were not completely unique to *Confidential* among '50s rags, yet Harrison's attention to detail guaranteed that his were some of the best examples of the technique.

Tom Wolfe came up with the phrase *aesthetique du schlock,* which has been endlessly reprinted ever since to describe

Harrison's oeuvre. What most of those quoting Wolfe fail to grasp is that in his own way, he meant it as a sincere compliment. He was clearly jazzed by how deeply Bob Harrison cared about the aesthetic of his magazines. The publisher may never have been driven by a passionate sense of the art of writing, exactly, but he knew what made a good story cook, and his vision of what his magazines could be was always fully realized. It all mattered so much to him, which is why he was better than his imitators. *Confidential* became his very own work of art. Within his own terms, and with only a smattering of hyperbole, it could be said that Harrison was every bit as successful and influential as Picasso. Or at least as Margaret Keane, who earned millions in later decades, painting large-eyed children who cry.

Confidential True Stories: The mob targeting Bishop Sheen, J. Edgar Hoover, Winchell, and McCarthy; the mob using F.D.R. as an unwitting tool of assassination in the planned murder of a Chicago mayor; how hoodlums are often behind the gowns you wear; the alleged murder of Countess Dorothy di Frasso, the Rubirosa murder case, a madman gunmen attacking Sugar Ray, the rampant problem of mink coat thefts, Hungarian Slave Women—Robert Harrison signed off on anything that could make someone take the magazine off a newsstand shelf and open it, and once opened, keep that person reading. If it popped it was newsworthy—as long as it didn't get him into trouble.

The Rubirosa Murder Case
July 1954

> *Some mighty strange fruit ripened on the Rubirosa family tree. It includes adulterers and smugglers—also numbers at least one murderer! The Rubirosa's are a clan whose exploits sound like titles for detective novels. Adultery is common, there's a dandy hijacking in the record, and a couple of bold smuggling raps... Convicted in $60,000 smuggling attempt, Profirio's brother*

Cesar must live in Greece until his stiff fine is worked out; maximum time, 95 years...
WANTED FOR MURDER: Notorious hoodlum Louis della Fuente Rubirosa, first cousin to Profirio Rubirosa is still sought for brazen political killing... the Rubirosa clan never said what happened to its trigger-happy relative...

Whatever Profirio Rubirosa's relatives did or didn't do, most of the events depicted in the article were already 20 years old. Rubirosa's own dubious celebrity was based not only on his playboy marriages and his physical endowment, but also on his glamorous indolence. Despite occasional ambassadorial posts over the years, polo playing and women remained his preoccupations. He was actually known for an overwhelming attentiveness to women, coupled with a kind of sweetness— both Robert Harrison attributes. He liked to say that gigolos leave their women having made them miserable and poor, while he always left them richer and happier. Another thing he shared with Harrison. Rubirosa's many advantageous marriages included not just one of the world's wealthiest women, but two: Doris Duke *and* Barbara Hutton.

Rubi must have had something. Many of his exes remained friends and financial supporters throughout his life. Apparently Rubi was the epitome of a Latin Lover, the kind of guy Ricardo Montalban, Fernando Llamas, and earlier, Cesar Romero, made careers out of pretending to be. Actually, by Esther Williams' account, her husband Fernando did do the Latin Lover trip for real. In her autobiography, "Million Dollar Mermaid," Williams describes his endowments and talents frankly, including his occasional physical abuse and obsessive need to control her every move—all Rubi behavioral tics as well.

Throughout the '50s Zsa Zsa was so smitten with Rubi she couldn't stand to be away from him, whether she was married to someone else or not. Rubi and Zsa Zsa were kind of like opposite-sex mirror images of one another—Barbie and Ken with genitals and nipples. When Marjorie first came to

Hollywood, Uncle Bob told her she should call Zsa Zsa. Marjorie did, and was invited by the clearly uninterested Gabor to tea at her Bel Air home. On the grand tour of the place, Zsa Zsa made a big point of showing Marjorie a room and saying it was where Rubi stayed on his numerous overnight visits.

Along with hubba-hubba pieces like "Pega Palo: The Vine That Makes You Virile," the magazine published other kinds of exposés that straddled the line of hype and public service, doing a little bit of good here and there in spite of themselves. These were the articles Harrison used to defend himself against charges from various quarters (including the Postmaster General) that the magazine was nothing but smut. He could point to pieces on children being poisoned by aspirin, the dangers to humans from household insecticides, Narcotics Anonymous, the hazards of Demerol, quack doctors, Polly Adler's Prostitute's Anonymous, the problems of parolees fitting back into society, and various other warnings of terrible risks in modern society.

How much good they ever did is debatable. The turbo-powered hype and cheesy scare tactics, not only in the copy itself, but also in the layout and photo choices, could put serious readers off, even as they lured curiosity seekers. And sometimes the information wasn't exactly new or particularly well-researched—the aspirin article, for instance, was lifted from a high school paper written by Marjorie—there had been a hole in the March 1955 issue, and Bob needed some filler.

A couple of decades later, once the Surgeon General mandated cigarette package warnings, and the link between smoking and lung disease became clear, Harrison was always proud to point out that warnings about cigarette safety first appeared in *Confidential* in the '50s. There were four articles about cigarettes during Harrison's run as publisher. The May 1954 article "Pills That Kill the Smoking Habit," was actually one of the most lucid of the bunch—it even credited *Time Magazine* with having the courage to be the first to break the lung cancer story. Rather than ramp up the hype, the piece was actually very informational. It established that if you are convinced smoking causes cancer, an assertion that was not yet universally accepted, you could get help by taking one of several kinds of pills that helped ease cravings for nicotine. The writer tried one called Flavette. There were positive reactions from some who had tried it, plus a stimulant effect which helped them keep from gaining weight. That last bit was a little fishy—this *was* the era of doctors handing out uppers like candy—and the efficacy, ingredients, and safety of the drug is lost to history. But it was clearly a positive story.

If you want to quit smoking, see your doctor,
maybe you can get help.

It even explored the fact that many magazines were reluctant to criticize tobacco companies out of fear of losing their advertising revenue—a problem for print media decades later as well, though never for *Confidential,* where the advertisers were more down-market. The article was most notable for the complete absence of the hysterical style that characterized other public service pieces.

The second cigarette story *Confidential* ran got more into the swing of things.

The Big Lie About Filter Cigarettes!
March 1955

Fear is driving millions of scared smokers to filter-tip cigarette for that promised "health protection." Here is the latest laboratory lowdown on the filter ballyhoo! Some filter cigarettes pass on more nicotine than unfiltered brands! When filters hit the market with the biggest advertising barrage in years, did you believe what the ads told you—that now you could smoke your fool head off—and forget what the doctors said about cancer and heart disease?...Well, you're in for a rough awakening, buster. You've been had!... Now a new and far more dangerous specter (sic) has arisen to haunt the industry...the killer role played by nicotine in over 800,000 deaths a year from heart disease— which makes lung cancer's 22,000 fatalities a mere drop in the bucket!

That was more like it. The panic. The paranoia. And along with the absolutely true exposé of Big Tobacco's lies about filters making cigarettes safer, a little gross oversimplification of science, drawing all sorts of false conclusions about nicotine. The biggest eye-opener in the article now is the relatively tiny number of lung cancer deaths. Yet even with the mistakes, it was still a piece with an inescapably true point: Filters do not make smoking any healthier. And in the ten months since the first article, the magazine had stopped qualifying the cancer link to cigarettes. Smoking could kill you. Period.

In September 1957 there was a similar, though shorter, piece, "The Shots That Cure the Cigarette Habit!," trumpeting a new drug called Lobelia that a Swedish doctor was testing on humans. Not content to promote the drug's use in kicking the coffin nail habit, the story cheerfully detailed how Lobelia was derived from an Indian herb white explorers took back to Europe that had successfully cured the "White Plague of Syphilis." Now that's a wonder drug. Lobelia is actually still available on websites, with the same history and claims *Confidential* reported in 1957. The article's layout and cheesy tone just made it *seem* like the whole syphilis and Native American connection must be a phony.

Unfortunately, Harrison couldn't ever resist a contrary, attention-getting story on any subject—as long as it could have a headline guaranteed to make you look. Later in 1957 he threw away every ounce of credibility he had built up about warning the public on the health dangers of smoking, and left a mixed legacy on the whole subject. How many among *Confidential's* millions of readers who had successfully kicked the habit, were only too happy to puff up again when they read this:

Cigarettes Do NOT Cause Cancer!
November 1957

Not long ago, in the midst of another flood of scareheads claiming that cigarettes cause lung cancer, a jittery chain-smoker was panicked into a desperate expedient. Having failed in previous fear-inspired attempts to quit smoking, he submitted to hypnotism. It worked! He found, when he woke up from his hypnotic trance, that he had lost the desire to smoke. But two weeks later he committed suicide! Literally as well as figuratively, cigarette smokers are being scared to death by a bogeyman that has no scientific reality!

The article ran on and on, basically telling the reader to go ahead and smoke. It was as breathtaking as those old commercials and magazine ads claiming a particular brand of cigarettes was recommended by doctors—for pregnant women no less—to calm their nerves. The writer missed the chance to add the historical perspective Harrison liked to have in his stories. In 1618 just before his death on the guillotine, Sir Walter Raleigh said of tobacco, "This is sharp medicine, but it will cure all disease."

Medicine also figured in a few other stories, frightening tales of how Demerol, Opium, and Dolophine, as well as aspirin, could kill. Lurid accounts of back-alley users were written with the sensational sizzle readers found addictive. The stories weren't bogus. The dangers were clear. The most prescient drug story had to be a July 1957 piece on how heart patients should be taking aspirin every day. They couldn't have been more ahead of the curve on that one.

Scare tactics were usually a part of the stories. How else could you get someone to read a boring piece on auto safety. Hospitals screwing up your surgeries, doctors killing you with untested drugs, labs criminally mixing up your results, the dangers of sitting in the wrong seat on an airplane if it crashes, spot removers that kill kids, questioning the safety of your bank... *You or someone in your family could die in any number of ways and you could lose all your money **unless you read this article!*** Anyone who watches the afternoon block of local news on any television station in America is acutely familiar with the technique. How many times is a little rain in Los Angeles promoted with teasers screaming, "Storm Front Warning! Coming up next!" How often does the prediction of a teeny tiny little snowfall in New York get a blurb between commercials as, "Overnight Blizzard? Get the latest!"

Sometimes second guessing a story seems easy, like the January 1958 "Warning! Coffee CAN Make You Fat!" One imagines it will be about the hidden calories and fat in cream and sugar. But no. The piece was an 800-word warning on how the caffeine in coffee could give you "nerves," which play a major role in weight gain, as could drinking too much of any liquid. Including water.

Now down to four cups of caffeine-removed coffee per day, not only has this housewife escaped her daily caffeine-poisoning but she has decreased her fluid intake by some 15 gallons per month!

Harrison's girlie magazine sensibility is clearly at work on a different category of story—the steamy sex exposé, where spicy photographs often contradicted any pretense of moral purpose. It's another area where a particular style prevailed from the beginning of his reign to the very end, from "Sex Styles Have Changed in New York," in December 1952, to "Tip to Railroad Cops: Keep an Eye on Those Club Car Chippies," in January 1958. The first used staged models and dubious attributions to report the new phenomenon of social register debs using phone answering services to facilitate fun forays into prostitution. Really. The second revealed a shocking new racket being used by America's call girls (presumably not the same debs of the earlier story) who would get first class berths and cruise club cars to solicit customers on night trains and trans-continental trips. A lot of the stories offered a good laugh, which was

Harrison's intention. And sometimes Hollywood and the "sexposé" happily coexisted:

Even the Cops Blushed When They Learned:
Where Marie McDonald Hid That Ring!
May 1957

When Marie McDonald was "kidnapped" awhile back and then returned under foggy circumstances, she was the darling of the front pages for quite a spell. And all during that spotlighted period a lot of questions were asked that never got answered. One of the biggest queries was this: What happened to the six-carat rock "The Body" was wearing at the time of the alleged **snatch***?*

According to the beauteous Marie, she was abducted and raped by two "Mexicans," and the pair of loving and looting Latins lifted the $8,000 ring, along with her honor. That is not so, we theenk (sic). The ring went south of the border, all right, but not to old Mejico. What the nation's press never told—and what the public will learn here for the first time—is this: The ring was found not long after Marie turned up. Where? You ask. Was the bauble on her body? No, it was not on "The Body," but hold your breath...It was in "The Body!"...Dr. Fisher decided to call in noted gynecologist, Dr. Kermit H. Anderson, to check Marie's "I wuz raped" routine. He might better have called in a jeweler with one of those glass things in his eye, or a diamond miner with a lantern in his hat. Or he might have asked for a professional opinion from Tiffany's or Cartier's.

*...in probing below the belt he'd found there were
diamonds in that thar "Body"—to be exact, an
$8,000, six-carat diamond ring!*

One would be hard pressed to find an article about a
woman hiding a ring in her vagina in any other mainstream
publication with *Confidential's* readership numbers. This was
just one of many stunts sometime actress and personality
McDonald pulled in the '50s. The anatomical angle placed it
squarely in *Confidential's* weird-sex story territory, giving her
non-existent career no momentum whatsoever. It was about
giving readers a sexual thrill, just as *Confidential* did with "Too
Hot To Print," "Hollywood Lonely Hearts Ads," "Call Boys of
Manhattan" (hetero, not homo), "Love In Africa! Savages Kiss
and Tell," "Eight Wives at Once!" "You Can Rent a Wife!" and
"The American Academy of Dramatic Art: School For Scandal!"
For the most part the stories seem geared to the nebbish
looking for a thrill or two and for a way of feeling superior to
someone, anyone. Sex, crime, and drugs. Fun for Harrison and
easier to do than Hollywood stories, since you could say just
about anything about kinks, gangsters, or pill popping with no
risk of libel. The only worry was whether an obscenity charge
could stick. But Bob faced that threat down over and over, and
would only admit to it once—just in time to save Marjorie from
prison.

Of course, the sex, drugs, and mob stories were downright
truthful compared to another Harrison genre.

...Two or three incisions may be enough to free a woman from her prison of frigidity...

TURN THE PAGE

Wacky In Wonderland
Truth Takes a Holiday

 Now It Can Be Told! Bat Boy, born in the pages of *Weekly World News* in 1992, measuring two feet long and weighing in at an impossibly hefty 19 pounds, is the true son and heir to Robert Harrison, lifelong bachelor, who never wanted children.

This tabloid saga of a boy found in a cave, with enormous amber eyes that see in the dark, and oversized ears that work like radar, is a perennial *Weekly World News* favorite, even inspiring an off-Broadway musical in 2001. In 12 separate stories over a decade, Bat Boy is found, escapes, is captured, is wanted by the F.B.I., attacks a 10-year-old girl, is sighted in Texas, endorses Gore in the 2000 presidential race, falls in love, gets sick, and is hit by a truck. The pictures of Bat Boy recall Harrison's history farther back even than *Confidential*. The Composographs from *The New York Graphic,* with their painted photos of angels mixed with real people. Harrison's entire oeuvre has come full-circle.

Oddball stories of seriously dubious origin, and even more dubious veracity, were a mainstay from the beginning, and continued throughout the run of *Confidential*. They ebbed a bit in 1955 and 1956 as movie star gossip started taking up more and more room, but made a huge comeback in Harrison's last few issues, after the trial. There is no evidence that anyone took them any more seriously then than they do now. It was all just a goof—something for a laugh between gossip and exposés.

American tabloid weeklies from the '60s to the early '90s relied on the same mix of generally accurate gossip (at least when it came to anything actionable—puff pieces were always more fictionally constructed) with wild stories of U.F.O. sightings, alien abductions, mutants, and the deformed. Slowly most, including *The Star* and *The National Enquirer*, began dropping the bizarre pieces in favor of Hollywood stories, and a new emphasis on scandal involving politicians. Now only *The Weekly World News*, or *The Globe*, would run anything as truly inane as this Harrison favorite:

Gangster Ghouls
August 1953

> *Grave robbing as a business went out of style some 50 years ago, but today underworld hoodlums and punks are plotting a fantastic scheme which, for sheer audacity, is unparalleled in the annals of crime. This new reign of horror is based on a daring plan to steal corpses and hold them for ransom!*

> *Looming large in the ambitious plans formulated by these crypt crackers are the ashes of persons who are known to have left wealthy and prominent survivors. The despoilers are certain that the living will ransom their dead for amounts from $10,000 to $50,000!*

> *The magnitude of their grandiose schemes is astounding. Not only have they laid plans to snatch the well-preserved and expensively entombed corpse of Evita Peron—on the theory that the nation of Argentina will pay a king's ransom for its return—they've even mapped a strategy for heisting the bones of South America's great Liberator, Simon Bolivar!*

There was even a supporting photograph with the article, of two "ghouls" trying to shield their faces from photographers. One of them was Robert Harrison. The other was a *Confidential* staff writer. Maybe the idea of gangster ghouls wasn't as outright silly as Bat Boy, but they both orbited stars in the same solar system. Proving these kinds of stories false is pointless since no one cares and no one is hurt by them, and no one is being libeled, so no one can sue.

Who exactly was going to take umbrage with "American Hoods Take Over Havana!"—Batista? Lucky Luciano? The faked shots of Havana in turmoil, with Harrison's girlie mag models running amok on New York streets seemed almost deliberately phony—as if he so wanted you to be in on the joke, that he was willing to show the theatrical underpinnings to anyone who would take the time to look. Anyone who got through the seventh grade without committing suicide would be totally unsurprised to read that "50,000 Insane Teachers Are In Our Schools!" and "The Black Market in Human Eyes," "Blood For Booze," "Gold For Ghouls," "Local Corpse Makes Good," and "The Black Market in Human Body Parts," were macabre enough to give a little shiver even as one tries to keep from giggling.

Who wouldn't be frightened of being "Shot By a Cufflink" or getting mowed down by "The Pen That Is a Lethal .38?" What sap would want to pass up reading about "The Case of the Attic Lover," "Arab Sheik Buys American Wife," "The True Case: of the Man Who Wouldn't Die," or "The Case of the Two Missing Heads?" The carny, freak show appeal is timeless, essential somehow to one's own sense of well-being.

Certain kinds of stories provide readers with a sense of empathy. Someone has lost a loved one and reads about a widow's grief, for instance, and feels connected and understood. Then there are the object lessons; usually boiling down to someone undeserving getting rich and/or famous, then losing everything through cheating or drug and alcohol abuse. There but for the grace of God... The strange-but-untrue tales are there to elevate the reader's sense of self-worth. Sure, the happily married guy who's a little bit of a nebbish feels *morally* superior to a two-timing tomcat, but with an article like "The Case of the Two Missing Heads" he gets a chance to feel intellectually superior as well. He can shake his head, laughing. *Who the hell believes this stuff?* Whoever the true believer may be, the reader knows his or her own I.Q. is higher by leaps and bounds. The rewards go beyond the little chuckle, giving the ego a boost, and making that reader feel less guilty for reading the rest of the gossip and innuendo the magazine provides, since it's infinitely more substantive.

Many of these articles had the same sense of dread and paranoia as some of the political exposés—like so many

Twilight Zone episodes of the era, with their paranoid Cold War, Duck and Cover explorations of fear of the Other. That mentality wasn't (and isn't) confined to the '50s, but it reached a kind of peak in the McCarthy era. What could be more frightening than the idea that someone might steal your dead loved ones? Or take your eyes and body parts once you die to sell them to the highest bidder?

Far From Heaven, Todd Haynes' 2002 drama sought to recreate a Douglas Sirk/Ross Hunter mood of tortured longing, its plot complex enough for at least three *Confidential* stories: "My Husband Is a Homosexual!" "My Wife Fell For a Negro Gardener!" and "Big Shot Exec Goes Bust!" It reached beyond sex, into a realm where the terror always comes from the unknown and the unsaid. Churning music. Churning stomachs. But Harrison didn't have time for that kind of pessimism. *Confidential* just wanted you to laugh. He made a living in a field that was, at best, parallel to the profession of journalism. He was a storyteller. The narrative arc he could create in a story about an Arab Sheik buying an American wife—the cultural clash, the powerful emotions, the shame, the violence—these weren't always possible with straight reporting. Essentially he was a dramatist, a filmmaker even.

True Case of the Man Who Wouldn't Die
January 1958

> *...A couple of nights later, after Malloy had cadged several drinks, Murphy slipped him a shot of automobile antifreeze. Malloy smacked his lips and asked for another... Malloy was still on his feet, begging for more, after he had consumed enough of the stuff to blind and kill half a dozen men... on about the tenth shot, Malloy went crashing to the floor. ...The three plotters sat around, breaking open a bottle, waiting for the Irishman to die. Toward dawn, Malloy's pulse was so faint death seemed a question of minutes.*

The boys were figuring what to tell the (life) insurance doctor when Malloy suddenly stirred, opened his eyes, and yelled: "Gimme another shot o' that good stuff, me boy!" ...He had been drinking rot-gut for so many years that his system had become inured to it.

Disappointed, but not dismayed, the three plotters now got busy on a plan to dispatch the Irishman with ptomaine poisoning. Murphy opened a tin of sardines and set it out in the sun until the fish were putrid. Then he had the can ground up and mixed some of the slivers of tin with the rotten sardines and made Mike (Malloy) a sandwich.

Malloy ate the sandwich with gusto, washing it down with more anti-freeze. Later, when nothing happened to Malloy, the master plotters could feel the first twinges of quiet desperation. But they hadn't seen nuthin' yet.

One of the plotters had once buried a man who had died from downing the combination of raw oysters and whiskey. So the boys went out and bought a dozen oysters and soaked them in anti-freeze. Then Murphy served them to Malloy on the half-shell, with generous shots of wood alky. At the end of the feast Mike smacked his lips and congratulated the astonished Murphy on the tastiness of the repast.

Plotting their fourth attempt to get rid of the durable Irishman, the boys remembered if a drunkard catches pneumonia he seldom gets well. ...A sleet storm was pelting the Bronx... They got Malloy tanked on anti-freeze, stripped him to the waist, and left him lying there in the park with the sleet bouncing off his chest.

Next afternoon, when the plotters foregathered in Marino's joint, all croaking from the bad colds they had caught in the sleet the night before... In walked the durable Mike Malloy. "The funniest thing happened to me, Red me lad," Mike chirped to Murphy, "I woke up in Claremont Park a little while ago half undressed. Lemme have a shot, me lad, for I think I might of caught a bit of a chill."

It went on and on. Malloy, the indestructible man, was hit by a taxi and bounced 50 feet through the air, survived skull fractures, disappeared, got caught up in a mistaken identity plot, gave up drinking, and was finally, mercifully, murdered by carbon monoxide asphyxiation.

These stories were dreamed up, written, and edited by a revolving group of writers. Staff members like Ernest Tidyman (who would later write *Shaft* and win an Oscar for *The French Connection*) and Howard Rushmore came and went; Al Govoni, a former editor at *National Police Gazette,* was a regular standby; and in the beginning Harrison relied heavily on Jay Breen, who used to write as much as half the magazine under various names.

Breen was one of the first to tire of a peculiar tic Harrison had of using a Reader for every issue. The guy Harrison hired was an out-of-work actor with a stentorian delivery, who read each article out loud to the whole editorial staff. Bob believed that hearing the stories was the best way of evaluating every word, every phrase, and making the final decisions about whether or not to use it.

Some writers bitched that the Reader didn't like them, and purposely mumbled their copy to help kill their stories, but Jay Breen was past that once the scandal rag was into its second year. He and his wife would sometimes even decamp to the next room during the readings—but they could usually still hear the guy anyway. Harrison valued Breen highly, but was hardly blind to his writer's foibles, revealing in a 1959 interview:

> *You know what ruined Breen? He was making*
> *too much money, and that started him drinking.*
> *He must have been making forty or fifty thousand*
> *a year, and he never had money like that before,*
> *and he was living high and he started drinking.*
> *The trouble was, I guess, he had it too good! After*
> *a while he was drunk all the time. I remember we*
> *put out one whole issue up in Memorial Hospital,*
> *I think that was the name of it. He was in one*
> *room, for treatment, and I took the room next to*
> *it, and we put out the whole goddamned issue up*
> *there.*

Breen briefly ended up at the truly low-rent 1955 start-up magazine *Exposed*, with an "as told to" story called "From Here to Paternity," before dying soon after. Once Breen was gone Howard Rushmore shouldered more responsibility for a while, but it was steadfast and unflappable Al Govoni who was with Harrison for the whole ride—sometimes credited as a managing editor, as editor-in-chief, or as just a plain editor. When Harrison put the magazine under Rushmore's editorial control in name, it was still himself and Govoni who did the real work, while the often erratic Rushmore followed the beat of his own increasingly cranky drummer.

Three of the more well known writers were William Bradford Huie, Frank O'Leary, and Harry Botsford. Huie specialized in "inside" pieces, and was the former editor of *The American Mercury*. He worked a lot for the major mass market magazines of the day, and was thought of as a thorough, if rather biased writer. Once he got an idea in his head, he wouldn't let anything contradict it. O'Leary was an ex-convict who while in prison was one of the writers and editors of "The

Dictionary of American Underworld Lingo." How he and Harrison first met is anybody's guess.

Other contributors were usually moonlighting reporters and rewrite men from many of the New York dailies, or formerly first-rate writers who, through booze or bad temperament, were no longer welcome at the popular family magazines. A lot of them did it on the sly, under fake names, not even telling wives or girlfriends about their clandestine forays into part-time peeping. There were also press agents working both sides of the fence, selling articles on their clients, either out of a need for cash or sometimes for a little revenge over ill-treatment or unpaid fees. The one thing about Harrison: Let other tabloids hire and fire on the cheap. He paid full market rates, and got good writers because of it. There's no mystery about why *Confidential* stayed ahead of all its later pretenders. It was better. Spicier. More imaginative. And that cost money. Besides, Harrison liked to discover people, as he did with Lorenzo Semple, the young *Confidential* writer who went on to become a major Hollywood screenwriter, whose credits include *Three Days of the Condor*, *Papillon*, and *Never Say Never Again*.

Uncle Sam Wants To Sue
Shams, Scams & Taxpayer Tortures

Howard Rushmore was usually responsible for the political articles that emphasized often previously published stories on supposed Communists. But other political stories were aimed squarely at the disgruntled—at the guy who was sure Uncle Sam was ripping him off somehow, or that he wasn't getting his fair share. The chip-on-the-shoulder martyrdom of the reader was given focus and heat by the magazine's outrage— which in some cases was certainly overstated, but could also be remarkably on target. Like with the health story on how aspirin could be good for heart patients, when the magazine got something right, it could succeed spectacularly. Putting aside Howard Rushmore's Communist fantasies, there was a real strain of anti-establishment anger in the rest of the political stories that made it to print: Your congressmen are wasting money on lavish foreign trips, the government is printing porn, diplomats get away with murder flouting our laws, Uncle Sam gets income from hookers, he's in the casino business, he makes illegal money from betting on horse races, the shocking bugs in Social Security, legal stock market gimmicks that cost you millions...

Harrison liked stories that were skeptical of government and the hidden agendas of our politicians. Regardless of Harrison's personal politics, which were basically, if haphazardly, liberal, the tone he strived for was outrage mixed with humor—but even that was fairly unusual in other publications of the era. The mainstream press didn't often seriously question the institutionalized lack of ethics among politicians until after Watergate. Tabloids in the decades that followed *Confidential* rarely followed politics, until June 1987, with the breaking of the Gary Hart "Monkey Business" story. Scandal sheet political coverage reached a fever pitch during the Clinton years—*Phony Land Deals! Mystery Suicides! Sex! Pot!* Mainstream newspapers and magazines, books, and the Internet are now overstuffed with political sleaze revelations.

In some basic way, however, even with the odd scandal coming along that consumes the public's imagination, the stylishness has gone out of it. The need for Harrison to clean things up enough to pass legal muster was probably responsible, in part, for a great deal of the creativity—the puns, the innuendo, the double entendres that make the stories still such lively reading. Today nothing is obscene, so everything is vulgar, with the lowest common denominator leading the way. Can anyone imagine Ike, Nixon, Kefauver, Adlai, or any of them, publicly having to define oral sex? Maybe Ike and Mamie had a fabulous sex life, who knows? The public had to wait until they were both dead to hear allegations that he carried on a secret affair with Kay Somersby.

The Million Dollar Scandal in Nixon's Backyard
March 1955

*Sunny California is the hot-spot for a new
'windfall' grab. It's a political bomb that will leave
a lot of red faces in Washington—and make*

millions of U.S. taxpayers boil! ...And when it erupts, the voters may see a scandal that will make the recent Federal housing swindle look like a Girl Scout's lemonade party. ...(The) Transportation Act of 1940 says that when a common carrier—a railroad, plane, ship, bus, or freight line—sends a bill to the United States government, it must be paid immediately.

Let's see what happens when a slick operator takes advantage of this hustle-bustle law. The Toot, Gasp, and Wheeze Railroad, as a figurative example, does $100,000 a month worth of business with the Army and Navy. But it mails out bills totaling $150,000 a month—an overcharge of $50,000!

Does anyone shout 'Whoa?' The shocking answer is, NO. The law doesn't allow enough time for an itemized checkup and the dough is shoveled out— no questions asked. The bill is paid, as presented, within six days of receipt. Our aforementioned railroad tucks a fat fifty grand in its pocket—to which it has absolutely no right—and it can do the same thing, month in and month out, for years, before it's called up for an accounting. In the meantime, the light-fingered corporation is actually being bank-rolled by Uncle Sam. Our afore-mentioned TG&W Railroad's tactics would give it $600,000 in tax money—your money—to play with in a single year. From where you sit, a dodge like that may look like nothing but polite robbery. But not in court. There, it's just 'sloppy bookkeeping,' regrettable, but no crime.

How far-flung is this 'free-ride' racket? It's hard to tell. GAO managed to recover almost $50,000,000 in overcharges last year and that agency estimates that Uncle Sam has at least another $100,000,000 coming for 1954 alone. Best estimates are that there are billions out on 'loan' in this weird operation—all of it at zero interest rates.

The article only hinted at the idea that Nixon might be keeping the gloves off, protecting California's huge trucking industry to benefit companies who had given him and his party large political contributions. Harrison avoided making the direct allegation in *Confidential* of political payoffs by a sitting vice president, which would have been a shocking charge to the public. Today no one truly believes what the government says anymore, so covering the lies and evasions doesn't pack the emotional wallop it used to. The country has grown blasé and unsurprised when presented with evidence of corruption. In Harrison's day the idea of distrusting your own government was in its infancy. He had his reasons, though, since the government tried to put him out of business constantly.

AUGUST 27, 1955—The Solicitor of the Post Office issued a "Withhold From Dispatch" order on *Confidential,* barring it from the nation's mails. It was issued without any notice to Harrison, without any specified charges, and without any sort of hearing whatsoever, and was designed to bar the November 1955 issue from being mailed anywhere within the United States. The Solicitor's Office had lousy timing. The great bulk of the November issue had already been sent by the time the order was put into effect, so the country's avid readers were still able to learn that Clark Gable's father-in-law wasn't at his latest wedding, that Elizabeth Taylor's husband was on the prowl, how Johnnie Ray broke down a man's door because he was so besotted with him, what Mae West used to do with her Black chauffeur, why Mrs. Jack Webb was crossing Friday off her calendar, how Terry Moore was a Turkish Delight, about the budding romance of Gloria De Haven & Jeff Chandler, and why and how a cheap chippie made a chump of George Raft.

Harrison and his legal team came out swinging and Judge Luther Youngdahl seemed fairly sympathetic. He enjoined the Postmaster from continuing its withholding order, judging the timing and manner of its delivery to be entirely against the law. But the news wasn't wholly positive for Harrison. The judge decreed that from that point forward, Harrison would submit each issue to the Post Office, starting with January 1956, within 24-hours of its printing and binding. The judge ordered that if the Post Office found anything objectionable, Harrison must be accorded a proper hearing, and he further ordered that the magazine had to keep going through the mails unless the Postmaster General obtained, after due and proper notice to the publisher, an injunction from the United States District Court for the District of Columbia barring it from the mails.

So it seemed clear. Harrison agreed to a little oversight. The Post Office agreed that while it might have the first shot in any war against the magazine, the court would have the final say—and everything would have to be strictly by the book. But the Post Office violated the court order repeatedly and dared anyone to stop them.

Each of the early issues in 1956 made it in the mail by the skin of Harrison's teeth. The legal case dragged on at various court levels, with *Confidential* often prevailing—but judge-shopping and the bottomless pocketbook of the Post Office always kept the case alive and the magazine's postal future uncertain. Harrison cried foul, accusing the government of throwing his business into turmoil, though to some extent, the danger to the magazine was overblown. Most of the five million copies of the magazine sold at newsstands were distributed by truck. Any ban on the mails wouldn't have affected those issues at all. A few hundred thousand arrived at various locations through the postal service, and those were the only issues at risk. But the principles involved, the vast amounts of money spent on attorneys, and the future battles to come on other fronts if this battle were lost, these were very real issues at stake. Even the A.C.L.U. got involved, solemnly disdaining the magazine itself while making First Amendment claims in support of its right to exist. As wily as the government got, attorney Al DeStefano was one step ahead, attacking them on procedural grounds (his strongest argument in light of prevailing obscenity standards of the day) as well as on Constitutional grounds.

This was a time that, in retrospect, turned out to be the beginning of the end of rigid obscenity standards. In Hollywood the Code was under serious attack—Otto Preminger's 1953 film *The Moon Is Blue* was released without Code approval and did just fine. Court decisions were starting to take notice of changing standards in literature. The Post Office got sick of the whole *Confidential* mess at the end of 1956. They never admitted being in the wrong, and reserved the right to continue acting as they wished, but backtracked, saying that since nothing in the magazine was actually obscene (this after claiming the opposite for years) there would be no further need for Harrison to submit the magazine to them before publication. They gladly washed their hands of *Confidential* and Robert Harrison, who would make great hay of the Post Office's "nothing obscene" decision in interviews he gave during the 1957 trial in California, when charges of obscenity were an important part of the case.

Never mind the Post Office, Harrison's business relationship with Uncle Sam grew more and more complicated with every issue he published.

So did his relationship with Howard Rushmore.

On Independence Day, 1955, Rushmore had been on a television show in Chicago, telling right-wing shill and talk show host Tom Duggan that he was in the Windy City on a secret mission to blow the lid off the cover-up of Navy Secretary James Forrestal's murder. Evidently he trusted each and every individual in Duggan's audience to keep said secret. Forrestal had plunged to his death six years before from the sixteenth floor of the Bethesda Naval Hospital. The authorities ruled it a suicide. Rushmore charged it was nothing short of a Red Menace murder. He told viewers he was in Chicago searching for an old New York Commie leader named William Lazarovich who was using the alias Bill Lawrence, and asked the audience for any information they had about his whereabouts.

As the story went, when Rushmore got back to the hotel, a mysterious message was waiting, proffering an early morning rendezvous at the corner of Roosevelt and Halsted with a guy identifying himself only by the name Larry. Local authorities told him not to do it. The address was dicey. The timeframe suspicious. Rushmore pooh-poohed them all and slithered off into the night. Two days later, *The Chicago Tribune* reported Rushmore had disappeared.

Back in the Big Apple, Harrison was said to be duly alarmed. Harrison called Duggan, who then called in the police. The story spread. Chicago police scoured the city, finding no real leads. They were suspicious that the whole thing was a publicity stunt, but Rushmore's wife, Frances, and Harrison himself assured them they knew nothing except that Howard was in Chicago working on a "really hot" story, that would blow the lid off the Forrestal "murder."

Rushmore's disappearance spiked *Confidential* sales. Extra copies miraculously became available immediately and arrived on newsstands. Newspaper and radio coverage verged on the hysterical. As Rushmore continued to fail to materialize, the authorities, including the F.B.I., developed three possible theories of the crime: Perhaps someone angry over a damaging story in the magazine had taken revenge; maybe the Commies got him; or maybe he was intentionally lying low so he could search for Lawrence undetected.

An anonymous tip-off spoiled everybody's fun. Rushmore was discovered checked in under an alias at a Montana hotel. It was a hoax, but Rushmore denied that until his dying day. He kept trying to get the F.B.I. to listen to him, but it had been an F.B.I. agent who ratted him out to the cops in the first place. Hoover labeled Rushmore a nut, and that was the end of it. The magazine's sales soared. Harrison was pleased about that, but he was also more than a little bit ticked off that his employee had garnered so much personal publicity—Harrison wanted the press attention for himself and he wasn't about to let Howard Rushmore become the public face of his baby.

Harrison had bent over backwards to make Rushmore happy, and he certainly could have cut him loose once the magazine was a solid success, since Rushmore's connection to

Winchell was no longer the driving force behind Winchell's embrace of *Confidential.* Over and over again Rushmore would have a tantrum, threaten and accuse, get drunk, go home, and show up for work the next day as if nothing had happened.

Rushmore was a fast writer and a top rewrite man, but Harrison's willingness to keep putting up with him came down to the fact that the publisher inherently wanted every situation to be win-win. Howard's depressive anger was impenetrably foreign to Bob, whose good humor was boundless.

Rushmore spent his stint at the magazine pretending to his newspaper pals at publications higher on the food chain that he had nothing to do with the magazine's more flamboyant stories. He took to repeating endlessly in interviews that one of his daughters criticized a story on a favorite star, arguing that the actor's private life was none of her father's business, and accusing Rushmore of being no better than a Peeping Tom.

After the story of Rushmore's "disappearance" in 1955, the relationship was souring, with Rushmore and Harrison increasingly at odds. Marjorie continued to loathe Rushmore. She didn't like what he did, what he wrote, and she usually opposed him. Her knowledge of Howard's political interests was murky, and she never had a clear sense one way or the other about his articles being fair or accurate—they just made her nervous. She never told her uncle what to do, but when he asked her opinion she was forthright, saying she didn't think it was good for the magazine to be so involved, that it would come back and get them in trouble somehow.

I don't know why I always perceived Howard as dangerous. I just never trusted or liked him, He wasn't warm, just sort of aloof and cool, though I was crazy about his wife, Francis. She was a lovely girl, beautiful and sweet. But Howard was always horrible, he gave a bad vibe to me. And he would get very, very difficult about stories he wanted to run. Without us he had no job, he had

*no money, no friends, he had nothing. So he would
do anything to get anything. He was desperate.*

Harrison agreed with Marjorie about the Red stories. They
were mean-spirited, boring, and unpopular with readers.
Rushmore publicly bitched and moaned about being assigned
celebrity scandal instead of important Commie articles.
Harrison had also started becoming friendly with Jimmy
Wechsler at *The New York Post,* Rushmore's arch enemy. Plans
were drawn up to have two liberal Post columnists, Murray
Kempton and Jimmy Cannon, do some work for *Confidential.*
Rushmore went insane, screaming bloody murder about the
idea of those Pinkos being on the same masthead with him.
Harrison was tired of trying to appease Rushmore. Soon after,
Howard Rushmore walked away "in disgust," saying that the
last straw, the thing that made him so sick he had to quit, was
when Bob Harrison tried to "force" him to write a story about
how Joan Crawford beat her kids and was an unfit mother, an
assertion Rushmore called a total lie, insisting that:

*Joan Crawford should get an award as Mother of
the Year!*

Ask her kids.

Harrison accepted Rushmore's resignation with an
extremely generous settlement offer: The magazine agreed to
assume any liability Rushmore faced for libel suits in which he
also had been named and to pay him $2,000 to settle his
contract. For his part, Rushmore pledged that he bore neither
Confidential nor Harrison any ill will—a breathtaking falsehood
in retrospect.

With Rushmore gone, Harrison turned to the trusty Al
Govoni to steer the magazine in New York—the same guy who
had warned Harrison all along about Rushmore's penchant for
making mistakes and his growing alcohol problem.

And *Confidential's* "Reign of Terror" continued.

But just how terrifying was it really? Closeted gay men and
lesbians were always scared of being found out back then—so

remembrances of George Nader, Jack Larson, and Sal Mineo, among others, about their fears of what might be revealed in the magazine have to be taken in that context. And Tab Hunter? Today he is mentioned more often than any other star written about in the magazine, often with overwrought assertions about him being stalked relentlessly. But Robert Harrison printed exactly one story about Tab Hunter in all of the issues of *Confidential* he published. One. The story about the gay pajama party. And even that article, while it insinuated a lot, didn't outright declare Tab Hunter to be gay.

In real terms, *Confidential* was only one of many ways a gay or lesbian star's cover could be blown. The mixed race pieces may have caused temporary problems but no one lost a livelihood. Modern stories about *Confidential* are almost always chock full of the same breathless absolutes that were mainstays in the magazine itself:

Careers Were Destroyed!

Lives Were Wrecked!

Sources Committed Suicide!

Whose career? Whose life? Whose suicide?

It certainly must be upsetting to read a negative story about yourself. But in a business that has evolved to the point where the stick-like remains of Joan Rivers confronts celebrities directly on the red carpet about their horrible taste; where each and every performance on television or in the movies is sliced, diced, and reviewed in hundreds of media outlets all over the country and on the Internet; where focus groups are asked to give numerical ratings to the physical and personal qualities of actors, and to tell how they would end the movie if they could only do it themselves—in this industry how much responsibility can one scandal magazine bear for the fact that being a star means living with negative press? Here's a relatively complete list of the magazine's assertions about Hollywood celebrities in the years under Bob Harrison and the Meades:

- Elizabeth Taylor's husband is cheating on her.
- Rita Hayworth is a rotten mother and she kicked Dick Haymes out because he is a two-timer who drinks.
- Grace Kelly may fool around a little, but she's not all that passionate.
- Clark Gable once had a few suicidal thoughts but he licked them. He was stingy with his first wife but he claims that he wasn't. Also, his new father-in-law didn't attend his latest wedding.
- Johnnie Ray is a gay drama queen.
- Bogart is scared to fight people in real life.
- James Dean had a death premonition.
- A girl said no to Michael Wilding.
- Pearl Bailey got tipsy one night.
- Tab Hunter was arrested once at a gay pajama party.
- Dean Martin is jealous of his ex-wife and he really loves his mother as a good son should.
- Mario Lanza eats a lot and is a little loony.
- Linda Christian and Ty Power aren't compatible.
- Anita Ekberg chills Ty Power.
- Billy Rose is cheap.
- Howard Hughes is something of a wolf.
- Jack Benny, Broderick Crawford, Robert Montgomery, and Mae West aren't always photogenic.
- Abbe Lane is trying to keep Xavier Cugat home at night.
- Katharine Hepburn is a tomboy.
- Van Johnson was gay but now he is cured.
- Lizabeth Scott might be a lesbian.
- Rex Harrison is sexy.
- Danny Kaye got laughs at Buckingham Palace.
- June Allyson is naughty and is cheating on Dick Powell.

- The Gabors are boring.
- Vivian Leigh is a manic depressive with tuberculosis.
- Paulette Goddard once slept with her director on a film.
- Groucho Marx isn't very nice.
- Red Skelton is cheap and mean.
- Douglas Fairbanks, Jr. isn't well-liked.
- Delores Del Rio can't get an American work permit.
- Susan Hayward swore at her husband in a pool.
- Sonny Tufts likes biting women.
- Vic Damone has a son born out of wedlock.
- Victor Mature met a man he thought was a woman.
- Mickey Rooney's wife cheated on him.
- Mrs. Jack Webb is mad at her husband.
- Gloria De Haven & Jeff Chandler like sex together.
- Kim Novak slept around to become a star.
- Josephine Baker is a Commie.
- Adultery split up John Derek and his wife.
- Edward G. Robinson's son is a criminal.
- Some men have said no to hot-blooded Jane Russell.
- Jeanne Crain's husband had an affair with a starlet.
- Bob Hope and Barbara Payton had sex together.
- Yvonne DeCarlo's mother was a stripper.
- Tommy Dorsey is on the wagon.
- Marie Wilson is torn between husband and boyfriend.
- Gary Crosby is angry.
- Esther Williams is mad at her husband.
- Gary Cooper slept with Prince Rainier's mistress.
- Orson Welles has sex with some of his hypnosis subjects, and occasionally he likes to bite women.
- Joan Crawford had an affair with a bartender.

- Diana Dors accidentally stole some clothes.
- Dan Dailey dressed as a woman at a costume party.
- Elvis signs his autograph on some women's breasts if they ask. By the way, he likes sex.
- Guy Mitchell cheats.
- Maureen O'Hara kissed a man in public.
- Danny Kaye paid for sex then just wanted to talk.
- Robert Wagner is a dud in bed.
- Mike Todd made a chump of Harry Cohn.
- Otto Preminger makes actresses get undressed for their screen tests and he likes sex.
- Marlene Dietrich likes sex with men as well as women.
- John Huston and Gene Kelly like to drink and have sex, but not with each other.
- Mickey Mantle and other Yankees like sex.
- Dorothy Dandridge likes outdoor sex.
- Frank Sinatra likes sex and Wheaties.
- Guy Madison and Barbara Payton like sex together.
- Tallulah Bankhead is a lush who likes sex.
- Sammy Davis, Jr. likes white women and sex.
- Spank Donald O'Connor because he likes sex.
- Fernando Lamas likes sex but his date didn't.
- Linda Christian likes sex.
- Edmund Purdom likes sex.
- Walter Pidgeon likes sex.
- Eddie Fisher likes sex.
- Marilyn Monroe likes sex.
- Lana Turner likes sex.
- Ava Gardner likes sex.
- Burt Lancaster likes sex.

- Corinne Calvet likes sex.
- Robert Taylor likes sex.
- Sterling Hayden likes sex.
- Jose Ferrer likes sex.
- Jack Palance likes sex.
- Peter Lorre likes sex.
- Tony Curtis likes sex.
- Frederic March likes sex.
- Glenn Ford likes sex.
- Melvyn Douglas likes sex.
- Anthony Quinn likes sex.
- Gordon MacRae likes sex.
- Jayne Mansfield likes sex.
- Dana Andrews likes sex.
- Joan Collins is a perfect hostess.

And that's about it. That's the Reign of Terror.

The Movieland Massacre.

Even allowing for massive societal changes in the last half-century, it's a pretty thin line-up of mortal danger to Hollywood studios and stars. No one's career was destroyed, no one's life wrecked, and no one died. No one.

But June Allyson, Dick Powell, and Dean Martin probably didn't care about that when their love lives were splashed across the pages of *Confidential*.

WHAT THE GOSSIP COLUMNS DIDN'T TELL!

...HOW LONG CAN DICK POWELL TAKE IT?

When married crooner Dean Martin went to Las Vegas to fill a club date, little June Allyson tagged along, and their after-hours shenanigans raised plenty of eyebrows.

Think June Allyson is too nice to be naughty? Dick's been hitched to her for 10 years but that doesn't keep June from busting out all over...

By D. LORING TAYLOR

IT WAS THE NIGHT of the Photoplay Awards and the big banquet room in the Beverly Hills Hotel was jammed to capacity with the great and near great of Hollywood, on hand to pick up new laurels or cheer those who did. But as it turned out, there was more on the program than handing out medallions. There was a choice bit of gossip that set tongues wagging all around the room.

Dapper Dick Powell started it, when he was asked to take a bow at the shindig. The one-time musical comedy singer made the usual thank-you comments and then snapped the big room to attention with a remark no one had anticipated. "For those of you who were worried," he said, "everything's okay again at the Dick Powells."

It was a double-action bomb because there were many at the party who had no idea they *should* have been wor-

34

197

It's been no surprise to 50-year-old Dick Powell that June chases after the boys—that was how she got Dick.

LITTLE MISS MISCHIEF

Her millions of fans think June Allyson is more sugar than spice, but Hollywood wives claim this blonde with the roving eye has far too much spice to be nice...

35

ried about the Powells. There were others, though, who knew just what his problem was. Whispered conversations started buzzing around the banquet hall like a rocket. The subject was June Allyson, that five-foot-one-inch, petite little blonde who looks nice enough for an angel award.

But she is one little book that can't be judged by its cover. Insiders know that Powell has been plucking his pretty bride out of tangles with other men for most of their 10 years of married life.

June's fans—and they number in the millions—will howl their heads off at the charge that the cutie with the page-boy bob and the Peter Pan collar could ever be a hubby-snatcher. Nor can they be blamed, after swallowing years of a publicity build-up typing her "as the girl next door," "cute as a button" and just too nice to be naughty.

Admitted it Publicly—OFF the Record

What they've never been told is that, of recent years, the syrup got too thick for even June to pour. The one-time Broadway chorus dolly is 31 years old now, a veteran of nearly 10 years marriage with Powell, and has an uncontrollable itch to push the sugar bowl aside and reach for the spice shelf.

It long ago reached the stage where she was admitting it publicly—although *off* the record. Sitting at a cocktail table with a few other Hollywood beauties—including a well-known reporter—she recently flipped a pretty finger at the little-girl frock her bosses like her to wear and declared: "I've had enough of all this. I'd like to land in the middle of a juicy scandal—just to prove I've graduated into a woman."

Judging by what happened next, she meant it. A couple of years ago, she hung her (Continued on page 58)

these occasions was that Marlene had gotten word that still another mannish maiden, Jo Carstairs, was available for diversion.

For the uninitiated, Jo is a Queen in more ways than one. A million-heiress many times over, she owns a sun-splattered island in the Bahamas, Whale Cay, where she rules some 750 natives with an iron hand. Her favorite garb is a pair of dungarees and a man's shirt. She's been known to take strong measures against men who make advances toward her, since she prefers to make the overtures herself—and not to males.

Before the outbreak of World War II, Queen Jo used to enjoy loading her ocean-going yacht with steaks and champagne and setting off for Europe. The No. 1 stop on the continent was a little known bay, the harbor of Villefranche, near Cap d'Antibes.

Notified by cable, Marlene would be on hand and would be driven in a private limousine to the dock at Villefranche, where she would be rowed out for cozy weekends on Jo's yacht.

These naughty nautical adventures may come as a painful shock to Frede. On the other hand, Marlene had nothing to complain about. Back in '38, while Marlene was alternating between Jo and Frede, the latter bashfully suggested she'd like to go into business. Frede and Marlene put their heads together and decided the best venture would be a nightclub, catering to dolls as uninhibited as they were.

Dietrich was the behind-scenes backer when Frede opened a rollicking spot known as "La Silhouette." It did so well that, after World War II, Frede was able to buy an even flossier place, "Carroll's." On opening night, Marlene was resplendently present and contributed to the gayety. Remarque was there, too. So was Jean Gabin. Also Chevalier.

They were a worldly-wise trio, but had they started comparing notes on Marlene, even they might have been confused. For sharing their friendship with her was Frede, their hostess of the evening, Jo Carstairs, lurking off Cap d'Antibes, Claire Waldoff in Berlin. Back in Hollywood, too, in the years that had rolled by, there was Mercedes d'Acosta, Cary Grant, Jimmy Stewart and Gary Cooper. All these—and a husband, too!

What had the boys mumbling in their cognac was the big jackpot question: How does Dietrich do it?

There can be only one answer. The very contradictions which add up to Marlene Dietrich are best summed up in Frede's own words: Marlene is "incomparable!" ▲▲▲

HOW LONG CAN DICK POWELL TAKE IT?

Continued from page 35

marriage on a hook while she brazenly cavorted with crooner Dean Martin.

June and another blonde bombshell were cutting up capers together when they met the singer and his zany sidekick, Jerry Lewis, when the comedy pair were working an engagement at Slapsie Maxie Rosenbloom's in Hollywood.

June became a regular ringsider night after night and capped it by going right along when the boys moved on to a nightery in Las Vegas. Citizens of that so-called sin-suburb of Hollywood tilted their eyebrows as June and Dean rocketed around town.

It can be presumed that Mrs. Martin is as long-suffering as Mr. Powell. There was a lot of shouting and hollering from said mates, but the noise died down and there was no public scandal. But June refused to stop kicking up her pretty heels. Every time they assigned her a new leading man in a movie, her flirtatious ways gave patient Powell something new to sit up nights biting his nails about.

Her favorite stunt at Hollywood parties, for instance, has been to latch onto some handsome actor—usually years younger than hubby Dick—and duck into a corner until her glowering husband came to take her home. Aided more by luck than brains, she managed to avoid the headlines and gossip columns—at least, until recently.

There've been a lot of Hollywoodites who have openly predicted that Dick—now graduated to a serious actor and director—would give June her walking papers. It hasn't happened, though, and the guess is that part of Powell's seemingly inexhaustible tolerance stems from his memory of the days when he was married to Joan Blondell. He was the gadabout then and Joan had to close her eyes to larks that would make most wives sizzle.

Even so, the hour of atonement may

be just about up for Dick. When he made that "all clear" announcement at the Photoplay party last February, he tipped off all Hollywood that he was wise to June's latest caper.

It had gotten the mystery treatment in your favorite gazettes, because the truth had been too sizzling to run through the presses. Alan Ladd and his wife separated—after 13 years of marriage, but *both* carefully refrained from naming the reason. Who was it? None other than that sweet little Allyson lass, who'd been assigned to make a movie with Ladd and — as usual — had gotten ideas that weren't in the script.

Among other things, wasn't it also true that June had cozy after-hours dates with Alan in her studio dressing room while they were both working on "The McConnell Story"?

For weeks the gossip columns hinted at an impending explosion but June still escaped the front-page notoriety she'd once said she was hunting for. What saved her was when the Ladds patched things up, for perhaps the oddest reason any marriage ever was rescued. Alan came down with a case of chicken pox and called his ever-faithful to help him.

She not only cured him of the chicken pox, she nursed away the chick, too.

Powell had swung into action by this time, and was all but keeping Allyson on a leash. He took his 20-years-younger bride for a "vacation" in the mountains of Idaho and apparently managed to cool her off.

But friends who've known June and Dick from the day they tied the knot are wondering how it can help from coming unraveled. They first kissed on the set of the movie, "Meet the People," and June pursued Dick relentlessly, insisting that their smooching should be on a legal basis. Powell complained that the 20-year difference between their ages was too much time for even the most devoted lovers to overcome. She won, though, with the argument that June and December can merge, if it's April in your heart. So far, it's worked.

But Dick's a tough daddy. That's why the rumors have been racing around Hollywood ever since that night he said everything's okay with his frolicsome frau. It may be all right now. But there are plenty of people wondering how long it will be before June starts busting out all over again. ▲▲▲

STRANGE CASE
OF WALTER
CHRYSLER JR.

Continued from page 33

arranged a meeting in Chrysler's home.

What happened at that meeting is still a secret. But rumors about the Naval Intelligence probe filtered back to reporters and inquiries were made at the Pentagon.

On December 16, 1944, newspapers carried the following story: "Lt. Walter P. Chrysler Jr. resigned his naval commission December 5th, the Navy disclosed today in response to inquiry. There were no details."

Curious as to why Chrysler, then 35, would resign at the height of hostilities, reporters pressed for explanation. The Navy had a curt "no comment."

Under regulations, an officer may resign from the Navy during war time for five reasons: If his service is causing acute economic hardship for his immediate family; if he is more essential to the war effort as a civilian; if he is discharged under a Presidential order; if he receives a medical discharge; and, lastly, if he

resigns "for the good of the service."

Obviously, Chrysler's service in uniform caused no hardship to his family. As a matter of fact, he was a divorced man with no children and an immense personal fortune. He took little interest in the Chrysler empire and the corporation got along very well without his services. There is no record of any Presidential order dealing with Chrysler's resignation. This leaves two possible reasons for his leaving the service during war time: medical, and "for the good of the service." The Navy gave no reason.

But from inside Washington sources, this reporter learned that immediately following Chrysler's resignation, Forrestal ordered all Naval Intelligence reports on the case delivered to his office. The Chrysler file was given to the Secretary and every trace of the official ONI report vanished. To this day, a search of the various files where the Navy *normally* keeps such reports turns up nothing on this

(Continued on next page)

59

Half-Cocked He-Man Shoots To Thrill

With Rushmore out of the way, Harrison was ready to shoot for the stars. Instead, he ended up shot in the back—with national headlines that dwarfed the stories about Rushmore's "disappearance."

There has always been suspicion about the "shooting", which started with Bob's search for Pega Palo, a magical virility vine, in the mountains of the Dominican Republic. He went on the hunt accompanied by blonde "singer" Geene Courtney (of *Confidential* "Show Girl Sells Shares in Self" fame). They were on safari when Harrison was shot by big game hunter and international playboy Richard Weldy. Weldy's ex-wife, Pilar Palette, soon to be John Wayne's wife, had recently been named an adulteress in a *Confidential* story—leading to speculation that Weldy shot Harrison on purpose. Another theory was a love triangle, with both men vying for Courtney's affections.

The dramatic tension caught fire when Weldy fled the scene, abandoning the bleeding, limp, near-dead Harrison and his hysterical yet beautiful companion. Then came a frantic, 48-hour search by 5,000 Dominican scouts and soldiers, called out personally by Trujillo himself and ordered to find the American publisher or die trying. The brave search and rescue battalion saved the day, rescuing everyone, saving Bob's life, and most importantly, leaving Geene Courtney just enough time to redo her make-up before posing for the cameras.

Never mind that Harrison and Courtney were never a couple, Weldy was in the Dominican Republic with his own female companion, none of them actually did any hunting, and most of the foursome's time was spent at the hotel keeping the cabana boys busy playing fetch. Also, the Pilar Palette, John Wayne, Richard Weldy story appeared in the November 1956 issue, which even with the advance distribution policies of *Confidential*, was probably not on newsstands by September 5, 1956, when the shooting happened, since the magazine actually had a September 1956 issue that would have been on sale then. The article itself was tame stuff, dwelling mainly on the alluring charms of the Peruvian Palette, and how funny it was that the hunky Wayne couldn't get arrested while trying to woo South American beauties, until he met his friend Weldy's beguiling wife. It's all extremely friendly, with Weldy and Palette on the verge of an amicable split anyway, with Wayne getting his pal's okay before he makes a move on Palette, and the happy ménage going about its business with no muss and no fuss.

Al Govoni went along for the ride to the Dominican Republic, and he confirmed the official version of events for decades, though not quite giving eyewitness testimony, since he claimed he tripped on a rock as the shot rang out, and didn't actually *see* Weldy fire.

This managed to make headlines around the world, not just in tabloids like *The New York Post, Daily News, Journal-American,* and *The Los Angeles Mirror-News,* where it was front page stuff, but even *The New York Times* covered it, though speculation that it was a publicity stunt was widespread. Marjorie and Michael both confirm, over 50 years later, that it was indeed a publicity stunt. No one knew the truth then, except Marjorie, Edith, Helen, and Michael Tobias. Not even Fred Meade knew at the time.

Of course, had Harrison really been wounded and missing, its likely that his sisters Edith and Helen, in order to find him would have made Trujillo's life a living hell, tearing apart every last inch of his country, browbeating him mercilessly, and doing bodily harm to anyone fool enough to get in their way. Uncle Bob may not have been in the kind of danger the bountiful news reports were breathlessly detailing, but Marjorie was plenty concerned.

> *It was all very scary. First of all, to go to Trujillo's place... He's not like a normal, 100% person. You never know what he's gonna do, and he runs the whole country! Then you have to hope that everything works, and that the shot doesn't hit you, that you get to the hospital, and then get back, and out of the country. I thought it was very, very dangerous. At that time, I mean, Haiti and*

the Dominican Republic were positively primitive. But I didn't say anything. I didn't feel I should since it was something Bob really wanted to do. It was all his plan, and a very unique idea, so I just didn't feel I should say anything against it. I really didn't — and so I didn't. But I mean, it was fantastic… And it worked! He got stories saying he was missing, stories saying he was found, stories he was wounded, stories saying he'd arrived in New York. So many stories! It was day after day… I think it was probably one of the greatest publicity stunts ever, I really do. To be on the front page of all these major newspapers. They put it in even though they thought it was probably a phony, because it made good copy. And they couldn't prove it wasn't true. Funny. Nobody ever tried to see the wound. Can you imagine that? There wasn't even a wound! There was nothing!

And as if the shooting itself didn't get enough ink, there was more to come. June Frew, Bob's increasingly unbalanced girlfriend, turned up with a posse of reporters for Harrison's homecoming at LaGuardia. She attacked him, screaming and hitting him for cheating on her. No one knows today whether she was in on the gag or going off the deep end. Not that it matters. A good story is a good story.

Then an amazing stroke of luck: During a Mike Wallace interview where Mike berated Harrison on camera, demanding that he admit the whole thing was a hoax, Bob lifted his shirt to show his bullet wound, but instead of zooming in on the birthmark Harrison had intended to stand in for his alleged wound, the cameraman went into extreme close-up on a weird looking mole. Apparently, on black and white television, the mole looked horrific—like a bullet hole from an elephant gun.

Mike Wallace and the entire audience were satisfied that Harrison had been shot.

Trujillo went along with the magic act (and paid for the whole trip) because Harrison promised him that Pega Palo, the Vine That Makes You Virile, would become famous in the pages of *Confidential* and in publications all over the world, giving a dose of Viagra to the island's tourist business. As an added inducement, the two men agreed that the spokesman for the product would be Profirio Rubirosa. *Confidential's* perennial "Cash Box Casanova" was also Trujillo's former son-in-law, and an on-and-off ambassador for the Dominican Republic to various countries, including Argentina, where he was purported to have improved Dominican and Argentine relations by sleeping with Eva Peron.

The eventual "obscene" article on Pega Palo was part of the 1957 case against the magazine. The surge in vacationers to the island never happened but Bob Harrison made out like a bandit. The headlines didn't stop for weeks. The man and the magazine were public property—and circulation received a healthy boost, passing the all-important five million mark. The mainstream press was skeptical at times but never came out and said that the shooting didn't happen. Leave it to the rumor rags. Just like Harrison always said, scandal magazines often covered the truth that highbrow news outlets ignored. In its March 1957 issue, a *Confidential* competitor called *On the Q.T.* put "The Great Harrison Hoax" on its cover, detailing how the entire Dominican Republic story had been a publicity stunt.

But even as Harrison gloried in his successful publicity stunt back in New York, on the West Coast eight studio publicity chiefs in Hollywood were having a meeting, largely about him. They determined that the problem of *Confidential Magazine* and its threat to business was so serious that Harrison had to be approached directly. Sam Israel, publicity director for Universal-International Studios, was sent to New York to plead with Harrison to focus on politicians, socialites, and athletes and to leave Hollywood alone. Harrison didn't mean to be rude, but he laughed in Israel's face at the sheer naiveté of the request—which ignored two realities: Magazines that attacked politicians risked losing their second class postal permits, and people wanted to read about Hollywood more than they wanted to read about politicians, socialites, or athletes.

Second Chance to Win $10,200 Blackout Prize

SOLVE THIS WEEK'S PUZZLE -- SEE PAGE 26

How Social Security Changes Affect You	Journal NEW YORK American	7TH SPORTS
For Details, See Page 20	AN AMERICAN PAPER FOR A THE AMERICAN PEOPLE	WALL ST. SPECIAL
	IN TWO SECTIONS—SECTION ONE	
	No. 24,993—DAILY WEDNESDAY, SEPTEMBER 5, 1956 5 CENTS	

Publisher of 'Confidential' Shot in Jungle 'Accident'

THE TRIANGLE ... In current issue of Confidential Magazine, John Wayne (left) is night-clubbing in Peru with his "buddy," Richard Weldy, and Pilar Palette, who, at the time, was Weldy's wife.

KEPT GOING ... In photo alongside, Confidential notes that Weldy is "going" out of the picture, as the developments show. He did. Pilar is now Wayne's third wife. For the latest developments.

(Another Confidential photo in Palette Section.)

PUBLISHER SHOT ... Dominican police report that Robert Harrison (above), publisher of Confidential, was shot, and Weldy is being questioned.

Santa Fe Chief Crashes Into Mail Train; 20 Die

SPRINGER, N. M., Sept. 5 (AP)—Twenty railway workers perished early today when the speeding Santa Fe Chief smashed head-on into a sidetracked mail train in northern New Mexico. Railway officials said the death toll may be higher when wrecking crews get pry into the twisted and torn cars of the Chief.

At least, seven were injured.

Santa Fe spokesman said that as far as can be determined, there were no passengers killed in the early-morning tragedy.

The Chief shot into the bypass where the last Santa Fe mail train No. 8 was waiting its turn for the main line to continue north toward Denver.

CREWMEN VICTIMS

The dead included the engineer of the mail train, the engineer, fireman and conductor of the Chief, and 16 waiters and lounge car attendants who were asleep in a dormitory car on the Chief.

All available officers, doctors and ambulances from Springer, Las Vegas and Raton were ordered to the scene.

Four dead units and six local cars of the Chief were derailed. Two diesel units of the mail train were derailed with one badly smashed and scattered.

Publisher Frank Pfeiffer of the Raton, N. M. Range, said: "This is a major disaster. It's a mess."

Special equipment was ordered to start lifting debris in the search for possible other casualties.

The collision was shortly after 2 a. m. (4 a. m. N.Y. time), five miles south of here at the community of Robinson.

2 NEWYORKERS HURT

SPRINGER, N. M., Sept. 5 (INS)—Among the injured in the collision of two Santa Fe trains near here today were Mr. and Mrs. Norman Rosen, passengers, of New York. They are in Colfax Hospital here.

Marine Skin-Diver Dies

CAMP COURTNEY, Okinawa, Sept. 5 (INS)—U.S. Marine corps headquarters on Okinawa said that Staff Sgt. James H. Tyson, son of Mrs. Effie Tyson, Philadelphia, drowned while skin-diving near Nago on Okinawa Monday.

Ex-Felon 'With Baby' Sought in Kidnaping

Special to the N. Y. Journal-American

HAMDEN, Conn., Sept. 5—A New Haven ex-convict today was sought for questioning in the kidnaping of six-week-old Cynthia Ruotolo from her carriage outside a store here five days ago.

A pickup order for him was sent out after a woman identified his picture as that of a man who told her "I have a baby if you want to take it."

She said she was approached on a New Haven street as she returned home from work.

Before she could find a policeman, she said, the man sped away in his car.

ABSENCE OF CLUES

Police, however, conceded that this was a slim lead in a case marked by a complete absence of worthwhile clues.

State Atty. Abraham S. Ullman said "we have absolutely nothing" to go on after FBI

TODAY'S PAPER

Bridge 15	Movie Clock 15
Dr. Brothers 17	Obituaries 24
Camera News 16	Jack O'Brien 24
Comics 38	35 Lipulla Parsons 16
Cross-Word 38	
E. V. Durling ... 21	Sports 24
Editorial 20	Places to Dine . 12
Financial 12	Louis Sobol 23
Fishing 15	George Sokolsky 20
Food, Cooking ... 8	Sports 24
Cale Middlecoff 23	Sports 24
Mary Haworth .. 9	Theaters 13
Horoscope 38	Want Ads 27 to 29
Dorothea Kilgallen 13	Weather, Wall .. 26
N. Y. JOURNAL-AMERICAN	
220 South St., New York 15, N. Y.	

Full services of Associated Press, International News Service, United Press, King Features Syndicate, Chicago Tribune-N. Y. News Syndicate.

Phone Your News and Photo Tips to COrtlandt 7-1212

Ike Opposes School Riot Intervention

(Photo in Picture Section)

WASHINGTON, Sept. 5 (AP). — President Eisenhower today said the Federal government would not intervene in racial disturbances arising from school integration unless the states are unable to maintain order.

Questioned at his news conference on disorders in Texas and elsewhere at the opening of integrated schools, Eisenhower said he believes the States may have handled their problems adequately.

Eisenhower said the meeting would be in a bad way if the Federal Government felt bound the practice of using its police power habitually and constantly.

SITUATION IN HAND

"Today the structure of our alliances is enfeebled—from Korea to Greece and from Turkey to Japan. Today people turn with derision and suspicion to Negro children who wish to gain integrated schools.

Slugs His Top Kick ... 39 Years Later!

ST. PETERSBURG, Fla., Sept. 5 (INS)—Robert Moon, 61, has an elephant-like memory an abuse he has taken. He explained his slugging of Owen Barnhill, 58, in St. Petersburg by saying: "I've been waiting 39 years to get even with Barnhill—he was my sergeant in World War One."

Guard Tenn. Town Against Mob March

CLINTON, Tenn., Sept. 5 (INS)—Heavily-armed Tennessee National Guardsmen kept a sharp lookout early today for a repeated mob march on Clinton to "get those Negroes" who were arrested in the wrecking of a white man.

Rumors were rife last night as a crowd of 600 white persons were gathered at Oliver Springs, 16 miles southwest of Clinton, and shouts of "Let's go get 'em!"

One report said that a motor procession of underworldified size had neared Oak Ridge, which is about halfway between Clinton and Oliver Springs.

Authorities were unable to locate such a movement, however.

(Other Stories on page 28)

Adlai Urges Draft Halt, Hits GOP's Defense Planning

By ROBERT G. NIXON

LOS ANGELES, Sept. 5 (INS)—Adlai Stevenson called today for an end to the armed forces draft "at the earliest possible moment consistent with the national safety."

The Democratic Presidential nominee, in a major address, prepared for delivery for the American Legion national convention in Los Angeles said:

"I subscribe with all my heart to this purpose."

Stevenson, highly critical of the Eisenhower administration's defense planning, also lashed out at Republican foreign policy, charging it has weakened American world leadership by "four years of boasts and bluffs."

He declared:

"Today the structure of our alliances is enfeebled—from Korea to Greece and from Turkey to Japan. Today people turn with derision and suspicion to

(For details, see Page 11)

Stocks Gain For 3d Day

The stock market continued strong today, advancing for the third session in a row. Trading volume was the highest in weeks.

Steels were once more the leaders, aided by the upturn in production and heavy orders.

What was interpreted as a more conciliatory tone in American world leadership by the dues crisis helped the situation. Gains ran in about $2 a share, although Union Oil shot up as on reports of a big oil strike.

Bumps 3 Autos En Route to Jail

Simon Dam, 42, a laborer of 715 Clinton st., Hoboken, was no cool color today in the Plainfield, N. J. jail but he may not have been as bad night. At 7:19 p. m. his car struck another in Keyport. At 9:08 he hit a second car at Union Beach. At 9:36, back in Keyport, he hit a third car. He was given a drunkometer test and arrested on charges of careless driving drunken-driving and leaving the scene of an accident.

Quiz Big Game Hunter Linked in Love Expose

(From the Combined Wire Services.)

CIUDAD TRUJILLO, Dominican Republic, Sept. 5. — Dominican police report that Robert Harrison, 51, publisher of Confidential Magazine, has been wounded in a hunting accident in a mountain area north of Ciudad Trujillo.

Break Floods Harlem Area

A break in a 48-inch water main today flooded a 20-block area in Harlem and caused traffic coming from the Bronx over the 149th st. bridge to be detoured.

The break occurred at 11:15 a.m. The main was not shut off until 6:15 o'clock, after 24 water gates had been closed.

A detail of 20 extra police set up barricades and detoured traffic.

Six families were evacuated, police said, but many tenement basement apartments were flooded.

Some of the water poured into the Lenox ave. station of the IRT subway, but was pumped out quickly. Service was not delayed.

Pair Grab $20 In Hotel Holdup

Two men, one with a pistol, held up Thomas Burns, night clerk of the Curt Hotel, 303 W. 46th st., today and escaped with $20.

THE WEATHER

NEW YORK, NORTHERN N. J.—Partly cloudy and warm tonight and tomorrow with chance of 65-70. High tomorrow in 80's, turning cooler in evening tomorrow night.

LONG ISLAND—Partly cloudy tonight and tomorrow with chance of showers late in day. Low tonight in 60's. High tomorrow in 80's.

CONN.—Partly cloudy tonight and tomorrow. Little temperature change tomorrow with chance of afternoon or evening showers.

WESTCHESTER and ROCKLAND—Partly cloudy tonight and tomorrow with chance of showers in afternoon and evening. Low tonight in 60's. High

OUTLOOK METROPOLITAN AREA—Friday fair, low humid and warm weather. Saturday fair and warm; slip cool.

A report from authorities in the Barahona region said Richard Weldy, a big game hunter, was being questioned.

They quoted him as saying he fired a shot that struck Harrison, but said it was an accident.

There was no indication here that Harrison was hurt seriously.

The police account said Harrison, Weldy and a North American copper named Denise Ozare—they were members of a hunting expedition in the northern resort area.

FIGURES IN STORY

In New York, Jay Breen, associate editor of Confidential said Weldy figures in a story in the current issue of Confidential that involves movie actor John Wayne in its current issue of the magazine.

Breen said today:

"After learning that Harrison had been shot I telephoned down there and finally got through.

"I was told that last Sunday in the gambling casino at the Hotel Ambassador, Harrison ran into game hunter Richard Weldy and that they had a native exchange of words—and that Weldy was invited to leave.

"Bad blood has existed between the two guys (Harrison and Weldy) because of a story Confidential published this month in the effort that Wayne

(Continued on Page 16, Column 3)

TRAINING OPENS THE DOOR

Don't wait for the "breaks," Decide now to train for the job ahead. Select the career training that best suits your needs from the many and varied courses offered in today's Journal - American.

See "Careers for Men-Women" Today on Page 28

Model Demands $100,000 for Fall

LOS ANGELES, Sept. 5 (AP)—Actress-model Susan Harrison, 18, wants $100,000 damages for the time she fell 10 feet out of focus. She said she broke her glamour picture-artistic arm, on a reed palm at the apartment of producer-writer Blake Edwards when she fell through a trapdoor and broke an ankle. The accident, she said, was

(Continued on Page 2, Column 3)

Harrison was nothing if not thorough. He planned every aspect of this publicity stunt, the largest hoax he would ever perpetrate. He correctly assumed there would be an insatiable appetite for photographs of the ill-fated hunting party, and made sure dozens of shots were available. One has to wonder if staging these adventure scenes in the "jungle" of the Dominican Republic with "Showgirl Sells Self" Geene Courtney was as much fun as spanking the lingerie models in his girlie magazines. Harrison's "shooting" was front page news across the country.

The original *Daily News* caption on this photo said, "Mr. and Mrs. Robert Harrison. Arm in sling, Harrison is recovering from being wounded in the shoulder by a blast from the shotgun of Richard Weldy in the Dominican jungles. He described the incident as an accident and absolved Weldy of all blame. Both admitted arguing over an article in Harrison's magazine concerning Weldy's ex-wife, now Mrs. John Wayne." June Frew is erroneously referred to as Bob's wife. She often told reporters they were married, though they never were. She was a brunette here, but she was usually a blonde.

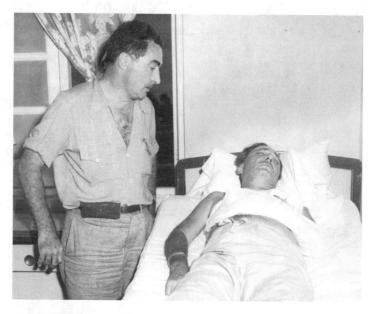

TOP: *Confidential* editor Al Govoni makes a hospital visit to the "injured" Bob Harrison. ABOVE: Govoni and Harrison consult with an actor hired to play the role of an attending physician.

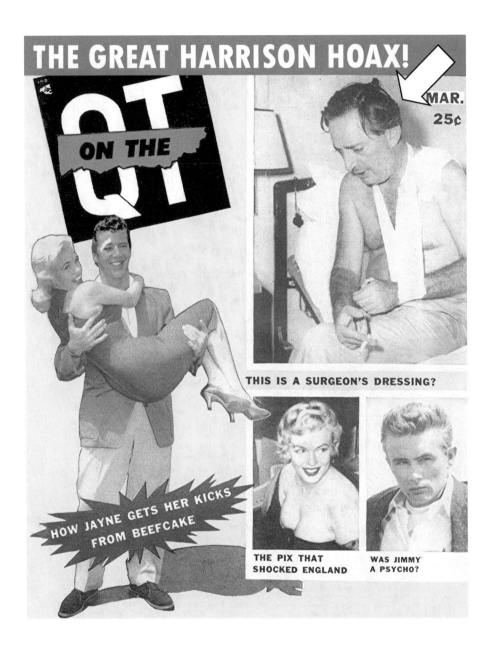

Q.T. EXPLODES THE GREAT HARRISON HOAX

Hunter-sportsman Dick Weldy confessed "accidental" shooting in fight over "spicy" story about ex-wife. The real dope: Weldy, Harrison often collaborated in gathering "inside" info for *Confidential* stories.

In the Excitement of the Harrison "Shooting," Newspapermen Forgot That *Confidential's* Ex-Editor Was Once "Kidnaped." Strangely Enough, Both Headline-Making Events Happened on the 6th of the Month—the Day *Confidential* Hits the Newsstands!

By CARLSON L. THOMAS

THE so-called "accidental" shooting of scandal magazine publisher Robert Harrison by big-game hunter Richard Weldy in the jungle wilds of the Dominican Republic will probably go down as the biggest publicity stunt in the history of lurid journalism. Those who closely follow the publishing business know it was no accident that the shooting scrape happened on September 6th—the very day a new issue of *Confidential* hit the newsstands with a story about Pilar Palette, Weldy's former wife. They also know that Weldy and Harrison have been friends

THE GREAT HARRISON HOAX

Actor John Wayne (with wife Pilar Palette, once Mrs. Weldy and subject of *Confidential* "expose") cracked: "I deplore the fact he (Weldy) is such a poor shot."

for a long time and Weldy has often collaborated with Harrison in gathering "inside" material for stories which have appeared in *Confidential*.

The entire incident had all the elements of a deliberately planned piece of publicity hogwash that brought together, as if by coincidence, several Broadway characters who had never been known to express the slightest interest in big-game hunting. Before they turned up in the Dominican jungle, Harrison and his managing editor, A. P. Govoni, had never ventured into a wooded area any wilder than New York's Central Park.

Harrison, riding the crest of a record-breaking newsstand sale of *Confidential*, had left New York with the announcement that he was going to the Dominican Republic to get some information for a story on Porfirio Rubirosa, the former husband of Barbara Hutton and Doris Duke. The reason for the trip in itself seemed phony —*Confidential* had already carried enough articles about Rubi to fill a small library of sin-and-sex books.

Before leaving New York he also told friends in Lindy's Restaurant on Broadway: "I'll crack page one before my next issue and it'll help circulation."

So when Harrison turned up with a rifle wound in his shoulder and a voluptuous blonde night-club singer deep in the jungle of a Caribbean island, it came as no surprise to a lot of people who were aware of his ability to grab headlines. And before the whole thing was over, the side squabble between the blonde, Geene Courtney, and the lady who calls herself Mrs. Harrison developed into a page one hassle all of its own.

As soon as the news splashed across New York tabloids in bold headlines, Jay Breen, *Confidential's* editor, called all the newspapers and leaned over backward in his eagerness to give out with details of the "shooting."

Harrison was still in the middle

Hearing Geene Courtney was on the trip, the lady who calls herself Mrs. Harrison said: "I'll tell that fifth-rate performer to stay away from my darling!"

Geene fired own big gun with retort that Harrison marital knot was never a knot to her. Said Bob: "Geene's been maligned and is entitled to her say."

of the jungle while Breen was peppering newspaper editors with up-to-the-minute details on the publisher's condition. No definite information was available from Ciudad Trujillo, the Dominican capital, yet Breen seemed to be a virtual storehouse of news. He told the press Harrison had been seriously wounded—something no one else could learn in Ciudad Trujillo, let alone New York City. It also seemed odd that Breen would be handing out detailed statements even before he cleared them with his own boss, the man affected most by whatever the headlines might say. Obviously, Breen was determined to give *Confidential* the maximum publicity mileage out of the shooting.

Some of the newspapers sensed that all didn't quite add up in the super sensational story. The New York *Daily Mirror* headlined it this way:

CONFIDENTIALLY—AN ACCIDENT OR A STUNT TO BUILD UP MAG

The *Mirror* went even further. Its story began with the suggestion that somebody was pulling somebody's publicity leg, stating: "Robert Harrison, publisher of *Confidential*, says that his wounding by big-game hunter Richard Weldy was accidental, as Dominican police began to (Continued on page 50)

GREAT HARRISON HOAX

(Continued from page 111)

wonder whether they were the unwitting parties to a carefully contrived circulation-building stunt."

In their haste to publish stories about the shooting, most editors forgot that Harrison had once before pulled a three-day front-pager with the "kidnaping" of his ex-editor, Howard Rushmore, by Communists in the mid-West. Rushmore "disappeared" in Chicago while "on assignment" to track down details behind the suicide-death of the late Secretary of Defense, James Forrestal. By some, strange coincidence Rushmore also vanished on the sixth of the month —publication date for *Confidential*.

There were several other unexplained aspects that made the Harrison shooting look like a well-staged performance. When the Dominican police arrested Weldy and hauled him into the town of Jaraboca, a photographer appeared from nowhere and took a picture of Weldy posing with, of all things, a copy of the current issue of *Confidential*, which carried the scandal story about his former wife, Pilar Pallette. How Weldy got his hands on a copy of the magazine so quickly has never been explained. It had appeared on the newsstands in New York the very day he was arrested down in the Dominican Republic!

It also seemed more than just a coincidence that Weldy and Harrison would locate each other in the same patch of dense forest, although they had left Ciudad Trujillo, ninety miles away, in different cars at different times.

The account of what happened during the few minutes after the shooting made the whole affair look even more phony. When Weldy's rifle "went off" and "wounded" Harrison, Weldy ran out of the woods to his car, intending, so he said, to go for help. But the car wouldn't start for one reason or another.

Govoni, who was with Harrison, also ran out of the forest to his car and drove off after help. But when he found assistance he couldn't find his way back to where he had left Harrison, wounded, with Geene Courtney. It seems strange that Govoni couldn't have taken Harrison and Geene out of the jungle in his car, since Harrison had suffered only the slightest kind of shoulder wound.

When Harrison was finally brought to a hospital the following day doctors described his condition as "a flesh wound, nothing serious at all." Moreover the Dominican police didn't question Harrison at all, which indicates they were in on the phony stunt.

Weldy, meanwhile, freely admitted the shooting, telling police it happened while he and Harrison were arguing over the "spicy" story in *Confidential* about his former wife, Pilar, who has since become the wife of actor John Wayne. Incidentally, the story in no way cast reflections on Weldy, except to say that he introduced Wayne to several girls in Peru and Wayne finally married Weldy's ex-wife.

In Hollywood John Wayne joined the act by saying the only thing true about the magazine story was that he had been in Peru. The movie star said he hoped Weldy wasn't in trouble because of the shooting, and added: "I deplore the fact that he is such a poor shot."

Weldy bristled over this. "Listen," he told police, "I could have broken Harrison with my two hands. If I had wanted to hurt him I would have used my fists. You know I'm a professional hunter and a good marksman. When I shoot I don't miss."

This presents another interesting point in the phony game of jungle hide-and-seek. Assuming Weldy is a good shot, if he deliberately aimed a rifle at Harrison's shoulder, the chances are excellent that the bullet would strike the shoulder, particularly if Harrison co-operated by standing perfectly still.

When the shooting occurred Har-

rison's lawyer, by a stroke of luck, happened to be in Ciudad Trujillo, too. He was able to answer legal questions and take care of other details brought on by the "unfortunate accident."

But the reaction staged by the gal calling herself Mrs. Harrison was the *piece de resistance* of the fantastic story. When reporters found June Frew in her Manhattan hotel suite, she was weeping. "I can't believe the shooting was an accident," she moaned. "Someone seized on the perfect opportunity."

When Harrison's sobbing June heard the news that sexy Geene Courtney was with her husband in the jungle, she exploded like a pretty volcano. "Is that Courtney woman really with him?" she screamed. "Why, that old bag! She's the one who ought to have been shot!"

Several days later, when Harrison returned to New York looking in fine fettle and none the worse for his "grueling experience," June Frew met him at the airport and kept giving out quotable quotes on Geene Courtney.

"I'm going to tell that fifth-rate performer to stay away from my darling husband," she cooed in a tone of velvet barbed wire. "People are worried that the shooting incident might affect her career. What's she got to lose?"

Then, back in New York only a few days later, Geene got into the act by firing her own big gun. She flailed June Frew unmercilessly by calling a press conference and dropping a bombshell about the scandal publisher's "happy home." "June Frew," said Geene, "is an imposter who is not now and never has been married to Bob Harrison. And Mr. Harrison confirmed this to me, prior to the issuance of this statement."

The gal who says she's Mrs. Bob reeled under the blow. "I'll sue

her!" she shouted. "This is preposterous."

For his part, Harrison meekly told reporters: "Leave me out of this. If Geene says I confirmed it, she says it. Geene has been unjustly maligned and is entitled to her say." Harrison seemed gallant, indeed, referring to someone as being "unjustly maligned."

The charges and counter-charges had the appearance of being clearly aimed at continuing the publicity buildup and focusing attention on Harrison, his magazine, and the hen fight over his affections. Newspaper columnists chimed in to keep the pot boiling. In his New York *Post* column Earl Wilson quoted Bob Harrison and June Frew as saying they were married in New York State eight years before. But Louis Sobol, in the New York *Journal-American*, quoted Harrison with something entirely different. Referring to his June's "outbursts" against Geene Courtney, Harrison told Sobol he had little to say except to confess: "Everybody knows that we're not married."

Harrison, of course, quickly forgot about the shooting. He confirmed that it was "all an accident" and insisted that he held no grudge against Weldy. As things turned out, everybody was very mixed up in the affair was very happy when the smoke cleared away, and it was hard to believe there could have been so much publicity over people who liked each other so much.

Naturally, the newsstand sales of *Confidential's* current issue boomed to even higher figures. And no one was surprised when Danton Walker carried an item in his New York *Daily News* column which disclosed: "Geene Courtney, the curvaceous blonde named in the Bob Harrison shooting, is now considering four-figure offers from Las Vegas night clubs as a result of the publicity."

How phony can a little shooting be?　　　　THE END

There are tales of a possible slush fund of up to $350,000 being considered by studio heads to finance an all-out war on Harrison, and of famous producer-director Mervyn LeRoy spearheading the effort. A few tabloid stories exist to support the idea, but no hard evidence of such a plot exists. Supposedly the Hollywood types chickened out before committing themselves, scared that any attempt at that kind of collusion could really turn around and bite them in the ass. The feeling was that the scandal sheets could be dangerous foes if taken on so directly. As an anonymous actor explained to *Time Magazine*:

> *You've got to have guts or your skirts have to be awfully clean before you mess around legally with these people.*

It wasn't just *Confidential*. Jerry Giesler and other Hollywood insiders felt as if they were under siege, as Harrison's hit inspired dozens of copycats like *Uncensored, Top Secret, Inside Story, Suppressed, On the QT, Inside, Hush-Hush, Exposed,* and *The Lowdown*. These publications really trolled around in the muck, at times making *Confidential* look downright prim. An unsuccessful competitor surfaced called *Confidential Love Secrets* (no relation) and it was a sort of hybrid, bridging the *McCalls/Good Housekeeping* "ladies" world and the sexual frankness of *Confidential*. The result was like *O* in a parallel universe, with surprisingly prescient, often candid, human stories on topics like Irene Selznick succeeding as her "own person" after divorcing producer David O. Selznick, and an over-the-hill hooker making no apologies for the life she lived–even going so far as to defend the cleanliness and good nature of the other prostitutes she had known. It disappeared without a trace, needing another half-century before Phil Donahue and Oprah would make the world ready for its kind of content, while the scandal mags conquered the world.

Then Giesler declared war:

These magazines are a major threat to the movie industry. They must be treated as such. My clients have decided to fight, which is more than I can say for the industry as a whole... We'll hound them through every court in the country. We'll file civil libel suits and criminal libel complaints... We'll sue publishers, the writers, the printers, the distributors. We'll even sue the vendors. This smut is going to stop.

Headlines in *The Los Angeles Mirror-News* and in *The Hollywood Reporter* declared that Giesler was going to ask Congress to ban the publications. He filed suit on behalf of Lizabeth "Baritone Babe" Scott for $2.5 million, filed for $1 million for Robert "Hot Dog" Mitchum, and $3 million for Doris "African Prince Lover" Duke. Harrison wasn't frightened by the Giesler lawsuits or other pressure from Hollywood. Each attack was another chance for publicity. He milked the controversy for all it was worth, with his many interviews casting him as confident, happy, and laughing all the way to the bank— clearing as much as $500,000 in net profit off every issue. He was clear: The scandal magazine wasn't going away.

The desire to know that which is not told—and that's Confidential—will continue. That I place my life on.

Aside from Giesler, the rest of Hollywood continued to dither, unsure whether to get involved in a fight against the magazine. Finally, some Hollywood power brokers, supposedly aware that Attorney General Edmund G. "Pat" Brown was considering a gubernatorial bid and would need their financial support, decided the time was right to approach him about their problem. A campaign against smut sounded like a sure thing with voters. In early 1957 Brown started working with the Los Angeles District Attorney's office to investigate *Confidential.*

Meanwhile, that 1955 "Wrong Door Raid" story was working its way into the consciousness of politicians in Sacramento. California State Senator Fred H. Kraft, a San Diego Republican, used the story as the basis for launching an investigation into private detectives—which was his way of trying to implicate *Confidential* in aiding and abetting private detectives in breaking state law and violating the terms of state-issued private eye licenses.

Frank Sinatra was anxious to testify since he wanted wholeheartedly to prove to the world that he never busted in on Florence Kotz. He maintained that he was minding his own business, waiting in his car, when the other three came out to the street and told him they had made a mistake. That's all he knew. Philip Irwin, one of the detectives who admitted breaking down the wrong door, testified under oath that Sinatra was lying through his teeth.

Whether or not Frank Sinatra lied about being at the apartment had nothing to do with the stated purposes of the hearings, which were ostensibly about discovering if private detectives were misusing their licenses. In the case of the "Wrong Door Raid" they were. One of the detectives was indeed using a borrowed license, from a detective named Jack Stambler, since his had lapsed, but that piece of evidence, likely proving that at least part of the accusations being made by committee members were true, didn't come up at the hearings. Actual evidence involving the stated mission of the hearings wasn't sexy enough once stars got involved. Fred Otash was working for Sinatra, trying to prove his version of events, which were in opposition to some of the claims made by *Confidential.*

The Senate hearings began in February 1957 and dragged on for months. Kraft's public-spirited piety took a major hit when his wife charged him with adultery in March, making headlines like "Wife Sues Wrong-Door Raid Prober." By May, the whole thing ran out of gas, ending inconclusively amid charges and counter-charges as to the veracity of Sinatra's testimony. By that point Sinatra himself probably didn't remember the real story. As the Senate hearings were winding down, California Attorney General Pat Brown denounced exposé magazines in general, and *Confidential* in particular, as a threat to the state's important movie industry. He empanelled a grand jury to hear testimony about the magazine's operations. Maureen O'Hara was chomping at the bit to testify. Other famous faces were also on the grand jury witness list, including Liberace, June Allyson, Walter Pidgeon, and Mae West. The acid man himself, Howard Rushmore, also volunteered to do his civic duty and expose the magazine's rotten core. So much for parting amicably with Harrison.

The grand jury returned indictments on May 15, 1957 against Robert Harrison, Marjorie and Fred Meade, Francesca de Scaffa, A. P. Govoni, Dan and Helen Studin, Edith Tobias, and her son and Marjorie's brother, Michael Tobias. The three charges were Conspiracy to Publish Criminal Libel, Conspiracy to Publish and Distribute Lewd and Obscene Material, and Conspiracy to Disseminate Illegal Information (about abortions and male rejuvenation). Ratcheting all three offenses up to the level of a Criminal Conspiracy was the only way to make the charges carry the possibility of hard time. The entire June 1957 issue of *Whisper*, and the May 1955, May 1956, and September 1956 issues of *Confidential* were listed in the indictment as lewd and obscene. Two articles charged in the indictment with violations of California's Business and Professional Code allegedly promoted abortion and deviant male rejuvenation, were "Beware the Newest Abortion Menace: The Pill That Ends Unwanted Pregnancy," and "Pega Palo—The Vine That Makes You Virile." Richard Kable and Richard Cox, two executives of the Kable Publishing Company, *Confidential*'s printer, were also charged.

Not one person on the list of indictments handed down in California was actually in the state at the time. The Meades had hustled themselves off to New York the minute the grand jury probe had been announced, and the rest of those on the list resided in New York. California prosecutors planned to extradite every one of them, vowing they would all face prison sentences. Assistant Attorney General Clarence Linn bragged to the press, "The jail doors are clanging for these people." *The Los Angeles Times* headlined a lead editorial, "No Compromise For Scandal."

TOP RIGHT: Frank Sinatra testifies at the Kraft Hearings about whether or not he stayed in the car during the "Wrong Door Raid" on Marilyn Monroe. BOTTOM LEFT: Attorney Arthur Crowley succeeded in quashing subpoenas for Marjorie and Fred Meade to testify at the Kraft Hearings, arguing that it would hurt their ability to defend themselves in the upcoming *Confidential* libel trial. BOTTOM RIGHT: Edith and her son Michael Tobias, Dan and Helen Studin, Al Govoni, and a clearly irritated Bob Harrison surrender to authorities in New York on the California libel and obscenity indictments.

Attorney Al DeStefano successfully fought their extradition, and none would ever stand trial; leaving California authorities with no one else to go after except California residents Marjorie and Fred Meade. Today Michael Tobias has no memory of ever having been indicted. He believes his mother, Aunt Helen, and Uncle Bob intentionally left him as far out of the loop as possible so he wouldn't worry about going to jail.

These were the two articles the California prosecutors found the most obscene of all the material in *Confidential* they found questionable. The top piece is strictly for laughs, while the bottom article warns AGAINST abortion.

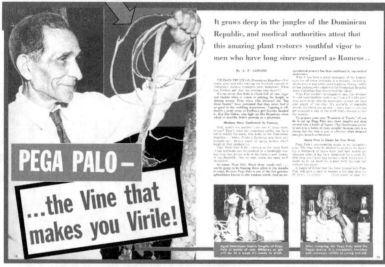

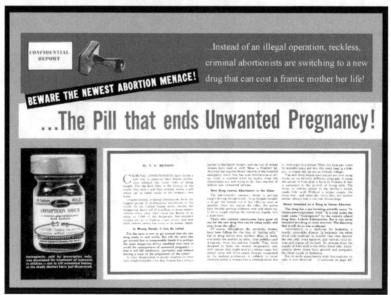

In New York Harrison was getting very nervous. Attorney General Brown had started pressuring California news dealers to stop carrying the magazine. The July 1957 issues of *Confidential* and *Whisper* were barred from distribution in California. They were all being threatened with prison.

Harrison had to work overtime to keep his paranoia in check—and he wasn't always successful. They were coming at him from every side. He was a man who loved a challenge, but this was something else. At night he paced his apartment, wondering where the knives would come from next. It all morphed in his mind, to the point where he sometimes had trouble sorting out truth from fiction—as if the bullet wound was real. People weren't just out to get him in New York and California, but back in the Dominican Republic too. How could a guy like him go to prison? He'd really have to make like Mitchum, be the bad guy, the heavy, the tough...

Harrison used the *Confidential's* September 1957 issue to speak to his five million readers in an unusual editorial.

He was in a fight for his life.

▼

Hollywood vs.

A Publisher's Statement:

California has accused us of a crime —the crime of telling the truth!

THAT THIS MAGAZINE IS UNDER ASSAULT in the California courts is, we assume, a fact known to most of our nine million readers. We have been indicted by a Los Angeles County grand jury on charges of:

1. Conspiracy to publish criminal libel;
2. Conspiracy to publish obscene and indecent material;
3. Conspiracy to disseminate information about abortion;
4. Conspiracy to disseminate information about male rejuvenation.

A California Assistant Attorney General has stated to the press: "In my opinion CONFIDENTIAL is finished."

This is a determined effort, initiated by a segment of the motion picture industry, to "get" this magazine.

We hold no secrets from our readers. In our first issue, nearly five years ago, we promised to "publish the facts" and "name the names." We have kept that promise; and our readers have made us successful. We have *the world's largest newsstand sale*. We sell more than three million copies per issue; and each copy, conservatively, is read by three adult, free Americans.

Nine million Americans are worthy of respect. We respect them. Our success is due to their appreciation of our efforts to establish the truth and to maintain *the right for them to have the truth*.

We deal only in truth; and here—frank and honest—is the truth about this effort to "get" us.

WE ARE *NOT GUILTY* OF "CONSPIRACY TO PUBLISH CRIMINAL LIBEL."

A precious and historic American principle is this: truth may be distasteful, but truth can *never* be libelous.

In an American courtroom, under the Stars-and-Stripes, thank God, truth stands as the unassailable shield against charges of libel.

Our readers will note that nowhere in the California allegations are we charged with falsehood. *We are charged only with telling the truth*. We are prepared to prove the truth; and the hope of those who would "finish" us is that they can persuade an American jury that truth can be libelous.

We don't believe they can do it.

We believe that the truths we have published — some of them unpleasant for certain people — have been in the public interest and in the best traditions of American journalism.

Not maliciously do we publish the truth about the homosexuality of a government official who held a a position of high public trust. We don't hate or despise such an official. We want only to keep faith with nine million Americans *who are entitled to the truth*.

Confidential

Free Americans have the right to know how, at a time of great danger, scores of homosexuals—admittedly grave security risks—came to infest our State Department.

Is an American jury going to "get" us for daring to tell that truth? . . . We don't believe so.

A portion of the motion picture industry has some political power because of dollar contributions. Why is this portion of the industry so anxious to "get" CONFIDENTIAL?

Our readers know the answer, but we'll state it briefly.

"Hollywood" is in the business of lying. Falsehood is a stock in trade. They use vast press-agent organizations and advertising expenditures to "build up" their "stars." They "glamorize" and distribute detailed—and often deliberately false—information about private lives.

Because of advertising money, in these "build-ups" they have the cooperation of large segments of the daily press, many magazines, columnists, radio and TV. They have the cooperation of practically every medium *except* CONFIDENTIAL . . . They can't "influence" us. So they want to "get" us.

The trouble with their "build-ups" is that they create a phony atmosphere which spoils some of those who are "built-up." From Fatty Arbuckle to Bergman-Rossellini, Hollywood has had trouble with its "spoiled darlings" who have decided that the rules for "ordinary" mortals don't apply to them.

Some of these spoiled people became Communists to show how big, bad, bold and unconventional they are. Others have flaunted their sexual depravity.

All we have done is "blow the whistle" on a few of these spoiled ones. We have given the truth to our readers who have wanted and were entitled to the truth.

And for this, Hollywood wants to "get" CONFIDENTIAL.

We know that an American jury will decide in our favor.

WE ARE *NOT GUILTY* OF "CONSPIRACY TO DISTRIBUTE OBSCENE AND INDECENT MATERIAL." Since its inception, CONFIDENTIAL has gone through the United States mails, a privilege that is denied to publications which are obscene and indecent. When has truth become "obscene and indecent?"

Is the book, *Peyton Place*, obscene or indecent when it details one sexual intercourse after another?

Is *Reader's Digest* obscene and indecent when it instructs women in how best to experience the act of love.

Is Hollywood being obscene and indecent when *Baby Doll* finds blessed release with the artful stranger in her husband's absence?

Obscenity and indecency depend on purpose. Our purpose has been to tell the truth.

WE ARE *NOT GUILTY* OF DISSEMINATING ILLEGAL "INFORMATION ABOUT ABOR-TION." Instead, in our only article on this subject we exposed the practices of criminal abortionists and warned women of the horrible risks and dangers involved.

And as to "male rejuvenation," our interest has been the same as that of other American magazines. Science is seeking to prolong male potency; and we have tried only to report the developments.

We do not underestimate this effort to "get" us. We concede that those who want to "finish" us are powerful and resourceful. They have some tricky arguments; they are artists in the old three-shell game.

But we expect to survive. For we believe that even those Americans who may not like what we say will, nevertheless, defend our right to say it.

We doubt that the time has arrived when Americans can be "gotten" for the crime of telling the truth.

—— ROBERT HARRISON

Blackout Prize NEW Jackpot $15,650
SOLVE THIS WEEK'S PUZZLE -- SEE PAGE 26

How Uncle Sam Makes You Pay	Journal NEW YORK American	7TH SPORTS WALL ST. SPECIAL

For Details, See Page 20

No. 24395—0683   Thursday, January 4, 1959   5 CENTS

CONFIDENTIAL'S EX-BOSS SLAYS WIFE. SELF

Publisher Robert Harrison and niece Marjorie Meade

SCANDAL CALLED 'FAMILY BUSINESS'

Los Angeles - August 13 - At the libel trial of *Confidential Magazine* continued yel Clarence Lin Harrison and something a labeling and t

including not just Mr. Harrison and his redheaded niece Marjorie Meade, but

FLAME-HAIRED FEMME FATALE IN DEAD FAINT

Bribery Attempt Charged

Confidential Witness
FOUND DEAD!

DRUGS FOUND AT CRIME SCENE
ROSECUTION CHARGES FOUL PLAY

Francesca de Scaffa

Sleaze Rag Snitch
Twice Tries Suicide

Mexico City - May 19 - Said to be "in despair" and "distraught" over allegations linking her to articles in *Confidential Magazine* that California state officials charge are "obscene and

Universal Studios star Tab Hunter

Judge Says Teen Idol Must Testify

Los Angeles - August 6 - Judge Herbert Walker declared today that Hollywood actor Tab Hunter must appear to testify in the *Confidential Magazine* libel and obscenity trial. This

MOVIE VIP's VOW RE 'DIRT-HAPPY' SCAN

Confidential Magazine New Yo
Publisher Robert Harrison:

'THIS IS WAR!'

PART THREE

TORRID TRIAL TERROR
Murder-Suicide Tragedy

Tinseltown Gets Tough
Lock 'Em Up And Throw Away The Sleaze

JULY 1957. The heat and smog over Los Angeles turned thick and black. The celebrating in Hollywood over Robert Harrison's indictment went limp when he, as well as every other New York resident who had been indicted, successfully resisted extradition to California. Libel was not an extraditable offense under New York law—a surprise to the California prosecutors, an unusual pairing of Assistant Attorney General Clarence Linn and Deputy District Attorney William Ritzi—who should have done their homework on the issue but didn't.

They couldn't even extradite Francesca de Scaffa, busy making headlines in Mexico for marrying famous bullfighter Jaime Bravo and then either trying to commit suicide once, twice, or not at all, saying she was distraught over being publicly named in the *Confidential* case. She refused to come back to California unless granted immunity from prosecution. Fat chance. The prosecution team wouldn't compromise. Ritzi was even a Sunday school teacher. They believed the articles in *Confidential* were nothing but filth and lies, and they believed wholeheartedly that everyone would see it that way.

When they failed to extradite, the disheartened prosecution team almost dropped the case altogether, but they didn't want to lose face, so they focused on the two California residents, Fred and Marjorie Meade—as well as on the obscenity charges, and the violations of state statutes that resulted from printing the Pega Palo and abortion pill articles. Pretty sad for a case that began with hopes of switching back the balance of power between Hollywood and the tabloid press.

From the get-go it was a downer for everyone in town. They all had hoped for Harrison's head on a platter—all except the hordes of folks up and down the food chain who were used to secretly selling stories to *Confidential.*

Harrison got the best legal help in California, Art Crowley of course, in addition to using DeStefano and one of the partners in his firm, Jacob Rosenbaum, in New York.

Marjorie and Fred returned to Los Angeles and made $25,000 bail. While Art Crowley was preparing his defense of the magazine, he was still advising and enlisting Fred Otash to aid Sinatra in the Kraft hearings. Crowley and Otash were FOR the magazine in the libel trial, but AGAINST the magazine's version of events in the "Wrong Door Raid."

At the Kraft hearings, Otash went to great lengths to prove Sinatra wasn't at Kotz's door. The whole drama of "was Frankie there or not" took up most of the time, even though it had no bearing on the hearings. Otash's vivid tales after the fact of Ruditsky being roughed up by P.I. license investigators, and of corruption and betrayal, never stuck, though back in New York, Al Govoni was sweating the whole thing out, since he was the one who wrote the story in the first place, under the pseudonym J. E. Leclair, the name of his brother-in-law.

The committee wanted to subpoena Marjorie and Fred Meade and Fred Otash, but Crowley successfully argued it could harm his clients' ability to defend themselves in the upcoming libel trial. Otash declared himself and Sinatra winners in the hearings since no indictment was issued against Sinatra for lying. That was true. But no indictment was issued against *anyone.* The hearings, as heavily hyped as a Miss America pageant, were a total bust.

But over on the trial side things were heating up.

Hollywood immediately went to pieces over Arthur Crowley's threat to subpoena first 100, then 200 stars. If the D.A. wanted to allege the magazine's stories were lies, then the people those stories were about should testify to that in open court—where Crowley made it clear, he would ask them about any and all aspects of their private lives that could have any bearing on the published articles in the magazine.

Suddenly the studio bosses wanted to back down. They nervously approached Attorney General Brown and the District Attorney about putting a stop to the case. The prosecution was unequivocal: They had launched an investigation and had made it this far. No turning back. Studio flunkies and studio heads alike quaked in their boots. It would be a bloodbath unless they got the stars out of town. Art Crowley jokes it was like the Exodus from Egypt. Fred Otash, armed with Crowley's subpoenas, combed Los Angeles. He caught up with Lana Turner at LAX and Dean Martin at a party. Dan Dailey saw Otash in the wings while onstage at the Hollywood Bowl. After the end Dailey leaped into the audience, escaping the subpoena by unwittingly inventing the mosh pit. The defense soon had 130 stars on enforced stand-by. When word reached Judge Herbert Walker that some planned to defy the injunctions, he warned, "They'll come to court even if I have to send officers with handcuffs to get them!"

Sensing the possibility of disaster in the air, Linn and Ritzi approached Harrison with a settlement. They would drop all charges if he agreed to pay a small fine and stop publishing Hollywood dirt. This was at the end of seven months of legal headaches. Bob was worried about Marjorie—she was showing the strain of her sudden infamy—and he felt guilty knowing he was the one prosecutors really wanted. Sales were still high but Harrison favored quitting while he was ahead. The country was growing saturated with Hollywood gossip. How long could *Confidential* lead the pack? Harrison agreed to the settlement.

The prosecutors and Crowley presented their agreement to Judge Walker. No trial, no stars on the stand, no Marjorie or Fred Meade threatened with prison. Both sides were completely flabbergasted when Walker categorically (and rather petulantly) refused to allow a settlement. He deemed the transgressions of *Confidential* far too serious to ignore. (Walker had started his working life as a child actor. Maybe he liked the limelight. His biggest moment in the sun would come a decade later when sentencing Sirhan Sirhan to death.)

Hollywood's initial misgivings about fighting *Confidential* seemed borne out completely. To make matters worse, Judge Walker turned down a request by Rory Calhoun's attorney,

Bernard B. Laven, to exempt the actor from testifying. He ruled that Calhoun, along with Maureen O'Hara, Dorothy Dandridge, Mae West, Robert Mitchum, Dick Powell, Corinne Calvet, Mark Stevens, and John Carroll had to remain on two-hour notice during the entire trial to appear in court. Across the country headlines screamed, "Stars Lose!" predicting that Walker's ruling would unleash a six-month parade of the biggest names in show biz being forced to dig their own graves under oath.

Marjorie prepared for the trial by buying a new wardrobe. Art Crowley wanted her prim and conservative, Peter Pan collars, that kind of thing. She got five outfits, one for every day of the week. She would rotate them as the trial progressed.

Maureen O'Hara launched her press offensive with unmitigated fury. All these years later, she still goes on about *Confidential*, devoting a whole chapter to the case in her 2004 memoir, each page filled with noble pride and factual errors. It makes for fascinating reading. Apparently O'Hara spent her life trapped by her own beauty and talent; she was single-handedly responsible for making Technicolor successful, because she photographed so beautifully in color that other screen queens decided to try it too; she changed U.S. immigration law to help the Irish; watched John Ford have sex with a man; and the trial against *Confidential* was entirely about her.

All because Harrison's magazine said she had fooled around in the back row of a theater. Not having sex, mind you, not drunk, not hopped up on goofballs. She was supposedly on a guy's lap being frisky. O'Hara had weathered other scandals, going through an ugly divorce and custody trial where she was publicly accused of adultery. But she wasn't even married at the time of the alleged petting incident. She was free to fool around (above the waist please) with anyone she fancied. Perhaps modern media in all its hyper-sexuality, irony, and mean-spiritedness makes it hard to put the article in context. Was it really all that bad? Not in comparison to a *Tempo Magazine* cover photo of O'Hara in 1954—a shot she posed for of her own free will—looking for all the world like a lioness in heat. The *Confidential* photo and story look downright sweet in comparison.

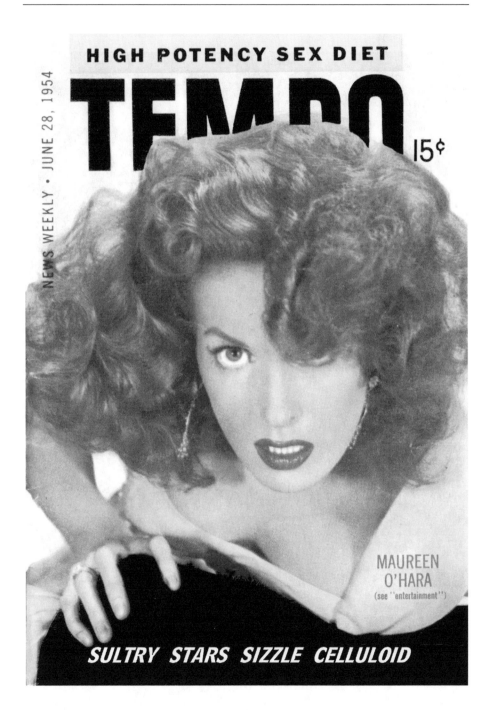

HIGH POTENCY SEX DIET

TEMPO

15¢

NEWS WEEKLY • JUNE 28, 1954

MAUREEN O'HARA
(see "entertainment")

SULTRY STARS SIZZLE CELLULOID

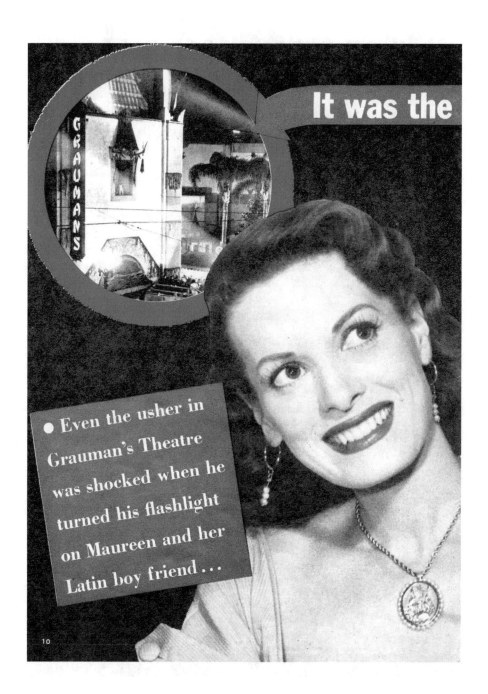

It was the

● Even the usher in Grauman's Theatre was shocked when he turned his flashlight on Maureen and her Latin boy friend...

hottest show in town when

MAUREEN O'HARA
Cuddled in

By R. E. McDONALD

ALMOST ANYONE who's ever been to the movies knows about Hollywood's famous Grauman's Chinese Theater. That's where the stars go to get their footprints recorded in cement. That's where they stage some of movieland's gaudiest premieres.

But you'd have to be an usher to get the real low-down on what goes on in this celebrated movie house. Garbed in your flashy uniform and equipped with your tiny flashlight, you'd discover something to make your eyes pop. Because Grauman's is also the theater where the stars go—not to watch the movie but to bundle in the balcony. And the show that goes on in the back seats often beats anything that's flickering on the screen.

No one can predict when an act along the aisle is going to produce more steam than the advertised attraction. For instance, a gentlemanly assistant manager at Grauman's didn't give it a second thought one November evening not so long ago when he greeted lovely, green-eyed Maureen O'Hara at the head of the main aisle.

Usher Got the Shock of His Life

Escorted by a tall and handsome Latin American, she looked as dignified as a queen. Politely murmuring that he hoped they enjoyed the picture, the manager turned them over to an usher, who led them to their seats toward the rear of the orchestra.

He'd had his share of troubles with over-amorous couples in Grauman's, but such a problem never entered his mind as he watched red-haired Maureen sweep down the aisle into the darkness. O'Hara necking in a public theater? It just couldn't be.

He got the shock of his life an hour later, though,

when the usher in charge of aisle "C" came rushing out to report that there was a couple heating up the back of the theater as though it were mid-January. Easing down the aisle, he saw the entwined twosome. It was Maureen and her south-of-the-border sweetie.

His eyes accustomed to the darkness, he saw even more than that. Maureen had entered Grauman's wearing a white silk blouse neatly buttoned. Now it wasn't.

The guy had come in wearing a spruce blue suit. Now he wasn't. The coat was off, his collar was open and his tie was hanging limply at half mast in the steam.

Maureen Made Movie-Viewing History

Moreover, Maureen had taken the darndest position to watch a movie in the whole history of the theater. She was spread across three seats—with the happy Latin American in the middle seat.

This is going to the movies?

The assistant manager coughed. Then he coughed again. For all the reaction he got from Maureen and her rumpled boy friend, he could have had double pneumonia.

What to do now? He was embarrassed at the prospect of having to walk over and tell them to break up the unadvertised love scene. On the other hand, what they were doing threatened to short-circuit the air conditioning system.

Luckily, the area they were capering in was surrounded by a wilderness of empty seats. Inspiration set in and he rushed back to the theater's foyer for a flashlight. Then, groping his way down the aisle as though searching for something, he kept flicking the light on the two until Maureen suddenly sat up, snuggled into one seat and the pair started to watch the movie.

Well, that was enough of that and the agitated assistant manager figured (Continued on page 46)

MAUREEN O'HARA *(Continued from page 11)*

he'd seen the last of such goings on. But was *he* wrong! So far as Maureen was concerned, this was double feature night and she was giving away more than dishes.

The manager had hardly returned to the candy stand out front before the usher from aisle "C" was on his heels with the breathless announcement, "They're at it again!"

They Were *Really* in a Cloud

This time, when he went to investigate, he found Maureen occupying one seat—her boy friend's. That is, they were *both* in it, and if she'd come to watch a movie she was wasting a lot of time and money. So was her sweetie. She was sitting on his lap, facing the *back* of the theater. Naturally, he couldn't see through her.

But neither seemed to mind. In fact, the kids were really in a cloud.

That was *too* much. The assistant manager turned his flashlight directly on Maureen and her Latin Lothario. Impaled by the beam of light, they froze—right in the middle of their clinch.

Flicking off the light, he marched over to the romantic duo and suggested, "Perhaps it might be best if you left the theater."

Well, Maureen and her petting papa were in no position to argue. They did as requested, but only after Maureen borrowed the guy's flashlight to help her back seat buddy find a diamond cuff link he'd lost during their torrid session.

Then, adjusting her blouse, Maureen led the parade to the little red sign marked "Exit." And to tell the truth, the manager was sad to see them go.

She Starred in Row 35

He's seen Maureen in Grauman's since—on the screen, that is. And he can tell you there's nothing she ever did for the camera that can match her antics in Row 35.

Matter of fact, there's something unfair about it. Because Grauman's has never even bothered to immortalize Maureen in cement outside the lobby. And her prints should be there ahead of everyone.

Of course, we *don't* mean footprints! ▲▲▲

Redheaded Maureen's blouse needed plenty of fixing after bouncing and bundling with that Latin lad in Grauman's Chinese Theatre.

Too many people are gone now and no one can definitively prove the story was true or not true. To this day Crowley swears it was. O'Hara can't prove it wasn't, though she maintains that she did show that she was out of the country during the time period the story gave for when the incident happened. Except of course for that fact that the story didn't give a specific date, and the main witness testified he may have been wrong by a month or so. A lot of people swore in court that they saw her at Grauman's doing pretty much what the article suggested. Chief among those supporting *Confidential's* version of events was Harrison's new head of European operations, a man living in London named Michael Mordaunt-Smith. The magazine was making huge inroads throughout Europe, achieving wide popularity in England, and Harrison wanted to take advantage of that by printing more stories about American stars in London for various reasons. That's how he got stories about Vic Mature mistaking a he for a she, Ava Gardner staying up all night with a band at the Savoy, and other tales of celebs who made the mistake of thinking they were free to cut loose, away from prying eyes in Hollywood.

Mordaunt-Smith was the one who had checked the sources for the Maureen O'Hara story while in Los Angeles, an article both he and Al DeStefano believed to be absolutely true. Marjorie had nothing to do with the story, but she also thinks it was probably true.

Smith's principal foot soldier in England was Lee Benson, a regular at seedy clubs, who made a point of cozying up to party boys and girls, and then seeing if he could tempt visiting American stars to snap at the bait—creating juicy stories in the process. Benson was called Little Mister Whisper, and was the English equivalent to Ronnie Quillan—definitely low down on the respectability chain. He would later pull a Howard Rushmore, and go to work for a newspaper called *The Daily Sketch* when they were working on an exposé of *Confidential* which intended to prove how false the stories were. A reporter named Victor Davis, on freelance assignment for the *Sketch*, was one of those assigned to call on each of the magazine's "victims" on Benson's list. He fact-checked the *Confidential* article about Ava Gardner taking a sexy but recalcitrant bandleader billed as Mr. Latin America back to her suite at the

Savoy Hotel, along with his whole band, where she ended up sexually frustrated. Davis went to interview Mr. Latin America himself, a handsome 32-year-old from Montevideo in Uruguay named Esteban Larraura, who was very embarrassed about the whole thing, but confessed in dribs and drabs that the story was accurate.

A jury of five women and seven men was impaneled on August 6, 1957 for the opening of *People of the State of California v. Robert Harrison, et al.* Even court veterans were stunned by the whole thing. The press was more intense than anyone had ever remembered for a trial. Each seat in the courtroom had the name of a publication on it, not just the American press, like *The Los Angeles Mirror-News, The New York Post, Time Magazine, The New York Times*, etc., but *Paris Match* and *The London Daily Mail* were front and center, heading up a huge contingent of foreign press.

Looky-loos were everywhere, sweating through the muggy days waiting around in the corridors of the Los Angeles Hall of Justice hoping to see someone, anyone famous. These weren't regular court watchers and most had no idea how to dress for the occasion. Some wore evening clothes. Shorts and Capri pants were seen. A few brought their ballet and tap shoes, practicing their routines, oblivious to anyone who wasn't a celebrity.

Ritzi and Linn prosecuted the case jointly, often working with as many as ten lawyers from the two offices. Clarence Linn opened with the prosecution making the "shocking" charge that the magazine hired "women of the night(!)" to entice Hollywood stars into compromising positions, who then supplied information for lurid stories. The Sunday school teacher seemed shaken, as if he couldn't believe what he had to say to the good people of the jury, when he charged that the magazine had published information about abortion and about remedying what is sometimes referred to as loss of manhood. He called Harrison the Mr. Big of the operation—a description bound to make Bob snicker just a little, safe and snug back in New York. Lots of pontificating about the terrible danger to the moral fiber of Californians, no, make that *Americans*, followed, with Crowley's (sustained) objections coming regularly. For his part, Art Crowley's opening statement was simple and categorical: The stories in the magazines were true, there was no malice involved, and the Meades and Hollywood Research were being unfairly targeted for matters that if legally debatable at all, should be tried in a New York court, since that is where Harrison lived and where the magazine was headquartered. He also brought up the fact that after years of struggle, the Postmaster General had declared that the magazine was not obscene.

Throughout the trial, Crowley, and by extension, the Meades, tried to separate Hollywood Research from *Confidential*. That was part of the argument against trying the case in California at all. In a corporate sense, Hollywood Research was separate, and the Meades didn't work directly for *Confidential* according to the paperwork. But when Fred Meade got on the stand and claimed he and Marjorie moved to California so he could go into the plastics business, and that Hollywood Research was an afterthought, a kind of busy-work assignment for Marjorie, financed with just $5,000 from her uncle, he was hovering dangerously close to outright perjury— and his testimony is directly contradicted by Marjorie's own memory of what really happened. Whatever the legal mumbo jumbo, Hollywood Research existed solely to service *Confidential*. The move was Uncle Bob's idea. And Marjorie and Fred received substantially more than $5,000 from him to start the ball rolling, well over $100,000.

Today Art Crowley readily admits this and has no memory of ever trying hard to separate the entities. Hollywood Research was all about *Confidential*. Period. He can't remember why Meade would have been testifying about money at all. But Marjorie remembers the separation issue as being important. It's hard to know for sure since no printed copy of the trial transcripts is known to exist anywhere in the world. The court system in California routinely destroys historical transcripts to make room for new cases. Crowley never saved his copy.

Judge Walker was a rather genial man, but intrepid "girl reporter" Theo Wilson, who became a legendary court journalist in the decades that followed (while also moonlighting with uncredited articles in *The National Enquirer*) worked the

Confidential trial for *The New York Daily News*, her very first. She liked to joke with the other press people and call Judge Walker "The Phumpfer," because of his tendency to mumble.

The British writers especially, couldn't understand a word he was saying. Overall a carnival atmosphere prevailed, especially since Walker's busy court docket couldn't just screech to a halt for *Confidential*. The Superior Court dealt then with over 10,000 felony cases a year, including grand theft auto, assaults, murders, rapes, arson, and everything else the human species dreamed up to do to one another. So Walker sometimes had to stop witnesses right in the middle of testimony to set a date, hear lawyers, or handle different phases of some of his other cases.

It scared the hell out of the poor non-*Confidential* defendants who were brought into the courtroom with no warning. Some guy attempted to strangle his wife. Okay, he was sorry. Whatever. Then he was taken downstairs in the Hall of Justice to a courtroom and confronted with what seemed like thousands of press, spectators, witnesses, and court personnel. He would practically faint from fear, figuring they must really be getting ready to throw the book at him.

Some of the *Confidential* trial jurors were just as confused. There they were, taking copious notes like good little boys and girls, and they would just keep going, taking notes on all the various defendants who paraded in and out, whether they had anything to do with the *Confidential* case or not. The foreign press was also mystified. The whole proceeding seemed so casual, with all the various defendants and attorneys wandering in and out, the mailman tramping right through the courtroom to deliver his mail, and even a tie salesman hawking his wares up and down the aisle during a recess. What would be next: Hotdog vendors? The ice cream man?

Judge Walker realized everyone was confused so he stopped to address the jury and the press. *Ladies and gentlemen, I suppose you're wondering why...* and he began his phumpf phumpf phumpf, earnestly going on and on about something or other, before leaning back with a satisfied grin. One British reporter leaned over to Theo Wilson, snickering, "Well! That certainly clarified everything, didn't it dear?"

As if that weren't entertainment enough, Walker then agreed to let William Ritzi read a ream of the magazine's stories into the record. So Ritzi began several days of Story Time, patiently, in his best Sunday school teacher's voice, all flawless diction and heated indignation. He began with "It Was a Hot Show in Town When Maureen O'Hara Cuddled in Row 35," before moving on to "Only the Birds and Bees Saw What Dorothy Dandridge Did in the Woods." Muffled titters from the audience and the press turned to outright guffaws as Ritzi droned on, replaced by Linn when his pedantic vocal chords tired out. Even Judge Walker started giggling a little.

The defense saw the laughter as a good thing: How could these stories be dangerous to anyone's morals when the whole courtroom was collapsing into such silliness? To Crowley it was clear:

An article can't be prurient if it makes you laugh. Laughing and sex aren't possible together. Later in his jury instructions Walker improperly told the jurors they could find something both funny and sexually prurient. He had it in for us, making it clear he thought we were scum and that we should lose. As the trial progressed Walker's judicial standards and ethics went out the window. And Linn? He was a pompous ass. They were obsessed with deviance, and so sure they were on the side of the angels that they didn't bother putting together a case. That was the thing. They had no case at all!

Things turned bitter when Rushmore appeared for the State. Even the prosecutors seemed a little wary of the lanky alcoholic with the sour disposition. He testified for three long hours of humorless rantings about the evils of Harrison's operation and the gossip biz in general—stating how humiliated he was to have ever been associated with the gossip game at all. (In the middle of all this, Judge Walker paused to rule that teen heartthrob Tab Hunter would have to testify, just like all of the grown-up stars.) Rushmore didn't seem to find any hypocrisy in condemning *Confidential*, saying he quit because he couldn't take it anymore, he couldn't stand subjecting himself to such a despicable endeavor. Never mind that Rushmore left *Confidential* and went on to report for not one, but at least four rival tabloids, including, *Tipoff, Scamp, Tipster,* and *Uncensored.*

Rushmore painted a picture of a lurid Harrison practically drooling with anticipation as he ordered an often unwilling staff to use any and all methods to dig up the dirtiest dirt around. Hookers. Drunks. Homos. Hotheads. Anyone was fair game in the endless search for the kind of muck that floated the perverted publisher's boat, as he overruled his editors and lawyers, printing lies with impunity, and attacking the good reputations of Hollywood's upright citizens. Like Mother of the Year Joan Crawford. Along the way Rushmore tried to implicate anyone and everyone with wrongdoing, alleging police corruption in Los Angeles and New York, payoffs to shifty sources, and immoral behavior from all concerned. The newspaper dailies reported his testimony as dangerous to the defense. Those who knew him considered him dangerous to everyone. And he was such a loathsome, unbelievable character that the prosecution started to wonder whether they had made a mistake. His bitterness lingered with the jury, basting the prosecution's case with bile.

Crowley put two of Harrison's New York lawyers, Daniel Ross and Al DeStefano, on the stand. Both lawyers testified to the exacting standards they held Harrison and the magazine to, saying that Harrison never overruled them on legal advice. Marjorie concurs even now, saying her uncle NEVER went against the lawyers. DeStefano admitted on the stand to advising against publishing the O'Hara story, but was careful to make it clear that his opinion in that matter wasn't a legal one—the story itself was fine—but a common sense one. He thought Maureen, as a "good Catholic woman" would blow her stack, and he was right.

Then Ronnie Quillan, the Soiled Dove, sauntered in, testifying for the prosecution. After riveting and horrifying the courtroom with her on-the-record admission of being a whore,

Quillan was questioned for what seemed like hours and hours about the boring details of when, what, how, and where she made it with Desi Arnaz ten years ago in the desert. *So what?* No one bothered to explain why a prosecution witness was testifying that the article she sold to *Confidential* was completely true. The mere fact of her being a hooker, and the indecency of anyone buying her story seemed to be the point Linn and Ritzi's were trying to make, which had nothing to do with proving libel. And she didn't say anything about her profession on the stand that she hadn't already said in print in her "Hollywood's No.1 Madam" story in *Whisper*. For his part, Desi was out of town and conveniently unavailable to testify, though he did issue heated denials—without ever having to be under oath.

Ronnie told a few fibs here and there, alleging, for instance, that Harrison sought her out, then admitting to Crowley that she was the one who pursued Harrison in the first place. She talked about the Meades wanting to equip her with that miniature watch tape recorder, then said that maybe it wasn't them, maybe it was von Wittenberg, the private dick, then not answering particularly clearly when Crowley asked if the tape recorder ever actually existed.

A whore and a bilious Commie-hater. The prosecution's two star witnesses.

Meanwhile, this just in from Paris: Errol Flynn trumpeted to reporters there that he was ready, willing, and able to tell all about how the magazine's scurrilous tale of his two-way sex mirror was nothing but a lie. It was all lies. Everything they said about anyone. Maybe he would sue. He flew into LAX with even more fanfare, his back up, spoiling for a fight. But Flynn did not appear in court or testify under oath about coverage of his peccadilloes in the magazine. Of course, for two decades he had been in and out of *other* courtrooms, accused by various under-aged girls and their mothers of statutory rape, so perhaps he had grown weary of courtrooms in general.

A few weeks into the whole trial drama it all seemed to be going wrong for the prosecution and for Hollywood. Over and over again, witnesses made allegations about things being untrue in the magazine, and were then forced by Crowley into admitting, under oath, that, well, maybe the stories were kind of true—but then hotly arguing that the *tone*, that was the thing, *Confidential* stories insinuated so much, it made it all *feel* like lies. But a snarky tone and an insinuating style do not a case for libel make. So Linn and Ritzi punted for all they were worth and introduced a surprise witness, producer Paul Gregory, who walked into the courtroom and called Marjorie Meade a blackmailer.

Marjorie keeled over in a dead faint—making headlines from coast to coast.

Gregory testified that a woman identifying herself as "Miss Dee" and an agent from *Confidential* had told him he could keep a "scandalously injurious" story out of the magazine by paying between $800 and $1,000. He pointed to Marjorie, calling her the mysterious "Miss Dee." Fred Meade had to be restrained from hitting Linn. Ritzi and Crowley almost came to blows. And Judge Walker adjourned, clearly alarmed by the violent turn of events.

Here's where deep pockets, ability, and determination came in handy. Otash went into overtime, looking for any way possible of disproving the details of Gregory's supposed meeting with Marjorie. Meanwhile Crowley hacked away at Gregory on the stand. Unfortunately for Gregory, he was a *Confidential* alum, having appeared in the magazine twice, once for co-hosting the Mitchum ketchup party, and the other time in a May 1956 story called "The Lowdown on Paul Gregory Himself!"—an article laying out the whole sordid saga of how he fleeced a love-struck old lady of all her money to help him on his rise to Broadway and Hollywood success. Hardly an unbiased witness. It got ugly. Crowley forced Gregory to admit on the stand to being a homosexual, as a way of proving he had other reasons for being afraid of the magazine. He brought into the record the fact that the *Confidential* story alleging the fleecing of the old lady left out the sworn affidavits Crowley had in his possession of witnesses who saw Gregory bringing sailors and other rough trade to the woman's house for the purposes of homosexual intercourse. Then Otash, with Marjorie's help, hit pay dirt. Not only was Paul Gregory's diary for the year, showing his meeting with Miss Dee, conspicuously blank on every other page of that year, but credit card records proved Marjorie wasn't where Gregory says she was. Then it came out that the place he says they met, a restaurant called Sherry's, wasn't even in business yet on the date he claimed she tried to shake him down.

Crowley also made hay out of the fact that Paul Gregory swore he had come forward at this late date because he had been unaware of the trial until he saw Marjorie's face on the evening news and put it all together. Unaware of the trial? Did the man live under a rock? Crowley was also able to score points by making the perfectly logical argument that trolling around for small change like $1,000 didn't add up for someone like the Meades, who were making buckets of money from the Hollywood Research business, and would have had no reason to jeopardize that for small amounts of cash. The defense had Gregory dead to rights. He had the motive to lie, and his story didn't check out. The prosecution backtracked. Ritzi said maybe the whole thing wasn't instigated by Marjorie, but by someone named "Miss Smith." He was in possession of a telephone recording of her voice but couldn't identify her by name except to say she had figured in the trial so far.

Maybe Ronnie Quillan was actually Miss Dee and perhaps Gregory made a mistake. Though their features weren't all that similar, Ronnie and Marjorie were both flame-haired beauties, at least at the time—sometimes Quillan's hair was black. And Ronnie Quillan was always on to the next deal, looking for an angle. Again the question arises: Is it possible she was on the take? Double-dealing? Crowley doesn't make any accusations, but he does laugh out loud.

Well, she was hardly a Girl Scout.

Michael Mordaunt-Smith took the stand to start the parade of witnesses attesting to the truth of *Confidential's* journalistic standards. The Irish reporter vigorously defended Harrison, the Meades, and the magazine. He bragged that every one of the 900 stories he checked out for Harrison had proven to be true. (In truth there weren't 900 stories in the entire run of the magazine under Harrison.)

The daily papers covering the trial focused more on the fact that Francesca de Scaffa was somewhere on the loose! Reliable reports indicated she had snuck back in from Mexico to see her daughter, keeping as low a profile as possible to avoid being served with her subpoena. The police went into action, chasing after her every step until she managed to hightail it back to Mexico, still a free woman.

Then even more drama: Chalky Wright died mysteriously in a bathtub accident, just after being issued a subpoena to testify for the defense about the Mae West story. Days later his former wife broke down in tears to reporters to tell of threatening calls and interrogations, gruff-voiced men warning her not to say what she knows about Chalky and Mae West's relationship. When pressed to tell what it is she wasn't supposed to say, she wouldn't say. Crowley had depositions from Chalky backing up his story in *Confidential.* Mae West's lawyers claimed Chalky signed two statements swearing the story was false but never produced them. None of it made it into the trial record. And any way you looked at it, Chalky was still dead.

Anthony Quinn's mistress, Mylee Andreason, was the next major witness. She was in the middle of telling the court how a steamy story about her and actor Mark Stevens was completely true when Judge Walker stopped her mid-sentence and dropped a bombshell: She was banned. No more stars could testify who were not in the six specific stories that had already been read into the record by the prosecution; including the articles on Maureen O'Hara cuddling, Dorothy Dandridge having sex outside, Robert Mitchum and the ketchup, Mae West and Chalky White, Gary Cooper having sex with Anita Ekberg, and "Little Miss Mischief" June Allyson stepping out on hubby Dick Powell—but THAT WAS IT! Calling 200 stars to take the stand just wasn't going to happen.

Suddenly there were celebrations all over town, with impromptu parties breaking out at the drop of a hat.

Meanwhile Ronnie Reagan and former alleged actor George Murphy announced a permanent committee of the Motion Picture Industry Council to combat attacks by scandal magazines. They studied the publications religiously. Both men later went into politics, where it would seem they used all the tricks they learned from scandal rags to their political advantage.

Then another *Confidential* Mystery Death. A woman named Polly Gould was found dead in her Bronson Avenue apartment in Hollywood. She had been a private investigator who had apparently refused to work for Harrison. Gould was on the prosecution's witness list and headlines cried, "Murder!?" She did die suspiciously, of an "apparently accidental overdose of barbiturates," according to *The Los Angeles Times*, but her entire testimony at trial would have been that she had not wanted to work for Harrison because she didn't particularly like the kinds of stories *Confidential* printed. That was it. Of course if *Confidential* had been covering the trial instead of taking the stand, they would have made Gould's death into a Malevolent Murder Mystery too. Neither Harrison nor the Meades saw irony in any of this.

Vincent P. Keuper, Monmouth County prosecutor in New Jersey, then made headlines by calling for 250 news dealers in the county's 53 municipalities to subscribe to a pledge refusing to sell any publications that carried indecent material or that glorified crime.

When Otash finally took the stand he blustered his way through a sort of defense of the magazine's practices, bragging that most of the time *Confidential* only printed half the story, cleaning things up so they weren't obscene, and echoing DeStefano's assertion that holding back certain information gave them leverage against lawsuits.

Linn caused a big brouhaha by accusing Otash of threatening one of their witnesses, alleging Otash was one of the gruff-voiced men who intimidated Chalky's ex-wife. Otash was so angry Marjorie thought he might actually get up and hit Linn, but the detective stayed in control of himself and denied everything, trying to deflect the attacks with sarcasm, while fingering Oscar-winning producer Mike Todd as one of the magazine's informants.

On August 26, 1957, Fred Meade took the stand to swear that all the stories were true, to swear that Hollywood Research was not part of *Confidential*, and to swear that he didn't move to California to work for Harrison. His temper flared, though, and things turned interesting again when he launched a passionate defense of his wife, hotly reiterating that neither of them ever had anything to do with blackmail schemes, and personally attacking the morals and credibility of the prosecution team.

Crowley felt the whole thing was farce.

At the time of the trial Louella Parsons was breaking the story of Ingrid Bergman leaving her husband for Roberto Rossellini. Just about every newspaper in the world picked up the story and ran with it, vilifying Bergman and printing all the lurid details. How was this different from 'Confidential?' No one ever gave me a satisfactory answer. And the tabloid press did to us what the state was accusing Confidential of doing to Hollywood. I read boldfaced quotes in the papers supposedly from me, printing things I never said. It was all a circus.

Harrison had approved the $10,000 settlement with Dorothy Dandridge, as long as there was no retraction or admitting of wrongdoing on his part, and as long as she agreed to stop attacking the magazine. She cashed the check then promptly signed on as a witness for the prosecution. DeStefano made angry noises about wanting the money back, since he felt she was violating their agreement, but as a matter of law, no civil agreement could bar her from testifying in a criminal trial. Harrison told DeStefano to leave her alone.

Would Sinatra talk? No. He quickly sailed his yacht into international waters. Clark Gable was sunning himself in Spain. And Lana, Ava, and Marilyn were nowhere to be found.

After Crowley rested on August 30, 1957, the prosecution immediately announced they would call Maureen O'Hara and Dorothy Dandridge.

Disproving the Maureen O'Hara story was the first order of business. She won't like hearing this, after all, it *was* eventually settled out of court, but from the testimony, all the available evidence, the numerous stories written at the time, and the conflicting recollections of everyone involved, at best the whole controversy comes out a draw. Many witnesses testified she was not there. Many testified she was, and make no mistake, a lot of people declared under oath that she was right there in that theater, and they described what she was doing in far more graphic detail than the magazine's article ever did. Mordaunt-Smith was especially blunt, basically saying he believed she was practically having sexual intercourse, right there on the Latin Lover's lap.

Then things really got positively giggly. There was so much conflicting testimony about the aisle and rows in the theater that one of the jurors asked if they could all go on a field trip and visit Grauman's. Maybe Judge Walker wanted to stretch his legs too. He agreed. They all traipsed down to the theater: The press, defendants, Walker, lawyers, court reporter, and the jurors, taking their tone from the solemn looking Ritzi, marching down the aisle in dead silence. They looked at the row of seats. It still didn't really compute for the jury. A bushy-haired juror with a large moustache named LaGuerre Drouet volunteered to stage a reenactment. He and a bailiff started tousling together in the back row, trying to approximate what the magazine alleged O'Hara was doing. Squirming around with his arms in the air as though he were cuddling a movie queen, the portly Drouet became wedged in the seat. The press and even the lawyers busted a gut, laughing as the red-faced Drouet (the same juror who suggested the trip in the first place) yelled at them that he was only trying to be thorough!

Then it was back to court for the main event. Finally, after all this time, two honest-to-God movie stars, right there on the witness stand:

Maureen O'Hara and Dorothy Dandridge.

TOP LEFT: Ronnie Quillan is arrested in Los Angeles several months after the trial, escorted from Hollywood Receiving Hospital, where she had been placed for psychiatric observation following a public brawl. TOP RIGHT: Marjorie Meade with Mylee Andreason during a break at the trial. Note Marjorie's prim dress and buttoned collar. BOTTOM LEFT: Maureen O'Hara and Liberace ostensibly compare notes on how she wasn't at Grauman's Chinese Theater cuddling in the back row, and he isn't now and never has been a homosexual. BOTTOM RIGHT: Errol Flynn makes his feelings for the magazine known. Happy to garner as much publicity as possible, Flynn steered well clear of the trial.

TOP LEFT: Prosecutors sort through a pile of "obscenity." TOP RIGHT: Howard Rushmore arrives to testify for the prosecution, betraying Harrison and the Meades. BOTTOM LEFT: Trial spectators wait to enter court. BOTTOM RIGHT: Jurors take a field trip to Grauman's Chinese to inspect the infamous "Row 35" where Maureen O'Hara was said to have "cuddled."

Looking up at husband Fred during a recess, Marjorie doesn't seem as demure as her Peter Pan collar is probably meant to suggest.

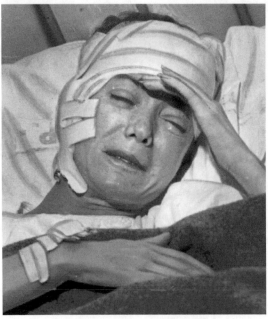

Key prosecution witness and prostitute Ronnie Quillan had a knack for getting into trouble. In early 1958, she was arrested yet again and suffered injuries while resisting arrest.

Many newspapers carried photos with captions identifying them as having been shot during the trial. Not true. Cameras were not allowed during court sessions. At recesses photographers descended. Often the principals would obligingly reenact the day's big moments. TOP: Attorneys Arthur Crowley and Albert DeStefano make a show of examining *Confidential*. BOTTOM: Fred Meade wipes a tear from Marjorie's eye. She certainly looks ready for her close-up.

Maureen O'Hara was so clearly furious that she scared the hell out of everyone. Look at the way she stares into the screen after John Wayne in one of those Ford epics and you'll get the picture. The fiery Irish lass (as all the newspapers endlessly called her in a number of variations) hotly defended her womanly honor, assailed Mordaunt-Smith, a fellow Irishman, no less, for telling fibs, and generally riveted the courtroom. Passport in hand to prove dates she was out of the country, witnesses lined up to confirm her story if the passport wasn't proof enough, she tore into the story about petting in the back row of Grauman's like a terrier shaking a rat in its teeth. She was an effective witness, indignation coming out of every pore. Crowley, however, was quick to point out to the jury that Miss O'Hara made quite a good living by making folks believe any number of things, that she was, in fact, an actress, and a very good one.

Miss O'Hara did not necessarily take this as a compliment. Miss O'Hara was furious. She was furious in 1957. She is still furious today.

Crowley had a few other tricks up his sleeve. He asked again and again how often O'Hara had been at Grauman's. She testified under oath that she had only been there twice, both times with her brother for premieres. Crowley had another witness though, a girl who worked behind the candy counter. She testified that not only did she remember Maureen O'Hara being there, but that all the ushers were talking about what was happening in Row 35. Was Miss O'Hara lying about having only been there the two times? Yes, the girl said. Ritzi snarled, asking the girl how she could be sure that it hadn't been a premiere when she saw O'Hara at the theater?

Because the candy counter was always closed for premieres.

Miss O'Hara stormed that the girl was lying, that Harrison was nothing but a scandal monger. (For the record, it would be interesting to know why O'Hara feels so above *Confidential* and its reportage, yet felt perfectly comfortable making the allegation in her memoir that John Ford was gay. Such a scandal monger is our Irish lass...) Crowley still has no idea why she has remained so enthralled with the story.

Maybe she likes the publicity, likes being a crusader, Joan of Arc. Who knows.

Dandridge was beautiful and poised on the stand. She stuck to the fact that race restrictions in Lake Tahoe made it impossible—not unlikely or improbable—*impossible* that she could have been arm-in-arm with a white man anywhere at that hotel at all. There were no people of color on the jury. No one on either side questioned the fairness of segregation, nor did any of the American press. The calculation for the prosecution was whether the jury was more likely to believe a White schlock-meister or a Black woman. No one in the courtroom (except possibly Dandridge herself) had been raised to accept a Black person's word over the word of a White man. The way everyone (except the Europeans) casually accepted the racism in the courtroom is breathtaking today.

Lost in all of this were any of the issues the trial was supposed to be about—such as the legal definitions and boundaries of the First Amendment, of obscenity, and of libel. Everything was dominated by emotion, by show biz, and he said-she said bickering.

Crowley made much of the public service articles in *Confidential*—correctly pointing out that the abortion article under fire in no way supported abortion (the advocacy of which was a crime in California at that time) but that the story actually warned women against the practice. For all his attempts at seriousness, though, the lurid nature of a lot of the so-called public service articles was readily apparent. Crowley even had passages from popular novels read into the record. If they weren't obscene, why should the magazine be?

The last gasp of energy provided by O'Hara and Dandridge quickly died as the trial petered off into its finish, with the prosecutors gamely trying to make their final arguments even as they absolutely must have been aware that if they managed to win there would be so many grounds for appeal that the win would be meaningless. The worst of Judge Walker's procedural mistakes was letting the surprise witness Paul Gregory allege blackmail in the middle of a trial that had nothing to do with blackmail. That alone would overturn a guilty verdict. Crowley had made mincemeat of him anyway but to this day he is flabbergasted that the prosecutors used Gregory, believing these holier-than-thou men actually put a witness on the stand knowing full well that his story was a lie. Just the sort of thing they believed Harrison and *Confidential* did all the time.

The People v. *Confidential* started out as a sham investigation, it opened up into a pointless trial, and it finished without proving much of anything about anyone. Sort of like the Clinton Impeachment.

Ritzi closed with a Bible story, about a character named Susanna who resisted attempts by the elders to seduce and then compromise her. He believed this to be somehow relevant in some way to something or other. Even the American press was baffled, never mind the Europeans, who thought the whole thing was just insane.

The six week "show" closed and the case went to the jury, who happily settled into a new life of room service and poolside dining at the Ambassador Hotel where they were sequestered. Happiness didn't last though. Deliberations were hostile and ugly. Some of the jurors refused to allow the foreman to read passages from the current literature Crowley introduced at trial, since they found the passages obscene (more grounds for appeal). They argued about anything and everything—except any issues having to do with points of law relevant to the trial. One juror asked Judge Walker to read an entire opinion by the Supreme Court defining obscenity, a request Walker deemed "impossible." At one point the personal attacks among jurors reached such a peak that bailiffs had to subdue one of them who threatened to throw a fellow juror out the window (further grounds for appeal). Still, they managed to keep it up for 17 days, a California state record at the time.

Marjorie and Fred waited it out in Palm Springs, distancing themselves from the tension and publicity surrounding the trial. As much as she was acutely aware of the stakes involved, and thoroughly indignant about Paul Gregory's blackmail allegations, Marjorie kept herself as unaware as possible of much of the controversy swirling around her. She didn't read the papers. Didn't listen to the news. On some level she was aware that the trial was getting massive attention, but she just blocked it all out, along with Rushmore's betrayal, Quillan's allegations, and as much of the rest of it as she could.

It was just the family business.

Marjorie had gone to work with her uncle. They weren't these *criminals*, creeping around in alleyways. They were fine, educated, sophisticated people. Café Society.

However the verdict turned out, it was clear there had been a real sea change in the public's view of *Confidential* and Robert Harrison. The trial became such a farce, that somewhere along the way the magazine and the man started becoming a joke too. Late night comedians took potshots constantly. Stan Freberg broadcast what he called "A Condensed Version of the *Confidential* Magazine Trial"—a 90 second series of clanging sound effects ending with a gasbag and a slow fizzle.

OCTOBER 1, 1957: The jury took its final vote and split seven to five for conviction. They informed Judge Walker they were hopelessly deadlocked and he declared a mistrial.

According to Crowley the vote should have been six to six. A female bailiff broke the law by telling the jurors she had heard that one of them was being bribed by the defense. Upon hearing that, one of the six who was voting to acquit switched sides and voted guilty (more grounds for appeal).

Harrison immediately declared himself the big winner, throwing a party for Art Crowley at Mama Leone's back in New York with a big banner saying "Crowley For President!" Harrison tried to give Crowley a new Lincoln, but his young lawyer turned him down.

> *I already had a new Cadillac. What did I need with two cars?*

Bob's ultimate tribute was picking up Crowley and taking him to the airport in his white convertible—with a violinist playing "Mr. Wonderful" the whole way—not just in the car—but through the airport as well. To this day Art Crowley can't believe how grateful and gracious Harrison was to him.

Of all my clients, and believe me, I've had a million of them, Bob Harrison was the most grateful. For years afterwards, anytime I was coming to New York he told me to use his hotel suite, he got me show tickets, anything I wanted. He was just a remarkable man. Amazing. Right after the trial he sent me a blank check, told me to fill in anything I wanted. I sent it back to him and told him, You fill it out. A blank check! Can you imagine? We stayed friends for years. He and I would have dinner with Winchell when I came to New York. But that had its drawbacks. Dinner with Winchell was always about Winchell. He had the most colossal ego of anyone I ever met. But Harrison? He was just great.

Assistant Attorney General Linn and Deputy District Attorney Ritzi were clearly losers. It was supposed to have been a very different case. Even as they publicly boasted of how they would win in the retrial, and even as Judge Walker seemed to take it on faith that there would be another trial, doubts surfaced immediately among the prosecution about whether to go for another round. They knew their best surprise, the illegal inclusion of Paul Gregory's testimony, wouldn't fly a second time.

Then on October 26, 1957, in a separate case entirely, the conviction of a boxer, Art Aragon, on charges of conspiracy, for fixing a fight, was thrown out of court on appeal. The unanimous ruling charged a miscarriage of justice marked by prejudicial actions on the part of both the judge and prosecutor: *Judge Herbert Walker and Deputy District Attorney William Ritzi.* Most of the legal issues were similar to the ones in the *Confidential* case, and many of Walker's rulings in both cases on questions of admissible evidence and law were equally similar.

If they attempted to retry the case against *Confidential* they would almost certainly lose. But all that moral indignation remained and the threat of another trial lingered. Harrison loved his magazine. He had created and nurtured it into a national hit. He believed wholeheartedly that he could win a retrial, but had to think long and hard about whether or not he could put Marjorie through it.

He had to make a choice—whether to keep protecting his beloved magazine or to protect his family.

Harrison settled the case with California, on the exact same terms they had agreed to before the trial ever started: Two $5,000 fines for indecency—one for the article on "The Abortion Pill" and the other for the story on the "Vine That Makes You Virile"—and Harrison agreed to stop aggressively pursuing Hollywood gossip. It was better this way. Harrison had never really developed a taste for prolonged animosity and trench warfare anyway. His five-year run had made him rich, famous even. That had to be enough.

All charges were dropped against Robert Harrison, Marjorie and Fred Meade, Francesca de Scaffa, Albert DeStefano, A. P. Govoni, Dan and Helen Studin, Edith Tobias, and Michael Tobias.

It was all over.

Except for the murder and suicide.

❯

PART FOUR

HUSH-HUSH HARI-KARI

ZEITGEIST GETS ZIPPERED

HUSH-HUSH HARI-KARI
Zeitgeist Gets Zippered

JANUARY 2, 1958. A frigid New York night. Blood is everywhere. The taxi driver is terrified. He slams his foot on the gas and shoots down the street. As he screeches to a stop in front of the nearest police station, the two dead bodies in the back of his cab fly forward and then slump backward again.

> *Why me, why tonight?! I was just minding my own damned business! And who's gonna clean up this mess, anyhow?!*

Howard Rushmore was back in New York when the trial ended in September 1957, flat broke and unemployed. No magazine would hire a writer who had just testified against his employer. The friends he thought he could count on, the right wing politicians, other conservative columnists—they all fell away, seemingly embarrassed to be seen with him. After all he had done for them. Now this.

Helping to "bring down" Harrison was supposed to have given him a clean start—allowing him to put the sleazy world of gossip rags behind him and be the hero to prosecutors and the public alike. Nothing ever worked out the way Howard thought it would, it never had, not really, not once in his life. He was freezing his ass off and Harrison had gotten off scott-free, with all his money, and the last laugh. The Meades were whooping it up back in Hollywood, and what did Rushmore have? Nothing. Not a damned thing.

His black mood chased him through the last months of 1957. Rushmore had always had problems with depression, but in the past he could beat it back somehow, move on to the next crusade, the next enemy—turn his inner bitterness and self-loathing outward instead of drowning in his own poison. He was sinking further, everything churning, the betrayals, the drinking, the drugs.

His marriage was in tatters. It had always been volatile, and Frances Rushmore had looked for a way out before. In September 1955 cops had rescued the suicidal Frances Rushmore by fishing her out of the East River. She was shocked and exasperated with them.

> *Don't you understand? I didn't fall, and I wasn't pushed. I jumped.*

Her own alcoholism worsened as Rushmore's beatings and threats grew constant. She couldn't take it anymore, and a few days before Christmas 1957, Frances Rushmore moved herself and her daughter into an apartment in Greenwich Village. She was determined to cut her ties to Howard. It was a difficult holiday for him. He spent it drinking alone. Somehow he made it through New Year's Day and set off the next evening for his old apartment on the Upper East Side, where Frances was packing up some remaining belongings. Perhaps if she hadn't picked that particular time to be there, things would have ended differently. The taxi driver, Edward Pearlman, recalled the couple arguing outside his cab when he pulled over to pick up Frances Rushmore on the night of January 2, 1958.

Both Howard and Frances entered the cab.

Moments into the ride, a gunshot rang out, and then another. The driver slammed on his brakes. Blood was everywhere. It was all he could do not to wretch. He stared for a split second in horror at the two twisted, lifeless bodies, there slumped in his backseat. He was no doctor, but he knew there was no reason to go to a hospital. With a screech of his tires he hightailed it for the police station.

> *What could make a guy do a thing like that?*

Frances Rushmore would be the last person Howard Rushmore betrayed.

Rushmore garnered the biggest headlines of his life with the murder of the woman he loved and with his own suicide. Marjorie will never understand or forgive him.

> *Frances was so sweet and kind. I just loved her. I knew she had a drinking problem, but she was never a mean drunk, not like Howard. She didn't have a mean bone in her body. It was just a tragedy.*
>
> *I mean, I've said it before, I never liked Howard... But to do a thing like that? Who would think, who could imagine...? Why? Was he just evil? I'll never understand it...*

Harrison had flown into New York that morning from a trip to Florida. When he got into a taxi, the driver turned and asked him if he'd heard the big news: The publisher of *Confidential* had just shot and killed his wife, and then shot himself, right through the head, in the back of a cab! Bob laughed and told the cab driver that he was not only very much alive, but that he didn't have a wife.

Everyone wanted quotes.

DeStefano said he was sorry, but couldn't stop himself from recounting how Rushmore had bitten the hand that fed him, even after Harrison had agreed to cover him for future legal claims.

Harrison was nicer, calling Howard a troubled man, and saying how sorry he was for Frances and her daughter, who now had no one.

Even Clarence Linn and William Ritzi got into the act, though neither one had anything particularly nice to say. An old friend was anonymously quoted as mourning him in a backhanded fashion:

> *I don't think he knew what he was doing these last few years. Yet once he was a gentleman.*

After all the hype, the whispered suggestions that maybe Chalky Wright was murdered, the phony reports of Francesca de Scaffa trying to commit suicide, the fabrications and exaggerations of wrecked lives and careers—after all that make believe—this was the real thing.

Jealous rage.

Betrayal.

Alcohol.

Drugs.

Two people dead.

Few today know Howard Rushmore's name but the Rushmore murder-suicide was almost certainly the seed of the sinister aura that would grow around tales of the magazine as the years went by. It made everything that was so funny just a few months earlier seem as ugly and misshapen as the thoughts boomeranging in Howard's head when he set out with a gun in his pocket on that cold night.

The Man, His Magazine & The Movieland Massacre That Changed Hollywood Forever

DAILY ☀ NEWS

FINAL ★★★★

NEW YORK'S PICTURE NEWSPAPER ®

5¢

Vol. 39, No. 166 · · · · · · · · · · · · · New York 17, N.Y., Saturday, January 4, 1958 · · · · · · · WEATHER: Fair, continued cold.

CONFIDENTIAL'S EX-BOSS SLAYS WIFE, SELF

Story on Page 2

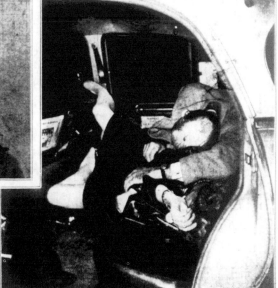

Death Rides Cab To Police Station

The body of Howard Rushmore, 45, former Red and onetime editor of Confidential magazine, lies sprawled across body of his wife Frances, 40, in cab near the D. 101th St. police station [→]. Two bullets hit her fine face through the roof of the cab. Rushmore then put a bullet in his brain. Mrs. Rushmore is shown in recent foto [▲]. Cabbie reported they quarreled bitterly during ride from 99th and Madison Ave. —*Story p. 2*

Harrison, flush with cash and looking for his Next Big Thing, still appeared in public with a succession of beautiful women at New York nightspots, he took to dabbling in the stock market, and plotting a comeback, testing the waters with one-shot magazines such as *Menace of the Sex Deviates* and *Naked New York*, before launching the little-remembered *Inside News*, with stories like, "Castro's Sex Invasion of Washington."

Not a step up in the world.

He settled the suits with Liberace, O'Hara, and Flynn in July 1958 for pennies on the dollar. Clean slate. But Harrison had lost the publication that guaranteed him the best tables at the Stork Club, the Harwyn Club, and El Morocco. Hollywood didn't bother with him now. Harrison said he didn't care. He still had a lot of money; he had his sisters; and the companionship of attractive young women. There would be an ugly bust-up with June Frew, but the lovely happenstance of meeting Regi Ruta made up for that.

For a while, as the '50s gave way to a new decade, Harrison didn't mind that things quieted down. So many storms had come and gone—1957 alone was like a series of recurrent hurricanes—that's what he believed finally wore him down, the drama, not the lawsuits. Within three months of Harrison's April 1958 announcement of a new "hands off Hollywood" policy *(Pssst! It's New!)* where in accordance with his settlement with the California Attorney General and Los Angeles District Attorney, Robert Harrison agreed not to cover celebrity scandal, he pulled the plug for good, selling the rights to *Confidential* and *Whisper* for a bargain basement $25,000 to writer-editor and self-styled entrepreneur Hy Steirman.

Back in Beverly Hills, Marjorie and Fred were out of a job, with two kids to support, and the upkeep of a home. They didn't worry about it. They hadn't exactly put aside any money for a rainy day—Marjorie remembers spending money like there was no tomorrow. In 1955 and 1956 cash practically rained down from back East—but when the end came, Uncle Bob came through again, with $150,000 as a thank-you for Marjorie and Fred's hard work. Fred would manage his growing real estate concerns and Marjorie set her mind into gear for her new incarnation as a Beverly Hills society matron.

For a time, the new *Confidential* owner Hy Steirman mandated more non-Hollywood stories and a softer approach to Tinseltown. An April 1959 issue, for instance, concentrated on the epidemic of bankruptcy, useless reducing pills, rabies, high television repair bills, fake diamonds, and bad dentists. The only two entertainment industry stories made the shocking allegations that Louella Parsons wasn't nice, and that Maria Callas was ambitious. Sales nosedived. The May 1960 issue led with "Castro Raped My Teenaged Daughter." Fidel wasn't likely to sue for libel in a U.S. court. But circulation continued to fall. A return to Hollywood smut in the '60s and '70s didn't help either, even with stories that ranged from a May 1962 article about an obscure actress confessing not just her sex change operation, but her affairs with Marlene Dietrich, Joe DiMaggio, and Bob Hope; to a May 1962 article about Elizabeth Taylor called "Tempest in a C-Cup"; and on to a January 1971 free illustrated swingers' manual. *Whisper* was reduced to stories about "Pagan Orgies of America's Voodoo Cults" and "Africa's Strangest Tribes"—with circulation nose-diving for it as well.

The trial settlement killed Harrison's magazine empire.

It killed *Confidential.*

But the planet kept spinning. Just as the *Confidential* era was ending, a new tabloid was born: *The New York Enquirer.* It would have a much longer shelf-life than *Confidential* once it became *The National Enquirer.* At the start there were no Hollywood stories at all. Gory police photos were its stock in trade, with headlines like "Mom Uses Son's Face as Ashtray," and "I Cut Out Her Heart and Stomped On It." It would be 20 years before the *Enquirer* would publish an issue that sold more copies than *Confidential* routinely sold in its heyday—it was the issue with Elvis in his coffin.

As Harrison thought up his next move, he and Walter Winchell liked keeping themselves busy riding around in police cars together at night, through the end of the '50s and beginning of the '60s—both contemplating new true-crime ventures that would never come to pass. Harrison maintained his man-about-town status, holding up his head regardless of how much the media sneered at the Sultan of Sleaze being forced into selling out.

CONFIDENTIAL'S NEW POLICY

Pardon us while we take a bow.

It's a proud bow.

We're proud because we like our new look which begins with this issue.

If CONFIDENTIAL seems changed . . . if you've noticed a new complexion, it's because we've broadened our outlook.

We're quitting the area of private affairs for the arena of public affairs. Some found fault with the private affairs. Some criticized.

But many eulogized and admired.

Where we pried and peeked, now we'll probe, and occasionally we'll take a poke.

If wiseacres say that we've retreated from the bedroom, we'll say yes, that's true . . . From now on we'll search and survey the thoroughfares of the globe for stories of public interest that are uncensored and off the record . . . It's a big world, a foolish world, a crazy world . . . and we'll be taking you on an inside tour, telling the facts and naming the names.

—ROBERT HARRISON
Publisher

Dear Reader:

As the new editors of CONFIDENTIAL Magazine, we promise to continue to fight the phonies in business and showbusiness, and expose the liars, cheats and racketeers who prey on the public — you and us.

The former publisher, Bob Harrison, in six stormy years, built a magazine that skyrocketed into the largest-selling newsstand magazine in the world. Its impact was felt by every person, newspaper and magazine in the country. It answered a need — for no magazine could sell over 4,000,000 copies per issue without reflecting what the public demanded.

Phase one of the magazine is over.

This is phase two of CONFIDENTIAL—with a new staff, two-fisted ideas and a renewed enthusiasm.

CONFIDENTIAL will be a journalistic gadfly!

We will print stories "too hot" for other publications. We will have a strong point of view. If we don't like the new cars, we won't be afraid to tell Detroit that the new autos are five feet too long, two feet too low and $500 too high.

We will expose the showbusiness phonies, like the untalented star who receives one million dollars a year. She is a tramp all the way from New York to Hollywood. While a person's sex life is his or her own business — this star is the example our teenagers try to emulate — and with disastrous results. This is the type of sanctimonious hanky panky that deserves a spanky — from CONFIDENTIAL.

And how about product misrepresentation! Aspirin companies give each other headaches. Tobacco companies put more nicotine and tars in cigarettes than they did five years ago. And stomach acids don't — we repeat — don't burn holes in handkerchiefs — regardless of what you see on TV.

CONFIDENTIAL will continue telling the truth. It will be positive in its approach. It will be a sensational magazine that reflects the best traditions of Joseph Pulitzer and William Randolph Hearst. It will publish stories that might never be told otherwise.

Our motto will be, "We will respect the respectable, love the lovable — but detest the detestable."

Hy Steirman
EDITOR AND PUBLISHER

For her part, Marjorie threw herself into the whole society thing with vigor and maybe just a little vengeance. She had always had the concentration of a method actress, jumping fully into whatever she did. When it was the magazine, that was it, the only thing in life. Now she decided hers would be a social existence and she flung herself into it with the same kind of drive and determination. And nobody said a word about her past, or if they did, it was never to her face. She turned up at every society event, every charitable fundraiser, every show business gala, remaking herself. Her life after *Confidential* was curiously devoid of any repercussions. She became fast friends with Eartha Kitt in the '60s, when they lived near one another in the Beverly Hills flats, and Eartha did take her to task once about the way she had been covered in the magazine. Marjorie denied any responsibility and the two remain very close, visiting each other often.

Marjorie's brother Michael relocated to Los Angeles about that time. For a variety of reasons, Marjorie and Michael don't speak now. But from the '50s into the early '80s there were still good times, mainly because they both adored their mother, their aunt, and their Uncle Bob.

In 1962 Michael was in Vegas on his first of three honeymoons, when Uncle Bob decided to kidnap him for a little fun: They took some guns and shot up a field next to a U.S. Army airport. Then they went for ice cream sodas. When they got back on the road, sirens and squad cars surrounded them. They were both held as possible U.S. saboteurs until the authorities could check with the Army to determine that none of their planes had been damaged by gunfire. Bob and Michael couldn't stop laughing, gleeful as little boys, then calling Michael's new wife to warn her that he might be a little late getting back to the hotel.

The living large way of life their Uncle Bob epitomized permeated every pore of Michael and Marjorie's lives. Marjorie never thinks of herself as much like her uncle, but they were always two peas from the same pod—which is probably why he was so proud of her and cared so much. Neither one wanted notoriety exactly, but they both liked getting attention. Both were able to focus every ounce of their energy on a single goal when the situation called for it, to the exclusion of all distractions. Marjorie didn't even let the avalanche of bad press during the trial enter her daily mindset. She knew who she was in the same way Harrison did, with little self-doubt or introspective dithering.

They both loved the magazine, and they loved working on it. That's part of why Marjorie is so flabbergasted by some of the things that have been said over the years and the way *Confidential* is portrayed. She is perfectly capable of recognizing that some of the stories weren't very nice. Reminded of the Errol Flynn article she laughs with that deep rumble of hers, readily acknowledging that it must have made him pretty mad. Ava Gardner's name comes up and Marjorie says she passes no judgment, even as she tells how she knows for a fact that Ava had to move to Spain so she could live her wild, sex-crazed life without any scrutiny or moral outrage. And Marjorie gives the whole public service argument in defense of the magazine sort of half-heartedly. She knows a lot of those stories were silly, but so did anyone with any sense. They were fun, that's all. She bursts into laughter when reminded of that article saying cigarettes don't cause cancer.

Oh. Well, that's bad. Did we really say that? I don't remember.

She knows how ridiculous it is. How could she not? (During the trial, Art Crowley had appeared on television and was asked about that story. The interview show's sponsor was Marlboro. Crowley pointed out that the article would make the show's sponsor very happy. The nervous host quickly cut to a commercial.)

Marjorie doesn't try to deny any of it or apologize. They had a blast—which is the part she wants people to understand. The whole notion of the sleazy Danny Devito character creeping around in "L.A. Confidential" is offensive to her.

Where did anyone ever get that idea? It was fun! The office in New York was always exciting, with

*this one doing this, and that one doing that, and
Uncle Bob running around doing ten things at
once. We laughed all the time. There was such
energy…*

*And we had a great life in California. We raised
our boys, we had good friends—some of them
famous too, but we kept it separate, we never did a
story about someone we only knew socially.*

*Our work was never, never some kind of secret,
shameful thing. Not ever. And not once, not when
I was young and Uncle Bob started with Beauty
Parade and not in all the years with
'Confidential,' did I or anyone in my family feel
ashamed of what we did. It was exciting.
Interesting. And it gave us a fabulous life.*

Giving up his baby was hard for Harrison. This was a lot
more unfair than a rainstorm spoiling the chances of an issue
of one of his magazines on the newsstand. He believed the
onslaught of bad press was hypocritical, and far more vicious
and conspiratorial than anything he had ever published. *The
New York Post* called him a "Freudian playboy caught in bed
with his own neuroses."

Suddenly he became one of his own subjects. It was as if
all the private dicks who gathered material for *Confidential*
were suddenly trailing him instead, rummaging through his
family closet, trying to get the inside skinny on what made him
tick, why he's always out with busty blondes, whether being so
close to his sisters is a little weird—and the whole thing made
Harrison furious. He lashed out in the pages of the *Post*:

*This is just a cruel way of getting at me. I'm so
sick of all the rehashing. God! The way the press
twists everything! It's so slanted and untrue.*

You don't even need to know how to *spell* Schadenfreude to picture the gleeful dancing in the streets across Hollywood and up and down Broadway at reading a quote like that. To the legions of those holding grudges this was tantamount to *Harrison* being the one accused of practically having sex in the back row of Grauman's Chinese, to *him* having to read about himself mixing races and having sex outside in Lake Tahoe, to *him* being publicly humiliated for drunkenly busting in on his movie star ex-wife and kicking the wrong door down, to *him* being the lavender lad shaking in his boots, hoping his career wouldn't go down the drain when his fairy frolics hit the headlines.

An obvious modern corollary is Martha Stewart, a woman whose fall made so many people so deliriously, and irrationally pleased with themselves. The general glee became so obnoxious that some who never cared for Stewart's dour precision found ourselves hotly defending her; mystified at how such a smart, talented woman could be made into a scapegoat for ills that infect every aspect of modern corporate life in America. It was like Harrison being blamed for everyone feeling ashamed of their own prurience in the '50s.

Along with all the snide stories, Harrison was angry and resentful that no one else in the media gave any support during the long fight in California, believing the First Amendment issues were clear, and that *The New York Times, Time, Look, Life, The Washington Post,* and every other news entity in the country should have rallied to his cause.

He was right.

There were Freedom of Speech issues, most of which got completely obscured by posturing and blustering on both sides, but even so, the stakes were real. Even the A.C.L.U., an ally in the battle with the USPS (though they made it perfectly clear that they did not condone the content of the magazine *at all*) failed to make much of a stink during the libel trial.

A lot of voices were silent during the trial, including the trades. Neither *The Hollywood Reporter* nor *Variety* gave the trial any coverage at all. Not one story. This when *The New York Daily News, The Los Angeles Times, The Los Angeles*

Mirror-News, and *The New York Post* were publishing daily accounts of each and every development.

Even the Grey Lady herself, *The New York Times,* and the oh-so-serious *Washington Post* provided heavy *Confidential* trial coverage through the end of July, almost every day in August, and during the first half of September in 1957.

> *Never mind the ruckus at that school in Arkansas and the Negroes, what did Maureen O'Hara wear on the stand?*

But no, the Hollywood trades stayed mum.

Even now Army Archerd is closemouthed about it when first asked.

> *I have nothing to tell you.*

He then rather kindly had a research assistant do a little digging and came up with the same conclusion: *Variety* never wrote about *Confidential.*

And that's the point.

When asked *why* his publication never wrote about Confidential or the trial, Archerd says he doesn't know, that the magazine was not at all a part of his world.

> *I never read it. I never had anything to do with them.*

But it was the biggest trial in Hollywood!

> *If you say so.*

Interview over.

The Hollywood Reporter made not one mention either, this despite the fact that "Rambling Reporter," one of their most popular columns, appeared every day; its 1,500 words written by Mike Connolly, the guy who took the Meades under his wing and introduced them to Hollywood society. So many words about so little. On August 13, 1957, for instance, *The New York Times* headlined, "Admitted Ex-Prostitute Says Publisher of *Confidential* Wanted Lewd Stories;" *The Washington Post*: "Clark Gable Linked to Party Girl Who Wrote for *Confidential*;" *The New York Daily News*: "Mag Trial Witness Drowns;" and *The Los Angeles Mirror-News* put, "Scandal Tip Methods Told," as their front page banner. On that same day Mike Connolly wrote about new movie projects for Alan Ladd and Barbara Stanwyck, the two-week trip to Hawaii taken by Rock Hudson and wife Phyllis, Cecil B. DeMille's birthday cake served on the set of his newest Paramount picture, Gary Cooper's desire to do another western, and Sterling Hayden's decision to act as his own agent for television roles.

And it wasn't as if the trades only printed fluff about the biz. One of the biggest stories through August 1957 in both *Variety* and *The Hollywood Reporter* was about the court case that had sprung up when the truth emerged about L.B. Mayer's secret plan to seize control of Loew's Corporation, which was the parent company to MGM. It was incredibly critical reportage of a man who was once the biggest powerhouse in Hollywood.

But the *Confidential* trial didn't exist.

The trades just went about their business, reporting on hirings and firings, box office grosses, looming strikes, and production deals. Talk about funhouse mirrors. It was like the biggest story to Hollywood in decades wasn't even happening, like putting their heads in the sand would make it all go away. They missed the big story. Even as they finally made mention of the agreement that ended the whole drama, breathing little sighs of relief that *Confidential* would stop digging in their celluloid garden, they showed no sign of understanding that it wasn't Harrison winning the battle and Hollywood winning the war, but just the opposite.

Robert Harrison changed press coverage of Hollywood forever. In fact, after selling the magazine, the new publisher figured out a few years later that he was free to resume printing trash about Tinseltown in the magazine, since he wasn't the one who made a settlement in California.

Confidential would never again be the shining star it was from 1953-1957, but it would go on dishing dirt all the way to the early '70s. The continued publication of *Confidential*, though, has little to do with Bob Harrison's true legacy, which is actually more about self-acceptance—though he probably would never have thought about it in that way, or perhaps even really comprehended the idea. There's a reason secular humanism is so frightening to social conservatives—because it's virtually unstoppable. For example, in a peculiar way, the Right is actually on target about the whole condom-in-schools issue. Not literally. There's little or no evidence that the availability of condoms causes anyone to become sexual earlier, or that it does anything other than protect kids from sexually transmitted diseases and pregnancy. But normalizing the idea of sex does have an effect. Something that used to be immoral is more acceptable, you can talk about it without shame. The secular humanist looks at that as progress. The social conservative sees it as a disaster.

Opening those doors, exposing how people really live, making the taboo commonplace—these are all paths that ultimately lead to self-acceptance.

Lots of people credit Robert Harrison with single-handedly tearing the veil off of Hollywood's hypocrisy, exposing her sordid secrets, forever ruining her façade of beautiful make-believe. He certainly had a huge effect on that process. Yet a wide convergence of societal and political events made *Confidential* possible. You can't credit the magazine with all of the changes in society that came afterward, with the swinging-druggy '60s, the sexy '70s, the selfish '80s, the reckless '90s, or this strange first decade of a new century that is only just now starting to be defined in the public consciousness.

Harrison didn't start the Cold War.

He didn't come up with Duck and Cover.

He didn't make penicillin available to the whole country, wiping out the fear of VD overnight.

He wasn't responsible for America's fascination with gigantic breasts in the '50s.

He didn't try to send millions of women who did vibrant, interesting work during World War II back to the dreamy torpor of suburbia in the '50s.

He didn't elect anybody, execute anybody, or make anyone rich, except his own family and friends.

But he did do *something.*

Harrison was both smart and lucky—a combination that has to be there for lightning to strike the way it did for *Confidential.* He was innovative and remarkably astute about what his readers wanted to read.

Part of his lasting contribution is how he opened a huge door for his readers into their own quirks and kinks. Ultimately it wasn't so much to do with what his readers thought about Hollywood or about Washington or High Society after gleefully tearing through an issue of *Confidential,* it came down to what they thought of *themselves.*

But even Harrison himself had it wrong. So did most of the people wringing their hands for 50 years over the tabloid terror he was supposed to have wreaked. They all thought the magazine was about the *What* of it all—*What* this star did, or *What* that politician got away with. And yes, on the literal face of it, that is indeed what the magazine reported. *What!??!*—the reaction Bob was always going for, that mixture of happy outrage and shock. However, in her own way, Marjorie is more on the right track when she emphasizes the fun they all had when they were doing the magazine, the spirit of optimism and playfulness. Because *that* was Uncle Bob's enduring legacy.

Not the *What.* The *How.*

Get past the politically incorrect language. Look deeper than the scandal. The tone of the stories is so childlike, so breathlessly excited yet alternating with tongue-in-cheek insouciance. It's that tone. The *How* made all the difference.

Once readers started laughing about sex, adultery, drunkenness, drug addiction, homosexuality, and anyone and everyone's libido—once that barrier was crossed—there was no going back. None of those taboos could ever be as frightening, and certainly never as hush-hush or shameful, not when the gods and goddesses of the silver screen, the carefully cultivated personalities the public were encouraged to love beyond reason, were having such fun doing it.

Whatever the story. Whatever the outcome.

The tone of the coverage changed how readers felt. It changed what they were willing to accept, in their idols, in themselves. That's Bob Harrison's true albeit unintentional legacy. No further hype, publicity stunts, or scandal necessary.

Harrison made a lot of money in the stock market in the years after he folded the magazine. He made a lot. He lost a lot, particularly by betting big on Studebaker. But he always came out ahead in the end. It definitely frustrated him that his various magazine ventures never took off, but Marjorie and Michael both brush off any idea of him as some sort of lonely has-been, mourning the loss of his tabloid empire. Life went on. The nightclubbing went on. The family got together. They went to the Jersey Shore. Everyone still had a blast—a quieter blast maybe—but a blast all the same.

Helen and Edith stayed with Bob, managing his various business ventures, shielding him from life's unpleasantness, and letting him know every single day of his life just how important a man he was. They didn't much like talking about the *Confidential* years, not after the fact, not to the media, their friends, or even their family. If the bad press hit Bob like a speeding train, it was almost unendurable to Helen and Edith. All of these horrible people attacking their baby brother, saying the most terrible things, making fun of him, ridiculing him and his family, and there didn't seem to be anything they could do about it. If they could have marched into every single editorial conference room of every publication that wrote about Bob and the magazine, and if they could have personally bawled out every writer and editor who had ever said an unkind word— well, they would have. It just got too big. Too messy. Too exhausting.

Winchell just faded away. In the late '60s he would hang around El Morocco jamming printed copies of his columns into the hands of startled patrons, bellowing: "This is the Walter

Winchell column for today! You don't want to miss this!" Liz Smith called it pathetic; truly the end of everything.

Most published accounts of Harrison's later years paint a similar picture of him. Tom Wolfe made hay out of Winchell abruptly dismissing Harrison one day at Lindy's deli in 1964 when WW was there with his granddaughter. His apparent snub is supposed to be evidence that post-*Confidential*, Harrison was reduced to overselling his own association with a better-known fellow has-been as a way of making himself seem more important. No other explanation is contemplated. Who knows? On that day maybe WW was preoccupied with his granddaughter; in a snit over something, which happened a lot; or wasn't wearing his glasses. The long friendship between the two men, particularly after *Confidential's* era of success finally ended, was witnessed by many—friends, foes, and family alike. Certainly Winchell's importance to the rise of the magazine is too well-documented to discount.

Marjorie is surprised now when asked about her own transition, about whether it was hard to segue into the quiet domestic thing after such an action-packed life of finding stories, checking sources, and meeting deadlines. To her it was simple. She just switched her focus. Yesterday was the past. Today is going to be great.

She and Fred were good partners during the magazine years, but even with the success and the excitement, she didn't feel as if her marriage was what a marriage was supposed to be. She wasn't passionate. Fred was great, a good man, a good father, but there wasn't the spark she felt there should be. During the whole crazy run, somewhere around 1955 or 1956, when she decided she wanted a divorce, Marjorie was shocked when Uncle Bob, her mom and dad, and Aunt Helen wouldn't support her in the decision. She's still shocked. They had never said no before, not about anything that mattered to her, not ever. Marjorie thought she would fly out to New York, get their blessing, return to California, and end the marriage. Instead, she found herself facing a wall of disapproval.

*Does he drink? Is he unfaithful? A gambler?
No? Then you have no business walking out of
this marriage!*

The magazine changed Marjorie forever. She became her own woman—growing up, accepting a larger share of responsibility, building a business, surviving the trial with her dignity intact. It was all part of a process of ripening. Though in truth, the biggest step for Marjorie had been moving away from home in the first place.

Being a whole continent away from the clan meant getting used to making her own decisions in a way she is positive she never would have done if she had stayed in New York. Never. It wasn't that her family was overbearing or controlling, it was that she never had time to question any of it. Life was too exciting, too fast. The Harrisons, Tobiases, and Studins were so sure all the time of what the right thing for her should be, that she didn't even think about it—she just went on to the next day, the next event, the next issue of the magazine. With physical distance came a different rhythm, even as the family stayed very close, very tight.

Marjorie didn't divorce Fred until the early '70s. It was amicable enough. Fred had turned away from the society life Marjorie craved. He wanted some peace and quiet— something that wasn't going to happen if Marjorie could help it. The kids were young men by then. Uncle Bob, Edith, and Helen left her alone about it. Her brother Michael never really understood what happened. He thought Fred Meade was great. She met her second husband, blue-movie distributor Bob Bernhard, at a party soon after. If her feelings about Fred weren't what she thought a marriage should be, several weeks of going out with Bernhard convinced her that he was the guy who could make it all different. They were happy together for almost three years before he had a massive coronary. Hoping to find a new focus, she opened a restaurant called Ruffage, at Richard Simmons' Anatomy Asylum, in partnership with Simmons and her brother Michael. It thrived for a time, but Michael in particular found the partnership with Simmons difficult, believing that they could have all made a fortune were it not for the infighting that ultimately destroyed the venture.

Michael went in and out of various business ventures. His luck with the ladies was always good, but maybe his experiences with Uncle Bob jaded him a little bit. His wife Barbara gasps and laughs as she tells friends how a few months after they were married in 1982 she met him at the door wearing nothing but stilettos, a push-up bra, garters and stockings.

He just asked her what they were having for dinner.

Garters and stockings? Michael had been surrounded by those kinds of accessories before he even started shaving.

Meanwhile Marjorie threw herself back into the charity party circuit. Her curiosity remained fully alive, leading her to travel, to read, to gossip, and to participate as fully as possible in life every day.

She met her third husband in the early '80s, veteran screenwriter Marty Roth. They held the wedding at the Friars Club in Beverly Hills, and Marjorie began her next great focus in life. They were terrific partners, and she easily became part of his business and social life. That helped her weather the accident that left one of her sons paralyzed, the deaths of her mother and aunt, and then of the paralyzed son. Then Marty died too in 2000.

When depression hit harder and deeper than it ever had before, Marjorie wasn't going to let that be the end of the story. She got some help. Her therapist advised her to throw herself back into things, going, doing, meeting—so once again she did the social butterfly trip, but this time it felt empty.

She has many friends and never lacks for activities, but it's the focus she misses, having something consume her totally.

FEBRUARY 19, 1978, NEW YORK. Michael Tobias was in New York with Edith, Helen, and Bob at the office. Bob called out to Edith to bring him a file. They heard him gasp and say, "Oh my..." Michael rushed into his Uncle Bob's office and found him slumped in his chair at his desk.

It was the end of the world.

There were obituaries that mainly mentioned the old scandals, the sense of *Confidential* as somehow being singularly sinister, the shameful legacy of a man who would do anything for a buck. But there were also hundreds of condolence letters from people who knew and respected him, and more than a few universities hoping to acquire his papers—knowing that love it or hate it, *Confidential* holds a unique place in the history of American journalism.

The funeral was small and it took place in New Jersey: Two facts that probably wouldn't have made Bob happy. Edith and Helen just stood there in shock, utterly unable to fathom the idea that their baby brother was gone. Michael kept remembering the sound of his uncle's last gasp in the office. Marjorie cried herself to sleep.

Dead. You just couldn't believe it. Uncle Bob was dead...

AUGUST 27, 2003, WEST HOLLYWOOD. FADE IN: At a booth in Mel's Diner on Sunset Boulevard, I was having lunch with Marjorie Roth. I gingerly approached her about whether she may or may not be interested in talking about *Confidential* and her uncle, in revisiting the whole story of the magazine's rise and fall. Marjorie was a bit ambivalent about a book being written. While she loved the idea of celebrating her Uncle Bob's achievements, the idea of bringing up the whole nightmare of the trial, of dredging up her past notoriety—that made her anxious.

So I started asking her about tiaras.

I'd heard stories about those women in the group Marjorie belongs to, the Crown Jewels, and I wanted the inside scoop. I imagined it as a cross between playing Barbies and being in a beauty pageant. But Marjorie was circumspect about the Jewels, and didn't want to invade the privacy of her friends.

For some reason, the Crown Jewels stayed on my mind, though, and I looked for other sources to fill in the blanks. I learned that apparently it all started when one day a few society women were sitting at lunch and one of them had an epiphany: All women love to wear tiaras. Why don't they start a group and throw a tiara ball! Then somebody else excitedly suggested they call themselves the Crown Jewels. Among a certain class of women, most of whom lived in Beverly Hills, the idea spread like wildfire.

The Tiara balls are usually held at the Beverly Hills Hotel or the Hilton or the Peninsula, with dinner and dancing. Men are encouraged to attend. The luncheons are for women only. At Christmas there's a ladies' tea, where money is raised and toys are collected for needy children.

The tiara buying expeditions must be every bit as entertaining as any scene out of *Quinceañera*. Imagine it. Beverly Hills society women, in their Chanel suits, heels, and Cartier watches, all piling into their cars and trouping downtown to the garment district.

There's a neighborhood there where stores line street after street, catering to Latina fifteenth birthday extravaganzas, when young women are welcomed into adulthood with as many rhinestones and seed pearls as their families can afford. Floor to ceiling, shelves and shelves, nothing but tiaras and scepters. The grapevine has it that the president of the Crown Jewels bought herself a daytime tiara as well as a more spectacular evening one. And when she crowns the "girls" she puts the scepter on their shoulders.

Like Queen Elizabeth brandishing a sword.

Or more to the point, like the New York drag balls documented in Jennie Livingston's 1991 famously non-Oscar nominated film *Paris Is Burning*. There's also an ironic coincidence in the name: One of the most elegant and discreet gay bars in early Hollywood happened to be called the Crown Jewel. Many of the Beverly Hills members of the Crown Jewels often attend their galas escorted by gay men, the fabled "walkers" of high society. This unacknowledged, and likely unknown connection with Hollywood's lavender and baritone past seems somehow fitting. And fun.

Even as Marjorie began to talk to me about the *Confidential* years, she still didn't want to breach the privacy of the Crown Jewels. But I did hear a story that had apparently made its way around the Beverly Hills cocktail circuit about Marjorie's enthusiasm for the group:

One day several years ago on *Good Morning America*, Diane Sawyer featured a group of women happily showing off their tiaras. They were from all over the country and talked about how they loved getting together and throwing fabulous, elaborate parties. I haven't been able to trace the actual broadcast itself, but it is likely that the GMA story was about the "Sweet Potato Queens" phenomenon.

I'm told that Marjorie got a bee in her bonnet and decided she should be on television too. Ostensibly with the Crown Jewels in attendance as well. Rumor has it that Marjorie sent in a picture of herself and her friends, all wearing their tiaras, all dressed to kill in their formal evening gowns—positive that one look would make Diane Sawyer book them for their own guest spot.

Evidently Marjorie never got a response.

It's not a huge leap of faith to suppose that Marjorie would have liked to have been on television—with or without her tiara. She has spent a lifetime flirting with fame, crossing over into her brief but sizzling notoriety during the 1957 libel and obscenity trial, but then reclaiming her identity, and fashioning her public persona safely into her current society lady niche. She likes the limelight, and she settles into it easily, wearing her status as a latter day belle of the ball with an easy, offhand grace that only occasionally slips into an imperious sense of entitlement.

Bob Harrison was a pea from the same pod. The idea of going on television with Diane Sawyer is not unlike the Café Society dreams that propelled Harrison to create his magazine empire. He and Marjorie both shared a fundamental, if unanalyzed, need to be center stage. Bob wasn't introspective or particularly interested in subtext, yet he could quickly size up a situation and see the whole story faster and more fully than most so-called serious journalists. He was always very clear about the role his magazine had to play.

> *Some of these people we wrote about would be very indignant at first, but I knew goddamned well it was a beautiful act. What they really wanted was another story in 'Confidential.' It was great publicity for them. The sad thing is that you couldn't put out a magazine like 'Confidential' again. All the movie stars have started writing books about themselves! Look at the stuff Errol Flynn wrote, and Zsa Zsa, and all of them. They tell all! No magazine can compete with that.*

Harrison would probably not have been surprised that his life's work is now remembered as something sinister. Since 1958 he saw glimmers of the writing on the wall. It all went back to Rushmore. Bob knew it that day in the cab at the airport, when the driver told him the publisher of *Confidential* had killed himself. The murder-suicide story would grow and multiply, tearing into public consciousness. And Bob saw it all, knowing instinctively that the horrific image of those two dead, blood-spattered bodies was going to stick to him like glue.

Robert Harrison died rich and happy, surrounded by people who loved him. So where's the sizzle? The rise and fall of a man and his most beloved creation should be a morality tale. Lessons learned. Paradise lost. Instead, we get an irascible charmer with a big bankroll in his pocket and a hot blonde on his arm.

But if you prefer, remember him as a murderous, suicidal sleaze-meister instead. Harrison probably wouldn't have minded. *Why spoil the story?* Better to be in on the joke. And best to have the last laugh.

▼

Later Years:

TOP LEFT: Bob in the early '70s, TOP RIGHT: Michael with his Aunt Helen in the late '70s, CENTER LEFT:AND RIGHT: Edith and Charles Tobias in the mid-'70s,

LEFT PAGE: Bob and Regi Ruta in the mid-'70s.

TOP LEFT: Michael and Barbara Tobias in the late '80s. TOP RIGHT: Marjorie in 1982. ABOVE: Marjorie and Marty Roth in 1988.

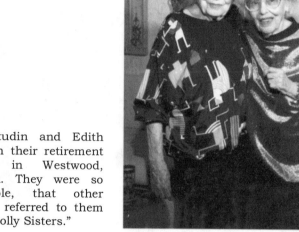

Helen Studin and Edith Tobias, in their retirement building in Westwood, California. They were so inseparable, that other residents referred to them as "The Dolly Sisters."

Michael Tobias with his mother Edith and Aunt Helen, in New York's Central Park in the late '70s.

Marjorie poses for a snap with First Lady (soon to be Senator) Hillary Rodham Clinton at a fundraising event that would become notorious for the fraud and financial shenanigans that sent the "King of Cons," Aaron Tonken, to prison.

December 1952

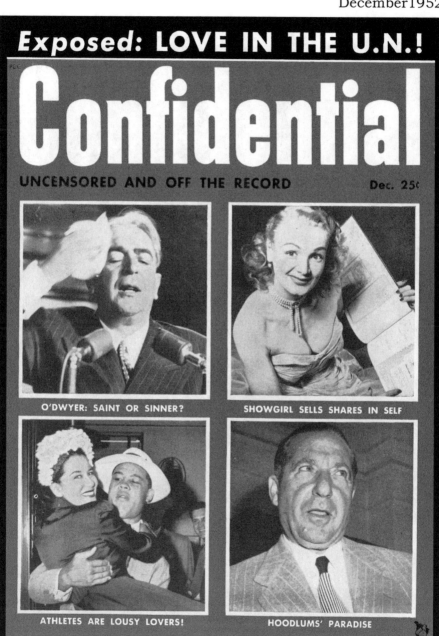

April 1953

THE JOHNNIE RAY SCANDAL!

PDC

Confidential

UNCENSORED AND OFF THE RECORD April 25¢

Exclusive!

JOHNNIE RAY: IS IT TRUE?

"I LIVED WITH TOMMY MANVILLE!"

THE MERRY WIFE OF WINDSOR

July 1953

NAMED: 1,000 'AMERICAN' NAZIS!

Confidential

UNCENSORED AND OFF THE RECORD   July 25c

BARRY GRAY: Broadway's No.1 Ingrate

BABS HUTTON: Platinum-Plated Brat

PEARL BAILEY and the Drummer Boy

DON'T MISS THE PICTURE A KING TRIED TO SUPPRESS!

See Page 12

August 1953

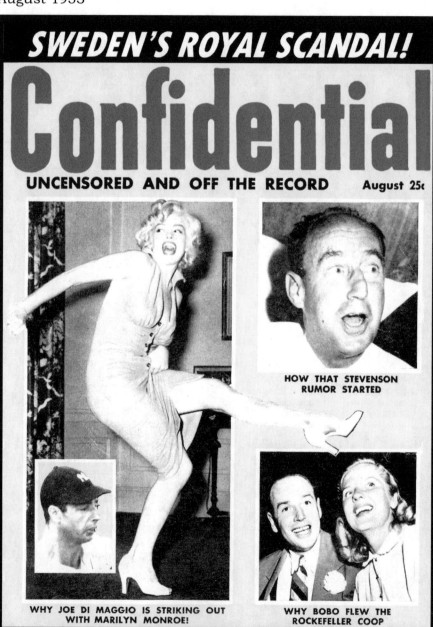

November 1953

WHY VIVIEN LEIGH BLEW HER TOP!

Confidential

UNCENSORED AND OFF THE RECORD

Nov. 25¢

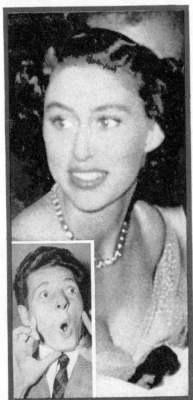

MARKED FOR DEATH!

Walter Winchell   Bishop Fulton Sheen

**What Happened When Danny Kaye
Played Buckingham Palace?**

**Shocking Lowdown on "Li'l Abner!"
What the State Probers Found**

January 1954

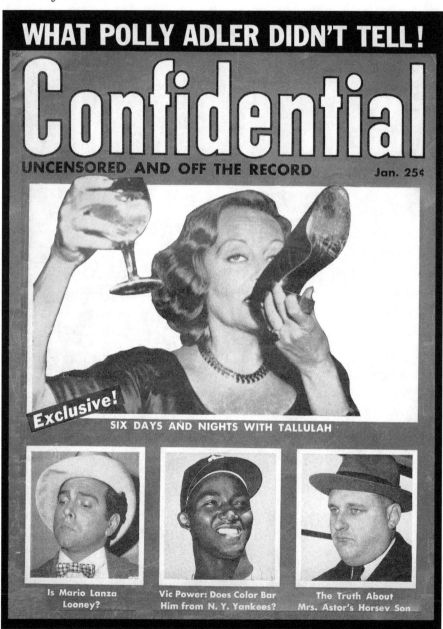

March 1954

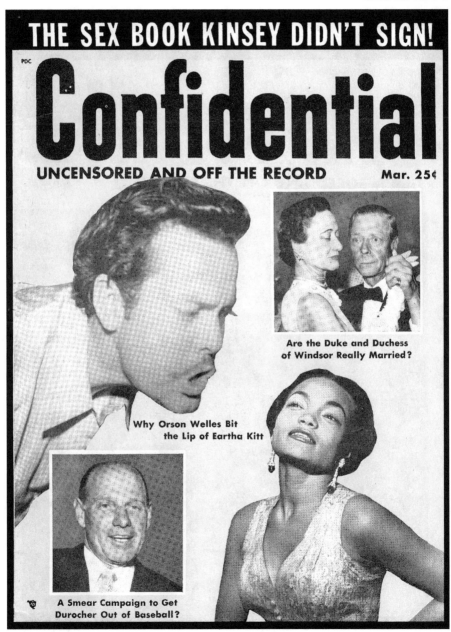

THE SEX BOOK KINSEY DIDN'T SIGN!

PDC

Confidential

UNCENSORED AND OFF THE RECORD   Mar. 25¢

Are the Duke and Duchess
of Windsor Really Married?

Why Orson Welles Bit
the Lip of Eartha Kitt

A Smear Campaign to Get
Durocher Out of Baseball?

May 1954

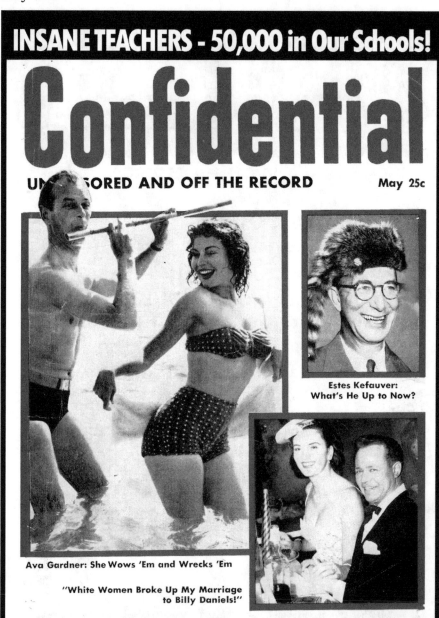

INSANE TEACHERS - 50,000 in Our Schools!

Confidential

UN[CEN]SORED AND OFF THE RECORD   May 25c

Estes Kefauver:
What's He Up to Now?

Ava Gardner: She Wows 'Em and Wrecks 'Em

"White Women Broke Up My Marriage
to Billy Daniels!"

July 1954

September 1954

November 1954

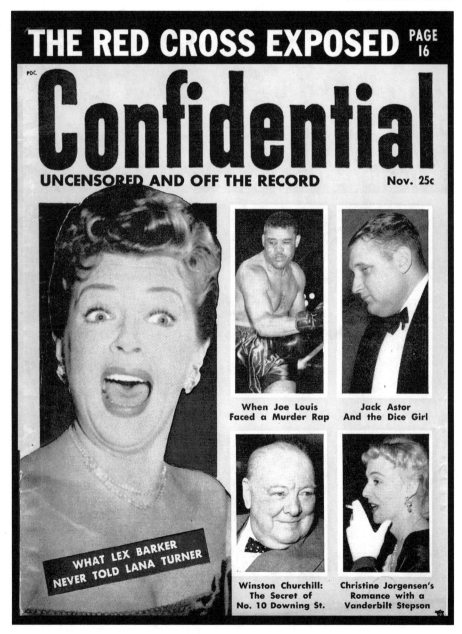

January 1955

TV's "STRIKE IT RICH" EXPOSED

Confidential

TELLS THE FACTS AND NAMES THE NAMES   Jan. 25¢

LOWDOWN: DOES DESI REALLY LOVE LUCY?

WHEN ROCKY MARCIANO
FAKED FOUR FIGHTS

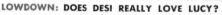

THE TRUTH BEHIND THOSE
SEN. SYMINGTON WHISPERS

EARTHA KITT AND HER "SANTA BABY"
ARTHUR LOEW JR.

March 1955

May 1955

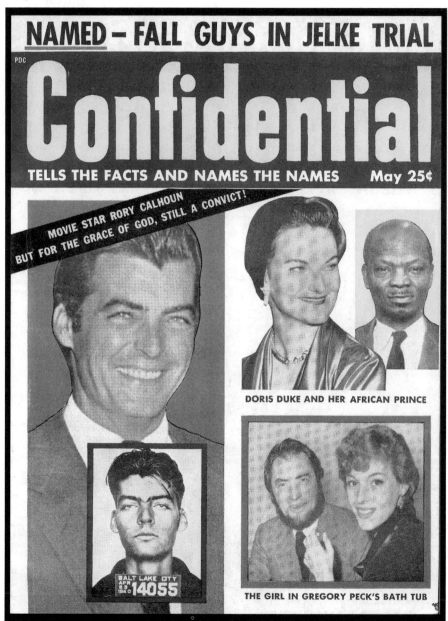

NAMED – FALL GUYS IN JELKE TRIAL

PDC

Confidential

TELLS THE FACTS AND NAMES THE NAMES   May 25¢

MOVIE STAR RORY CALHOUN
BUT FOR THE GRACE OF GOD, STILL A CONVICT!

DORIS DUKE AND HER AFRICAN PRINCE

SALT LAKE CITY
APR 23 1940
14055

THE GIRL IN GREGORY PECK'S BATH TUB

July 1955

Confidential

TELLS THE FACTS AND NAMES THE NAMES July 25¢

THE WIFE CLARK GABLE FORGOT

THE UNTOLD STORY OF
MARLENE DIETRICH

THE STRANGE CASE OF
WALTER CHRYSLER JR.

BILLY DANIELS AND
HIS BLONDE BABY-SITTER

September 1955

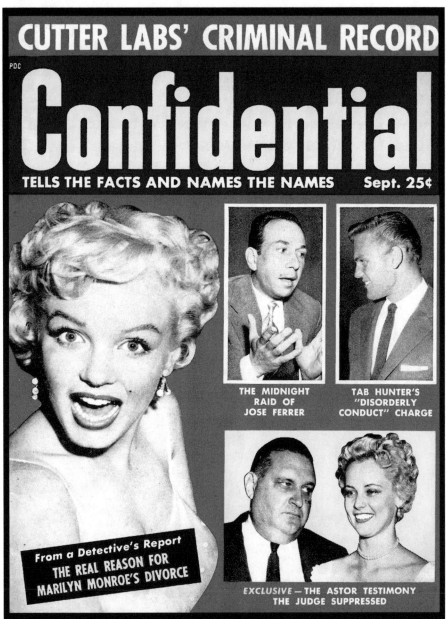

November 1955

THE ONE-HOUR PREGNANCY TEST

Confidential

TELL_ _S A_ THE NAMES Nov. 25¢

WHEN LIZ TAYLOR'S AWAY, MIKE WILL PLAY

THE DIRT KEFAUVER MISSE_
IN HIS OWN BACKYARD

HOW TERRY MOORE
BECAME A
TURKISH DELIGHT

MAE WEST'S OPEN DOOR POLICY—FOR MUSCLE MEN

January 1956

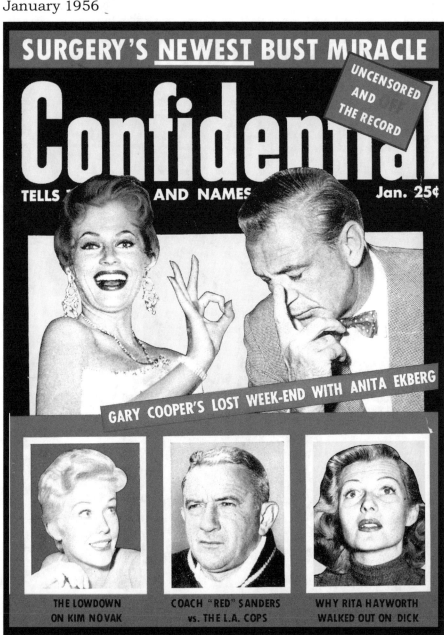

March 1956

May 1956

July 1956

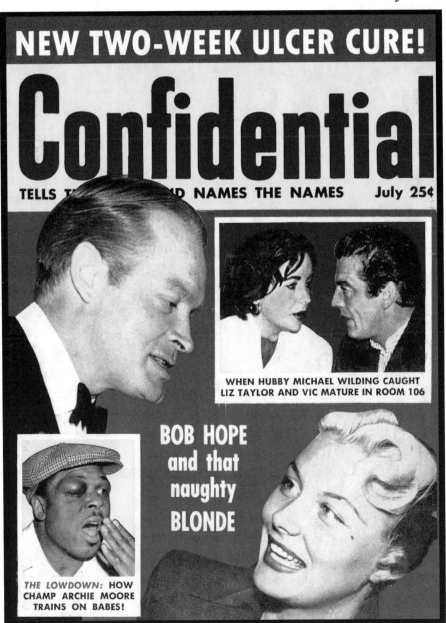

NEW TWO-WEEK ULCER CURE!

Confidential

TELLS T... ...D NAMES THE NAMES   July 25¢

WHEN HUBBY MICHAEL WILDING CAUGHT
LIZ TAYLOR AND VIC MATURE IN ROOM 106

BOB HOPE
and that
naughty
BLONDE

THE LOWDOWN: HOW
CHAMP ARCHIE MOORE
TRAINS ON BABES!

September 1956

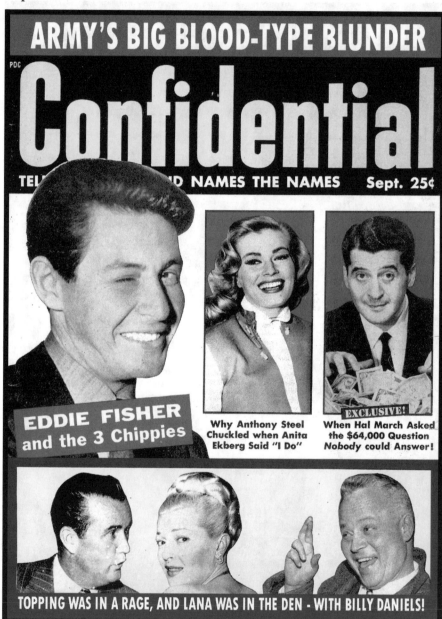

November 1956

January 1957

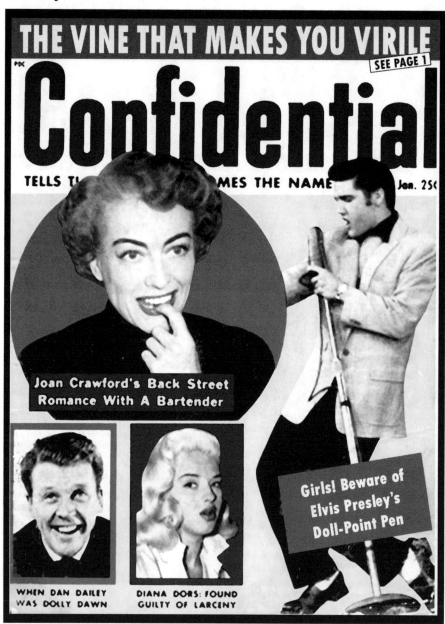

March 1957

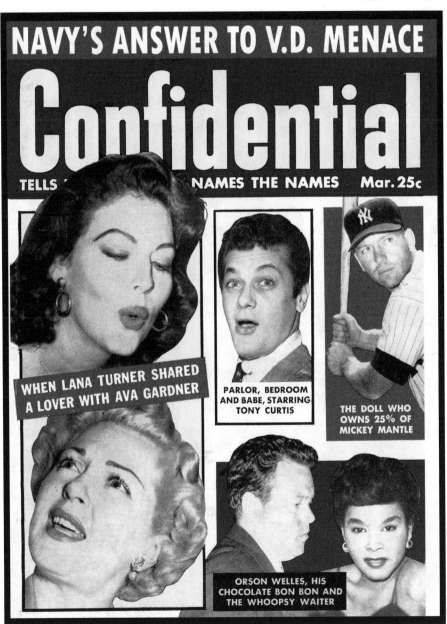

May 1957

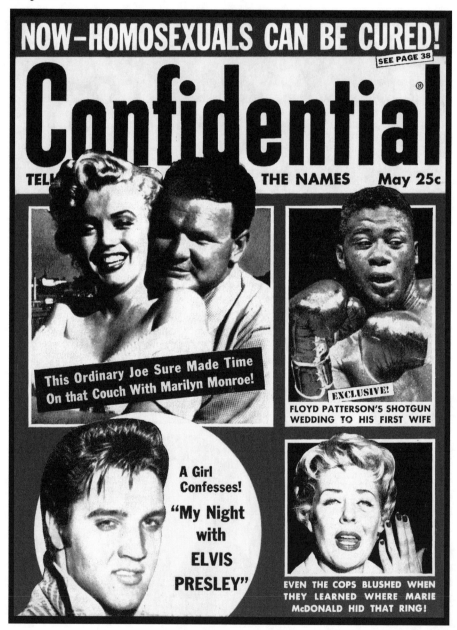

July 1957

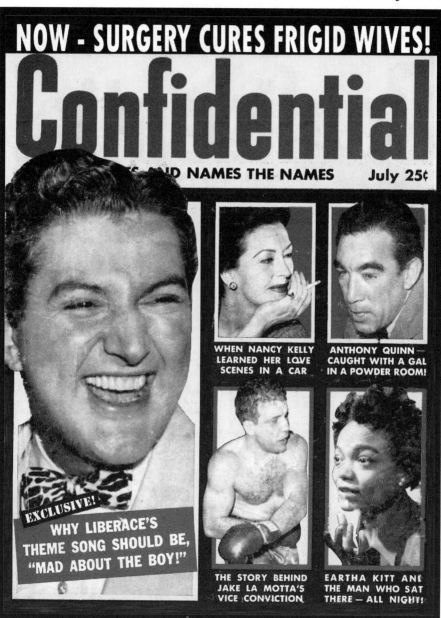

September 1957

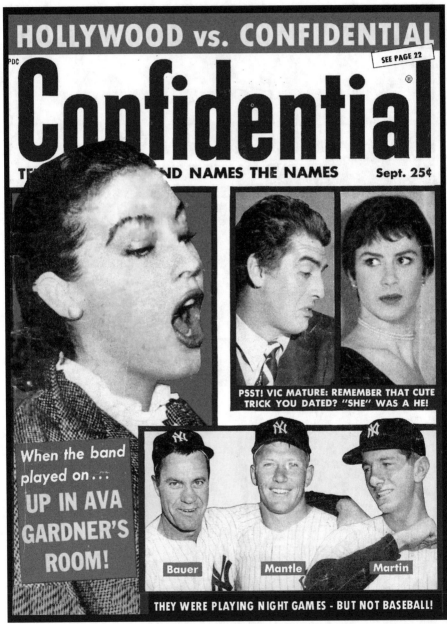

November 1957

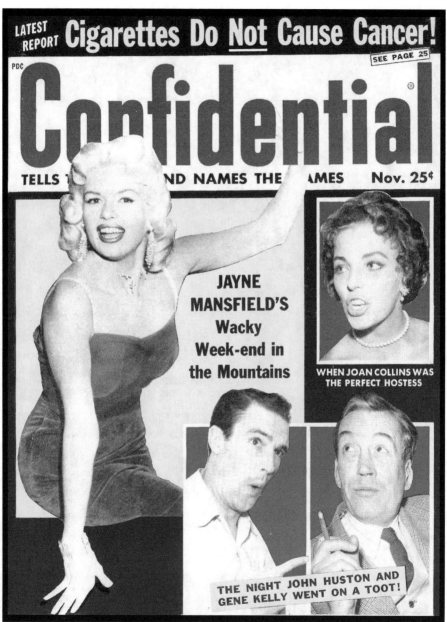

January 1958

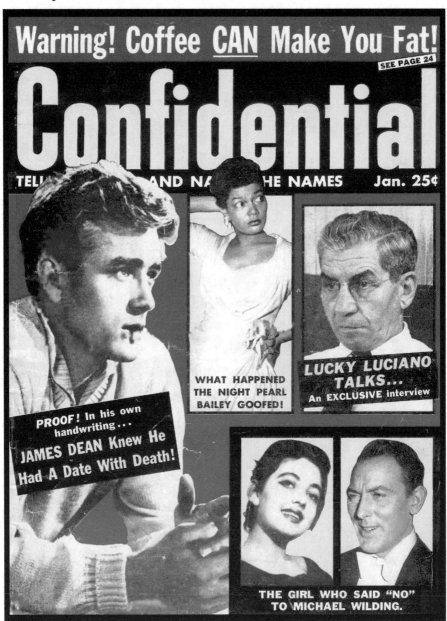

Harrison's last issue before selling the magazine—April 1958

Confidential

TELLS THE FACTS AND NAMES THE NAMES April 25¢

Psst!! It's NEW

› Billionaire J. Paul Getty
   Answers Elsa Maxwell
› Negroes Can Elect
   The Next President!
› Who Shot Walter Reuther?

June 1958—Hy Stierman's first issue as publisher

Still being careful/almost no celebrity dirt—August 1958

Celebrities abound/back to normal—October 1958

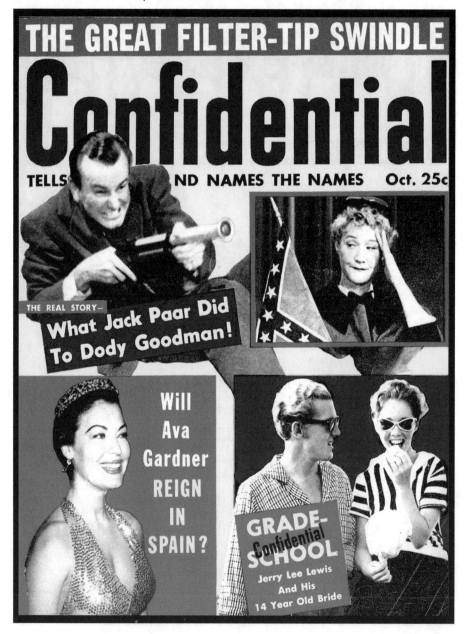

December 1958

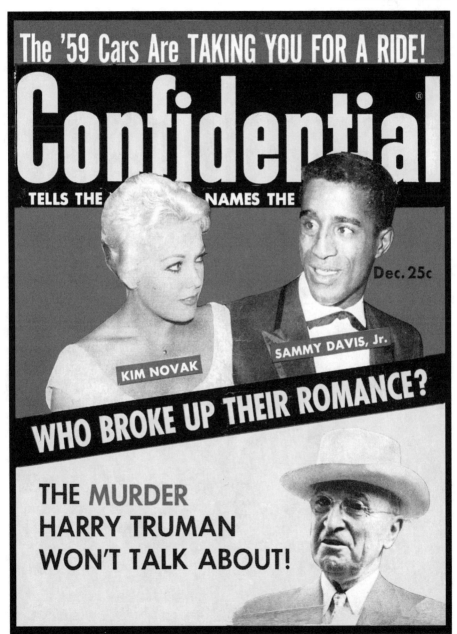

April 1959

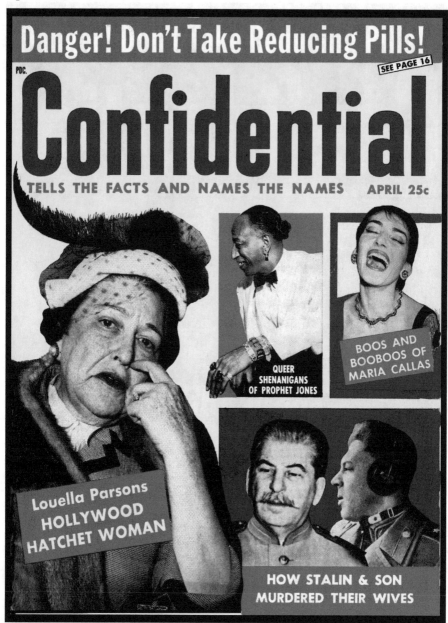

October 1959

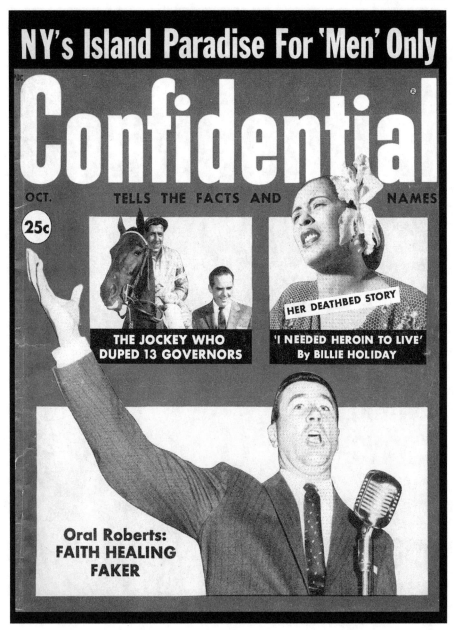

March 1960

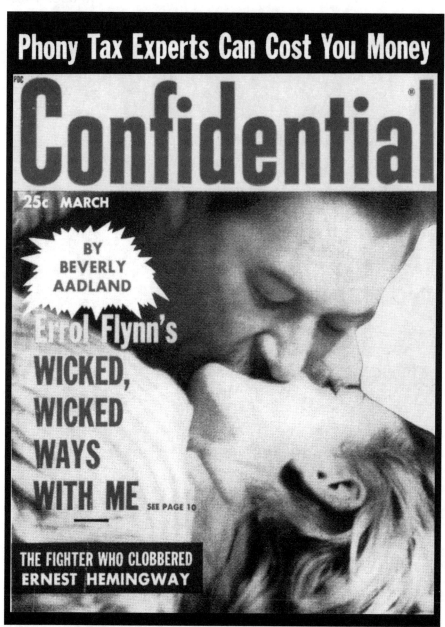

May 1960

May 1961

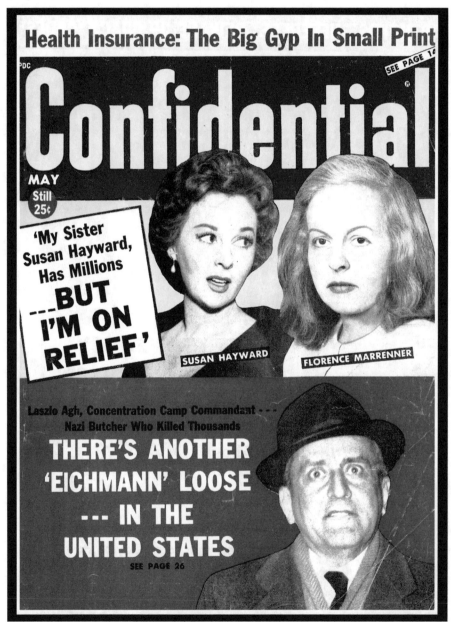

June 1961

October 1961

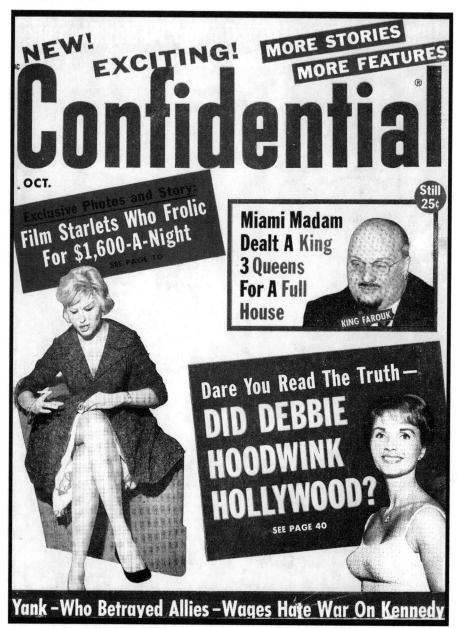

May 1962

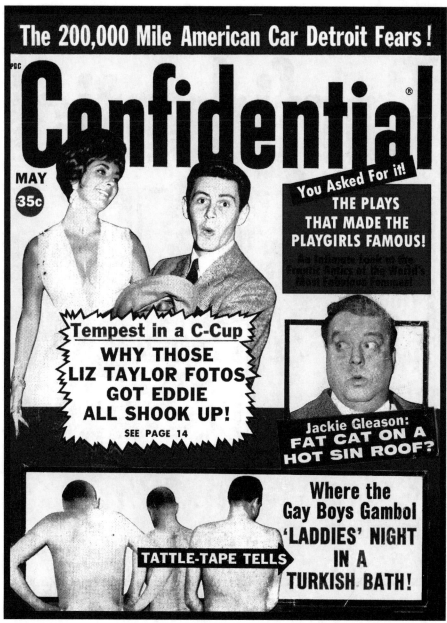

July 62

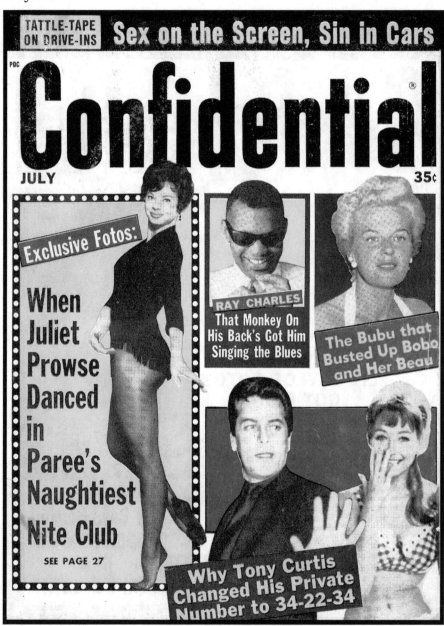

August 1962

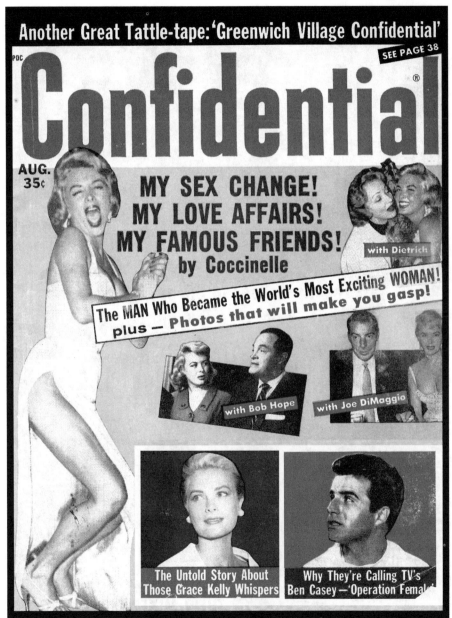

December 1962

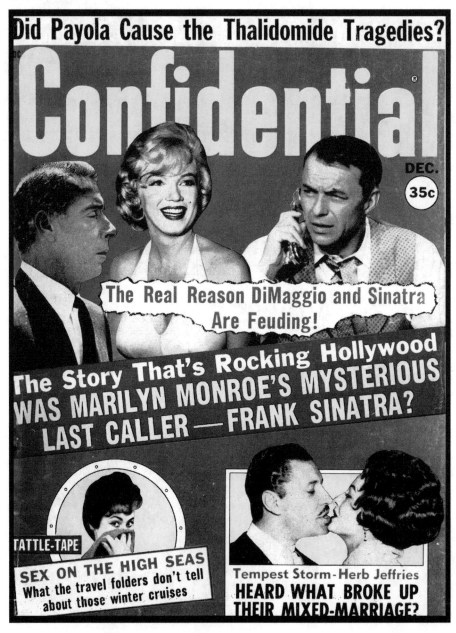

January 1963

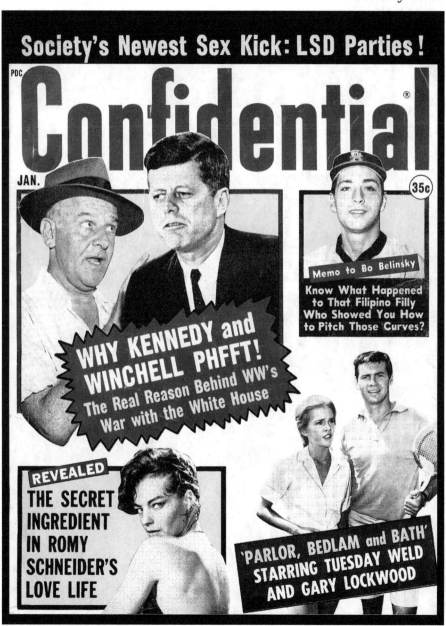

October 1964

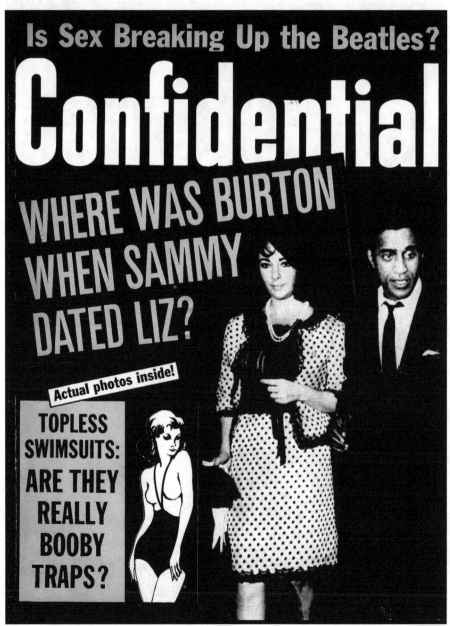

May 1965

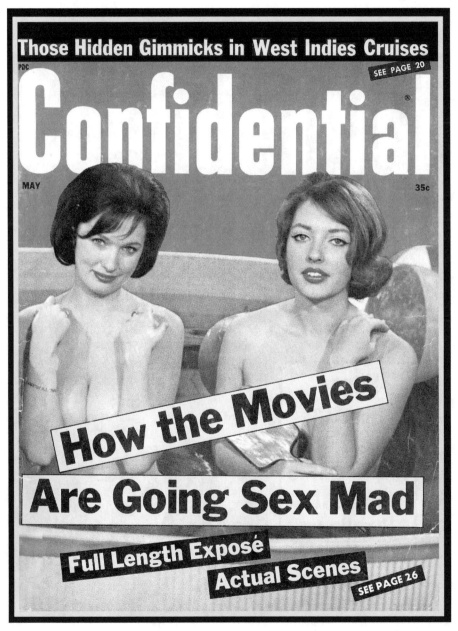

January 1968

Totally new look/nearing the end—March 1969

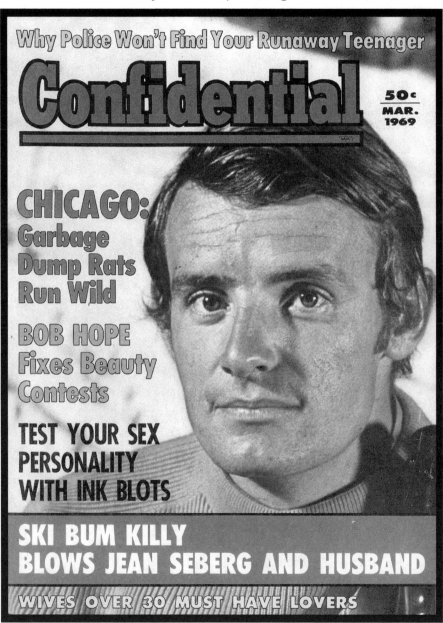

January 1971

September 1951

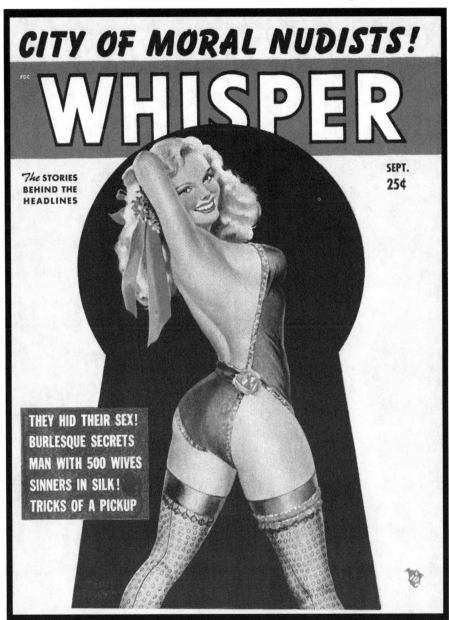

November 1952

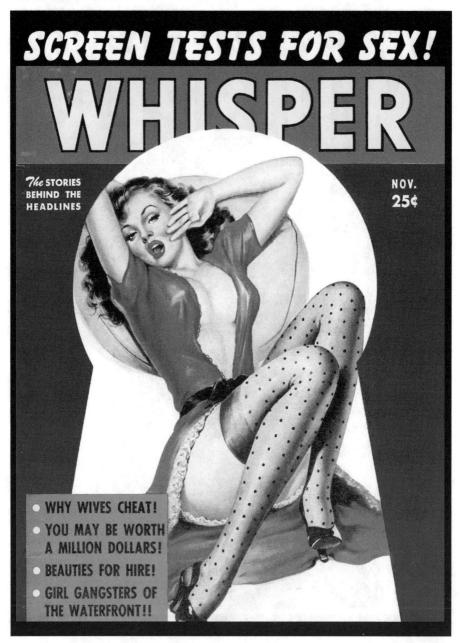

March 1953

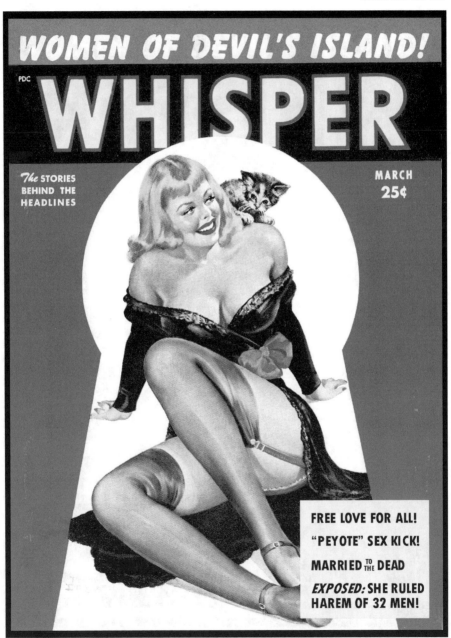

September 1953

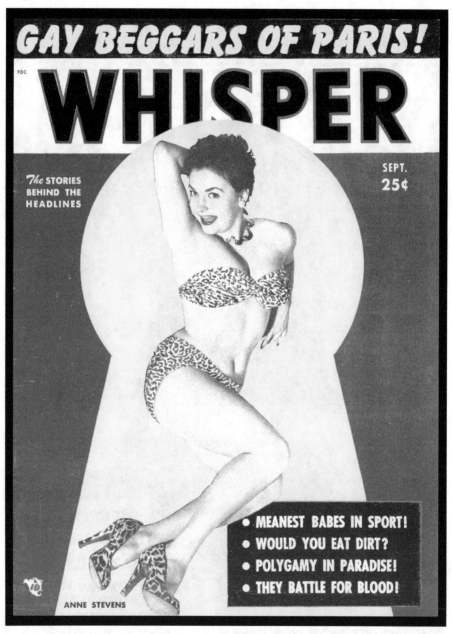

March 1954

THE MAN WITH SIX BRIDES!

WHISPER

PDC

THE STORIES BEHIND THE HEADLINES

MAR. 25c

PUNCHIN' JUDYS: Europe's New Kick!

EXCLUSIVE

WIVES ON THE LAM

DANCING HOUSE BOYS!

May 1954

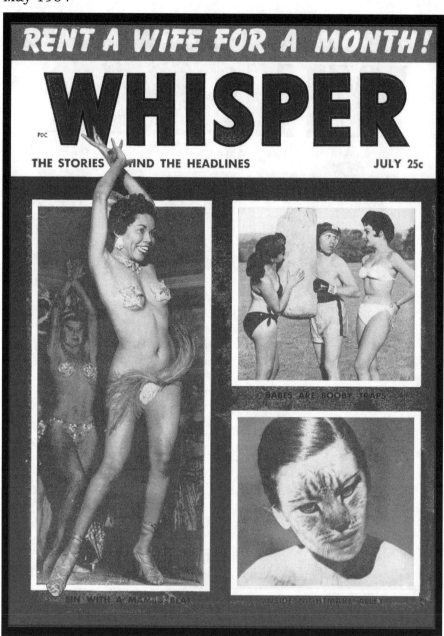

September 1954

April 1955

June 1955

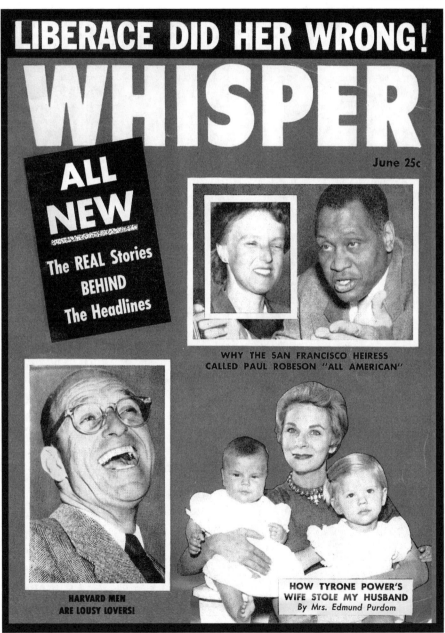

LIBERACE DID HER WRONG!

WHISPER

June 25c

ALL NEW

The REAL Stories BEHIND The Headlines

WHY THE SAN FRANCISCO HEIRESS CALLED PAUL ROBESON "ALL AMERICAN"

HARVARD MEN ARE LOUSY LOVERS!

HOW TYRONE POWER'S WIFE STOLE MY HUSBAND
By Mrs. Edmund Purdom

August 1955

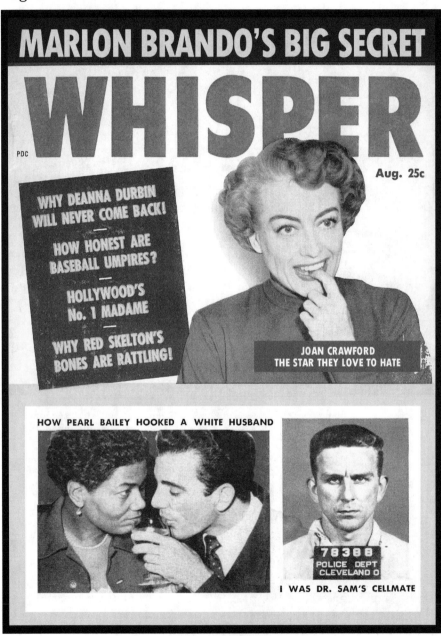

October 1955

January 1956

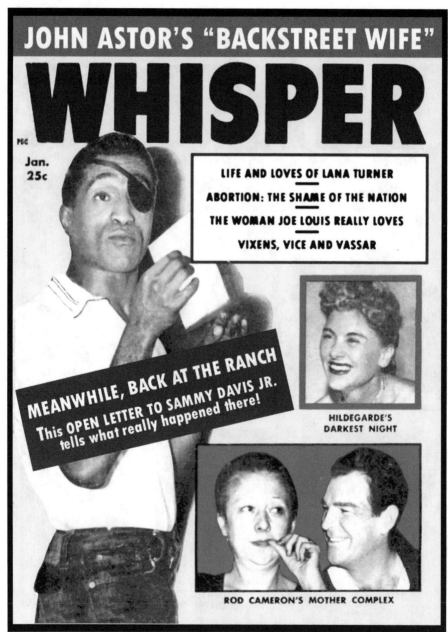

March 1956

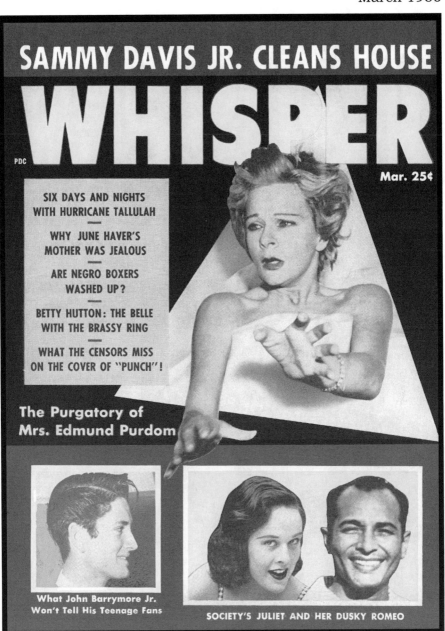

April 1956

JAMES DEAN'S FANS TALK BACK

WHISPER

PD6

April
25c

JOHN AGAR'S NIGHT OF LOVE
—
PREP SCHOOLS: HOTBEDS OF SCANDAL
—
RITA HAYWORTH: THE CHICK WHO
KEEPS LAYING EGGS

EXCLUSIVE: What Her PRINCE
Doesn't Know About GRACE KELLY

ATWATER KENT:
GOODBYE, SUCKER!

HERB JEFFRIES and BETTY HAYDEN
MISBEHAVIN' AGAIN!

December 1957

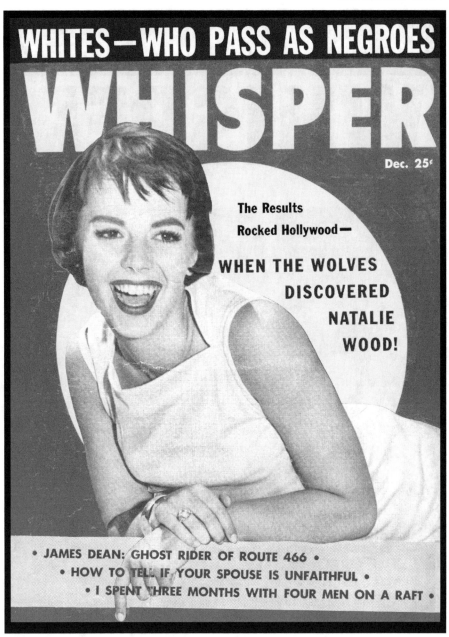

July 1959

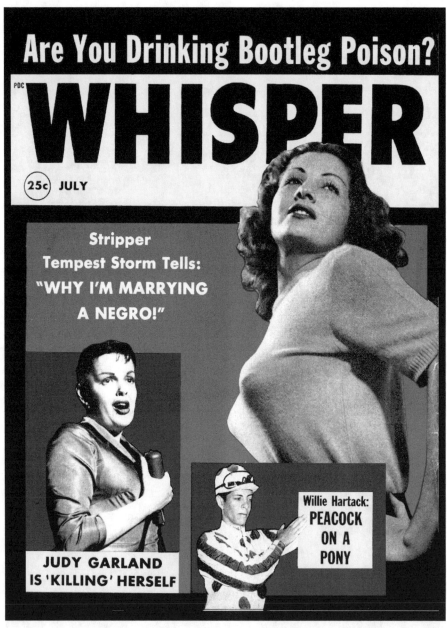

January 1960

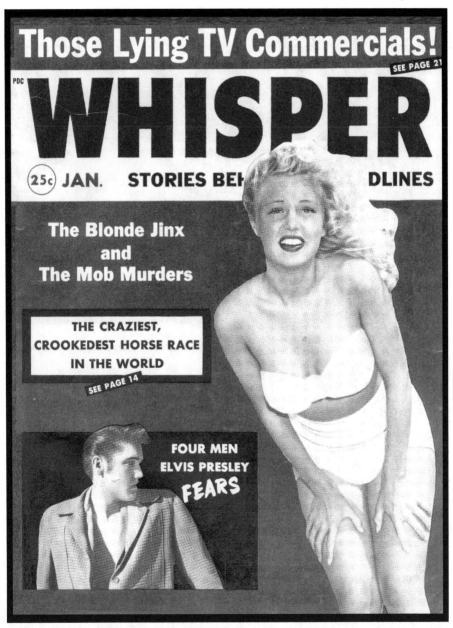

January 1966

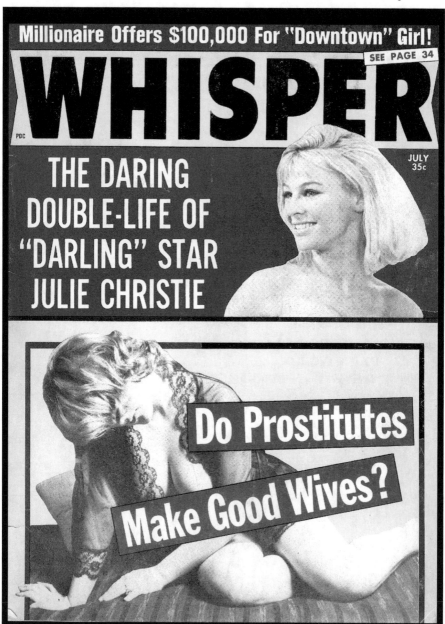

October 1941

February 1948

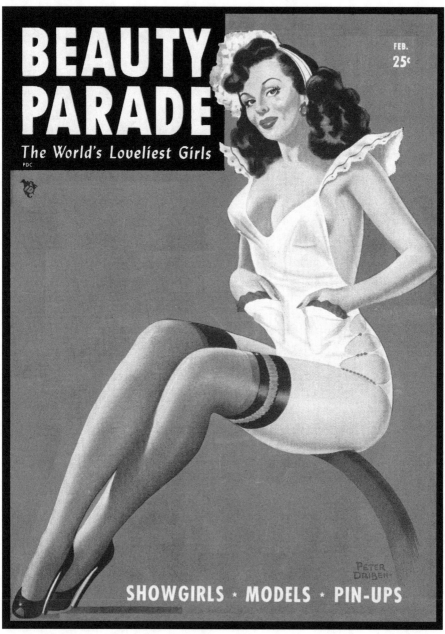

May 1950

February 1949

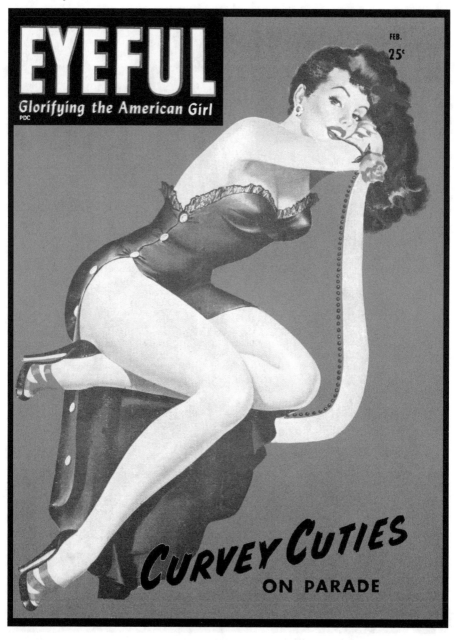

August 1950

October 1952

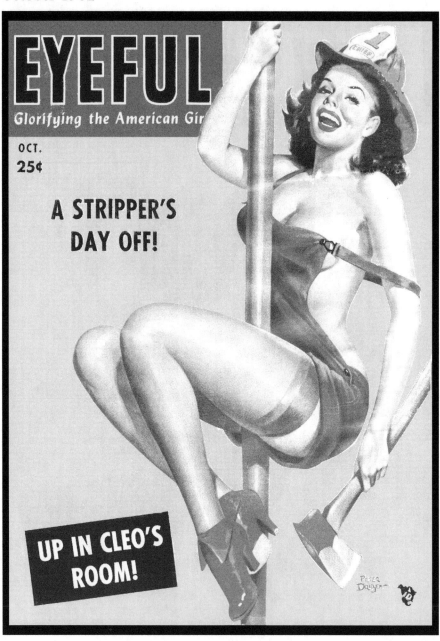

December 1947

December 1954

December 1949

April 1950

June 1950

August 1951

October 1952

October 1953

April 1950

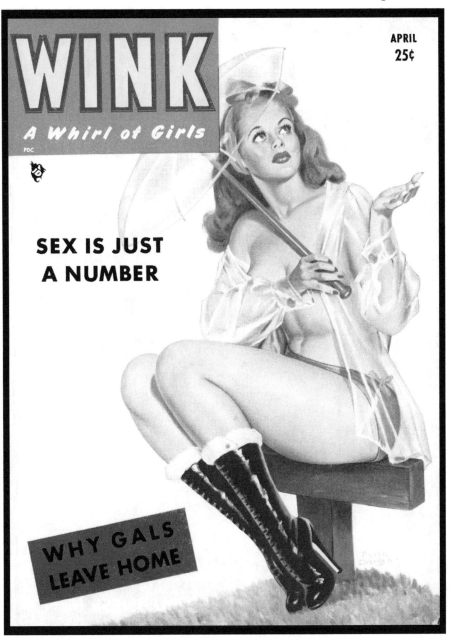

December 1954

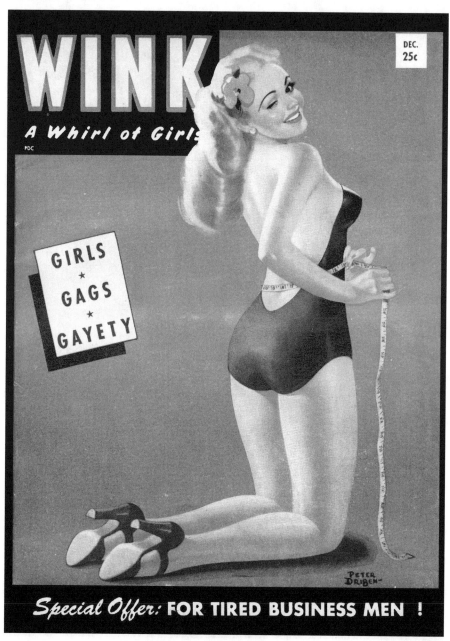

April 1955

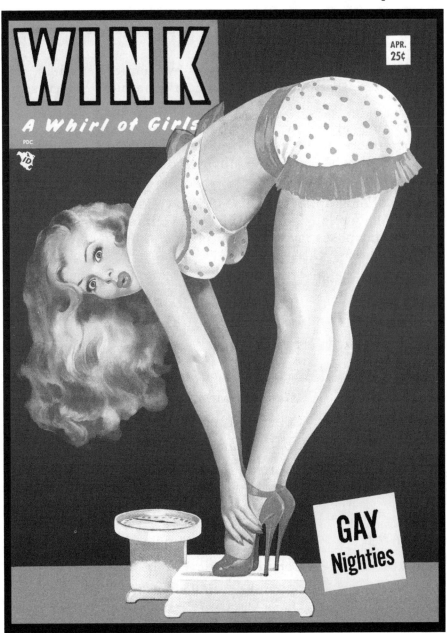

Photo Credits

All materials in *Confidential, Whisper, Wink, Titter, Flirt, Eyeful, Beauty Parade, Tempo, On the Q.T.,* and *The New York Journal-American* are in the public domain. Copyrights lapsed for these publications on various dates in the '70s.

Graphic design for interior montages by Samuel Bernstein, using material from the above publications unless otherwise noted.

When names are known photographers are credited. No photographers were credited by name in Harrison publications. Files that may have indicated their credits were destroyed after Robert Harrison's death.

Specific photographers are also unknown for Harrison and Tobias family photos, and for photos taken in the '50s for publicity purposes, as well as for photographs taken at various public events.

Page 18	*Titter* December 1949
Page 19	*Titter* December 1949
Page 20	*Wink* December 1954
Page 32	*Beauty Parade* October 1941
Page 33	*Whisper* covers various dates
Page 34-35	Courtesy Tobias Family
Page 40	*Confidential* November 1953
Page 45	Courtesy Tobias Family
Page 46	Courtesy Tobias Family
Page 58-59	*Confidential* various dates
Page 66-73	Courtesy Tobias Family
Page 91	*Confidential* May 1956
Page 92	Mitchum *Confidential* July 1955, Sammy Davis, Jr. *Confidential* March 1956

Newspapers

The Hollywood Reporter
> 07-29-57, 07-30-57, 08-01-57, 08-02-57
> 08-05-57, 08-06-57, 08-07-57, 08-07-57
> 08-07-57, 08-12-57, 08-13-57, 08-14-57
> 08-15-57, 08-16-57, 08-19-57, 08-20-57
> 08-21-57, 08-22-57, 08-23-57, 08-26-57
> 08-27-57, 08-28-57, 08-29-57, 08-30-57
> 08-31-57, 09-03-57, 09-04-57, 09-05-57
> 09-06-57, 09-09-57, 09-10-57, 09-11-57
> 09-12-57, 09-13-57

The London Daily Mirror
> 09-26-56

The Los Angeles Mirror-News

07-26-55, 02-18-57, 02-19-57, 02-18-57
02-19-57, 02-20-57, 02-21-57, 02-22-57
02-26-57, 02-27-57, 02-28-57, 03-01-57
03-05-57, 03-08-57, 03-09-57, 03-12-57
03-13-57, 03-14-57, 03-15-57, 03-18-57
03-19-57, 03-22-57, 03-27-57, 06-05-57
07-30-57 ,07-31-57, 08-01-57, 08-05-57
08-06-57, 08-07-57, 08-12-57, 08-13-57
08-15-57, 08-16-57, 08-17-57, 08-19-57
08-20-57, 08-21-57, 08-22-57, 08-23-57
08-24-57, 08-26-57, 08-27-57, 08-28-57
08-29-57, 08-30-57, 09-02-57, 09-03-57
09-04-57, 09-06-57, 09-11-57, 09-12-57
09-13-57, 09-14-57, 09-16-57, 09-17-57
09-18-57, 09-19-57, 09-20-57, 09-21-57
09-23-57, 09-24-57, 09-25-57, 09-26-57
01-04-58

The Los Angeles Times

03-27-57, 05-16-57, 05-19-57, 05-28-57
05-29-57, 06-12-57, 06-20-57, 06-26-57
07-02-57, 07-19-57, 08-18-57, 08-19-57
08-20-57, 08-24-57, 08-26-57, 08-27-57
09-10-57, 09-14-57, 09-17-57, 09-18-57
09-19-57, 09-21-57, 09-24-57, 10-02-57
10-03-57,11-13-57, 12-03-57, 12-19-57
05-17-58

The New York Daily News

09-06-55, 09-07-55, 05-20-57, 07-30-57
08-10-57, 08-11-57, 08-12-57, 08-13-57
08-14-57, 08-15-57, 08-16-57, 08-17-57
08-18-57, 08-19-57, 08-20-57, 08-21-57
08-22-57, 08-23-57, 08-24-57, 08-25-57
08-26-57, 08-27-57, 08-28-57, 08-29-57
08-30-57, 08-31-57, 09-01-57, 09-03-57
09-05-57, 09-06-57, 01-05-58, 01-06-58

The New York Journal American
09-05-56, 09-06-56

The New York Post
09-14-53, 09-15-53, 09-16-53, 09-17-53
09-18-53, 09-20-53, 09-02-57, 09-03-57
09-04-57, 09-05-57, 09-06-57, 09-07-57

The New York Times
12-22-39, 12-24-39, 12-28-39, 09-23-49
06-06-54, 09-04-55, 09-10-55, 09-05-56
09-07-56, 02-28-57, 03-01-57, 03-02-57
03-08-57, 06-07-57, 06-12-57, 06-14-57
06-15-57, 07-19-57, 07-24-57, 07-30-57
08-01-57, 08-03-57, 08-04-57, 08-06-57
08-07-57, 08-08-57, 08-10-57, 08-13-57
08-14-57, 08-15-57, 08-16-57, 08-17-57
08-18-57, 08-20-57, 08-21-57, 08-22-57
08-24-57, 08-26-57, 08-27-57, 08-28-57
08-29-57, 08-31-57, 09-04-57, 09-07-57
09-11-57, 09-12-57, 09-14-57, 09-16-57
09-17-57, 09-18-57, 09-22-57, 10-02-57
10-04-57, 10-06-57, 10-11-57, 10-15-57
10-27-57, 11-08-57, 11-13-57, 12-06-57
12-19-57, 01-04-58, 01-05-58, 02-20-78
07-02-58, 07-09-58, 07-16-58, 11-23-76
07-24-94

The Valley News
10-15-57

Variety
07-29-57, 07-30-57, 08-01-57, 08-02-57
08-05-57, 08-06-57, 08-07-57, 08-07-57
08-07-57, 08-12-57, 08-13-57, 08-14-57
08-15-57, 08-16-57, 08-19-57, 08-20-57
08-21-57, 08-22-57, 08-23-57, 08-26-57
08-27-57, 08-28-57, 08-29-57, 08-30-57
08-31-57, 09-03-57, 09-04-57, 09-05-57
09-06-57, 09-09-57, 09-10-57, 09-11-57

Variety (continued)
09-12-57, 09-13-57

The Washington Post
07-10-55, 07-19-55, 09-26-55, 10-08-55
10-30-55, 09-06-56, 09-07-56, 09-06-56
05-18-57, 06-02-57, 06-26-57, 07-21-57
07-30-57, 08-03-57, 08-10-57, 08-13-57
08-14-57, 08-15-57, 08-17-57, 08-20-57
08-21-57, 08-23-57, 08-23-57, 08-24-57
08-26-57, 08-27-57, 08-28-57, 08-30-57
08-31-57, 09-11-57, 09-14-57, 09-15-57
09-18-57, 10-02-57, 10-03-57, 01-04-58
01-05-58, 05-18-58

Magazines

American Film
"Now It Can Be Told" (Steve Govoni) February 1990

Beauty Parade

October 1941	February 1948	May 1950

The British Journalism Review
"The Father of Scandal" (Victor Davis) 2002

Confidential

December 1952	March 1956	April1959
April 1953	May 1956	October 1959
August 1953	July 1956	March1960
July 1953	September 1956	May 1960
November 1953	November 1956	May 1961
January 1954	January 1957	June 1961
March 1954	March 1957	October 1961
May 1954	May 1957	May 1962
July 1954	July 1957	July 1962
September 1954	September 1957	December 1962
November 1954	November 1957	January 1963
January 1955	January 1958	October 1964
March 1955	April 1958	May 1965
May 1955	June 1958	January 1968
July 1955	August 1958	March 1969
September 1955	October 1958	January 1971
November 1955	December 1958	
January 1956	February 1959	

Esquire
"Confidential File on Confidential" (Gehman) November 1956
"Public Lives" (Thomas K. Wolfe) April 1964

Eyeful

February 1949	August 1950	December 1952
April 1950	October 1952	

Exposed
Premiere 1955   March 1956   October 1957

Flirt
December 1947   December 1954

The Gay & Lesbian Review Worldwide
"Breaking the Code"(Carol Lemasters) March 1, 2001

GQ
"Confidential" (Sam Kashner) March 2000
"L.A.'s Dark Places" (James Ellroy) March 2000
"The Trouble I Cause" (James Ellroy) March 2000

Hollywood Confidential
Vol. 1, No. 5, 1956

Hush-Hush
January 1956   March 1956   September 1958

Inside Story
May 1955   August 1955   April 1956

The Lowdown
February 1956   September 1959

On the Q.T.
March 1957

Private Lives
June 1955   October 1955   February 1956

Revealed
"Miss Scandal of 1957" (Malcolm Morgan) December 1957

Salon
"Ask Camille" (Camille Paglia) September 1997

Sir!
February 1956

Supressed
July 1955

Tempo
"Maureen O'Hara: Sultry Stars Sizzle" June 1954

Time Magazine
"Success in the Sewer" July 11, 1955
"Sewer Trouble" August 1, 1955
"Cat-o'-Nine Tale" August 8, 1955
"Lid on the Sewer" September 19, 1955
"Confidential Wins a Round" October 17, 1955
"Ssh!" April 2, 1956
"Confidential Revisited" March 18, 1957
"Black Eye" May 27, 1957
"Technical Surrender" June 24, 1957
"The Woes of Confidential" July 22, 1957
"Putting the Papers to Bed" August 26, 1957
"Stalemate" October 14, 1957
"High Price of Virtue" May 26, 1958

Titter

| December 1949 | June 1950 | October 1952 |
| April 1950 | August 1951 | October 1953 |

True
"Who's Who in the Secret F.B.I. Files" January 1974

Uncensored
February   December 1956
1956   January 1958

Vanity Fair
"Confidential's Reign of Terror" (Neal Gabler) April 2003
"The Legend of Rubirosa" (Gary Cohen) December 2002
"The Golden Fleece" (Bryan Burrough) August 2003

Whisper
September 1951   August 1955   July 1959
March 1953   January 1956   January 1960
September 1953   March 1956   July 1966
March 1954   April 1956
June 1955   December 1957

Wink
April 1950   December 1954   April 1955

Books

"1, 000 Pin-Up Girls"
Benedikt Taschen,
Taschen, 2002

"Ava, My Story"
Ava Gardner
Bantam, 1990

"The Bad & The Beautiful: Hollywood in the Fifties"
Sam Kashner and Jennifer MacNair
W.M. Norton & Co. 2002

"Behind the Screen: How Gays and Lesbians Shaped
Hollywood"
William J. Mann
Penguin Books, 2001

"Dear Muffo: 35 Years in the Fast Lane"
Harold Conrad
Stein & Day, NY, 1982

"Dish: The Inside Story on the World of Gossip"
Jeannette Walls
Avon Books, 2000

"Florence Lawrence, The Biograph Girl"
Kelly R. Brown
McFarland & Co., 1999

"From the Glitter to the Gutter:
The Rise and Fall of Barbara Payton"
John O'Dowd
Unpublished, 2003

"The Girls: Sappho Goes Hollywood"
Diana McLellan
LA Weekly Books, 2000

"Grossed-Out Surgeon Vomits Inside Patient!
An Insider's Look at Supermarket Tabloids"
Jim Hogshire
Feral House, 1997

"Headline Justice"
Theo Wilson
Thunder's Mouth Press, 1996

"Hollywood Babylon"
Kenneth Anger
Straight Arrow Books, 1975

"The Hollywood Book of Death"
James Robert Parish
McGraw-Hill, 2001

"The Hollywood Book of Scandals"
James Robert Parish
McGraw-Hill, 2004

"I Watched a Wild Hog Eat My Baby!"
Bill Sloan
Prometheus Books, 2001

"Investigation Hollywood!"
Fred Otash
Regnery Co., 1976

"King of Cons"
Aaron Tonken
Nelson Current, 2004

"Lana, the Lady, the Legend, the Truth"
Lana Turner
Dutton, 1982

"Let's Go to Press"
Ed Weiner
G.P. Putnam's Sons, 1955

"Lost Hollywood"
David Wallace
LA Weekly Books/St. Martin's Press, 2001

"Man of the World"
Cornelius Vanderbilt
Crown, 1959

"The Million Dollar Mermaid"
Esther Williams, Digby Diehl
Simon & Schuster, 1999

"Miss Manners Guide To Excruciatingly Correct Behavior"
Judith Martin
Warner, 1989

"Mommie Dearest"
Christina Crawford
William Morrow & Co., 1978

"My 20 Years Running the National Enquirer:
The Untold Story" Iain Calder
Miramax Books, 2004

"Natural Blonde"
Liz Smith
Hyperion, 2000

"Past Forgetting:
My Love Affair with Dwight D. Eisenhower"
Kay Somersby
Simon & Schuster, 1976

"The Sewing Circle: Sappho's Leading Ladies"
Axel Madsen
Kensington Books, 2002

"Social Studies"
Fran Lebowitz
Random House, 1981

"Speaker's Electronic Reference Collection"
AApex, 1994

"Times We Had"
Marion Davies
Ballentine Books, 1985

"Tis Herself"
Maureen O'Hara, John Nicoletti
Simon & Schuster, 2004

"U.S.A. Confidential"
Jack Lait & Lee Mortimer
Crown Publishers, 1952

"Webster's Electronic Quotebase"
Keith Mohler
Webster, 1994

Other Source Materials

"The Casting Couch"
Lumiere Video
John Sealy Productions, Alan Selwyn/Selwyn Ford, 1995

"Slander"
Metro-Goldwyn-Mayer
Armand Deutsch, Roy Rowland/Jerome Weidman, 1956

"The Stan Freberg Show"
Smithsonian Historical Performances
CBS Radio 09-08-57

"Walter Winchell Radio Reports"
Walter Winchell
Sponsor: Kaiser-Frazer, 1949

VANDERBILT v. VANDERBILT
354 U.S. 416—United States Supreme Court No. 302.
Argued April 22-23, 1957.
Decided June 24, 1957 1 N.Y.2d 342, 135 n.e.2d 553,
AFFIRMED.

Other Interviews

Army Archerd, Janet Charlton, Robert Chmiel, Arthur
Crowley, Bill Dakota, Jack Martin, Marjorie Roth, Stella
Stambler, Lyle Stuart, Barbara Tobias, Michael Tobias

Websites

1955 Top Ten Stars
reelclassics.com/Articles/General/quigle
ytop10-article.htm

20th Century Box Office Champs
threemoviebuffs.com/archives/boxofficechamps.htm

Bat Boy

weeklyworldnews.com/batboy/index.

Batista

historyofcuba.com/history/batista.
htm

Confidential Magazine

catalog-of-cool.com/harrison.html
bjr.org.uk/data/2002/no4_davis.ht
m
bbc.co.uk/bbcfour/documentaries/
features/hollywood-
confidential.shtml
themediadrome.com/content/article
s/film_articlesvintage_smear.htm
abilenechamber.com/RonaldReagan
Tribute.html

Consumer Price Index Conversation Table

http://oregonstate.edu/Dept/pol_s
ci/fac/sahr/cv2002rs.pdf

Crawford, Joan

universalstudios.com/homepage/ht
ml/inside/history.html

Drugs: Dexamil, Dolophine, Demerol,
Thalidomide
rxlist.com/rxboard/ritalin.pl?read=259drugs.co
m/index.cfm?pageID=0&brndDolophineruralnet.
marshall.edu/pain/demerol.htmdermatology.cdl
ib.org/93/reviews/thalidomide/hsu.html

Eisenhower, Dwight and Mamie

arts.mcgill.ca/programs/history/fac
ulty/TROYWEB/WithIkeRumorsWer
eSteamierThanFacts.htm
dailyillini.com/feb_00/feb24/opinions/colJanua
ry.html/eisenhower.utexas.edu/ohfa273.pdf

Events of the Fifties
    paulsgoldenoldies.com/

Films and Actors, Various
    hollywood.com
    imdb.com/
    infoplease.com

Gangsters and Crime, Various
    crimemagazine.com/eboli.htm
    carpenoctem.tv/mafia/guzik.html
    wikipedia.org/wiki/Lucky_Luciano
    glasgowcrew.tripod.com/costello.ht
    mlangelfire.com/mo3/mullenfamily
    /wynona3.htmlcrimelibrary.com/g
    angsters_outlaws/outlaws/karpis/
    5.html?sect=17gambino.com/bio/f
    ranknitti.htm DEAD
    mugshots.com/Outlaws/Alvin_Kar
    pis.htm
    spartacus.schoolnet.co.uk/USAcap
    one.htm

Gay and Lesbian
    gaytoday.badpuppy.com/garchive/
    viewpoint/120897vi.htm

Glossary of Hard Boiled Slang
    lospadrescounty.net/et/inflation.html

Great MGM Musicals
    members.aol.com/mgmfanatic

Harrison, Robert
    catalog-of-cool.com/harrison.html
    bjr.org.uk/data/2002/no4_davis.h
    tmbbc.co.uk/bbcfour/documentari
    es/features/hollywood-
    confidential.shtmlthemediadrome.c
    om/content/articles/film_articles/
    vintage_smear.htm

Hart, Gary
>
> miami.com/mld/miamiherald/406
> 9344.htm

Inflation Conversion Chart
>
> lospadrescounty.net/et/inflation.ht
> ml

Keane, Margaret
>
> keane-eyes.com/

Kefauver Hearings (including Life magazine quote)
>
> history.acusd.edu/gen/filmnotes/k
> efauver.html

Kitt, Eartha ("Eartha, Moved")
>
> aarp.org/mmaturity/mar_aprJanu
> ary/droppingby.html

Lawrence, Florence
>
> northernstars.ca/actorsjkl/lawrenc
> ebio.html

Libertarianism
>
> lp.org/organization/history/liberta
> rian.org

Lobelia
>
> viableherbalsolutions.com/singles/
> herbs/s4May.htm

Lost Mind-Entertainment Awards Database
>
> lostmind.100megsfree2.com/

McDonald, Marie
>
> movies.yahoo.com/shop?d=hc&id=
> 1800073521&cf=biog&intl=us